P9-CEB-620

EXPLAINING CONGRESSIONAL-PRESIDENTIAL RELATIONS

SUNY series on the Presidency: Contemporary Issues
John Kenneth White, editor

EXPLAINING CONGRESSIONAL-PRESIDENTIAL RELATIONS

A Multiple Perspectives Approach

STEVEN A. SHULL
and
THOMAS C. SHAW

Whitaker Library
Chowan College
Murfreesboro, North Carolina

State University
of New York
Press

NO LONGER
the property of
Whitaker Library

Published by
State University of New York Press, Albany

© 1999 State University of New York

All rights reserved

Production by Susan Geraghty
Marketing by Anne Valentine

Printed in the United States of America

No part of this book may be used or reproduced in any manner whatsoever
without written permission. No part of this book may be stored in a retrieval
system or transmitted in any form or by any means including electronic,
electrostatic, magnetic tape, mechanical, photocopying, recording, or otherwise
without the prior permission in writing of the publisher.

For information, address State University of New York
Press, State University Plaza, Albany, N.Y., 12246

Library of Congress Cataloging-in-Publication Data

Shull, Steven A.
    Explaining congressional-presidential relations : a multiple
perspectives approach / by Steven A. Shull and Thomas C. Shaw.
        p.   cm. — (SUNY series on the presidency)
    Includes bibliographical references and index.
    ISBN 0-7914-4273-X (hc : alk. paper). — ISBN 0-7914-4274-8 (pb :
alk. paper)
        1. Presidents—United States. 2. United States. Congress.
3. Political planning—United States. I. Shaw, Thomas C.
II. Title. III. Series: SUNY series in the presidency.
JK585.S44 1999
328.73′07456—dc21   98-45327
                                                               CIP

10 9 8 7 6 5 4 3 2 1

Dedicated to
Janice and Merritt

CONTENTS

TABLES AND FIGURES

PREFACE

This book examines four government activities involving direct interactions between presidents and Congress and considers whether they are influenced by executive, legislative, or exogenous factors. Several studies analyzing presidential-congressional interactions attempt explanations of one of the Congressional Quarterly, Inc. (CQ) measures of presidents' support or success in Congress, occasionally with minor variations thereof. Sometimes using multivariate analysis, these authors seek to explain a single phenomenon, such as vote congruence. Although important efforts, CQ indicators of actor preferences based upon executive and legislative vote positions are limited. Indeed, support (the most commonly used indicator) is merely one aspect of presidential-congressional interactions and may not even be the most important one.

Explaining Congressional-Presidential Relations encompasses three additional aspects of presidential-congressional interactions apart from vote congruence or support: presidential position taking on legislative votes, presidents' propensity to veto legislation, and budget agreement between the two actors. Each of these four activities is an element in the adoption of public policy. We consider the relationships among these four interactions and then posit a general model of determinants of all four interactions. Our analysis covers an extensive time series (1949–95) and is more complete than has occurred heretofore. Within the multivariate time series analysis employed, we also control for policy area and aspects of political time.

These four government activities involving presidential-congressional interactions probably are related to one another in general as well as across time. Therefore, we expect them to reflect a dynamic temporal process in presidential-congressional interactions. For example, presidential position taking should relate to legislative support, while the veto should relate most directly to budget agreement. They seem to occur temporally within a given year but are not independent of each other. An emergent process among these variables would reveal a further complexity in presidential-congressional relations. Thus, we posit a cyclical process in which activities are related and influenced by those that precede them temporally to better understand why and how interactions between Congress and the president occur.

Explaining Congressional-Presidential Relations enhances the theoretical and empirical development of the existing literature in several ways. First and foremost is to understand the multifaceted nature of relations between the first two branches of our national government. The analysis begins by studying four direct interactions between presidents and Congress. Although prior research has examined each of these activities to varying degrees, no one has examined them *together* as interdependent phenomena. Lagged models of the interrelationships among them will improve our understanding of such activities. We are quite convinced that the legislative support or success that presidents obtain is not the only important element in the adoption of public policy.

Second, it is important to study whether policy area differences help us understand presidential-congressional interactions. If differences between foreign and domestic policy are observed, then the "two presidencies" represents a valid typology of policy content. Third, our analysis also incorporates several groupings of these data by political time: overall and by trend analysis, dichotomized by early versus late eras, by selected year in presidential term of office, and by presidents individually (from Truman to Clinton). Fourth, we model the explanatory factors differently than has been attempted heretofore. Three broad environments, containing both activities and resources variables, are used to tap the relative explanatory power of the environments on each of the four actor relations variables. We call this model a multiple perspectives approach, which contributes to theory-building in studying presidential-congressional interactions. Thus, assessing the interplay between Congress and the president separately and as they influence one another, comparing the explanatory role of three environments, and controlling for policy areas and time periods help facilitate greater understanding of the first two branches of our national government.

ACKNOWLEDGMENTS

This project began as a follow-up to an earlier volume by Shull entitled *Presidential-Congressional Relations*. Clay Morgan, then editor at State University of New York Press offered us an advanced contract based upon a prospectus only and we are grateful to his confidence in our work. Subsequent to Clay's departure, Zina Lawrence took over and continued to encourage our efforts. We are proud that John White, editor of an enviable series entitled "The Presidency: Contemporary Issues," saw promise in this book and supported its publication. The faculty board for the Press, including Bob Spitzer, an author in this series and editor of another with State University of New York Press also supported this project. We received assistance in coding data from Rosalind Cook and in data collection from Brad Gomez. Jeffrey Cohen, Chris Day, Martha Gibson, Dennis Gleiber, Janet Martin, and Lance LeLoup read all or most of the manuscript and we are grateful for their helpful suggestions. In addition, we are pleased that four outside reviewers all liked the volume and recommended its publication. In many instances, they had helpful suggestions, several of which we incorporated. We are convinced that the final product is much improved from the constructive advice from all above.

ABOUT THE AUTHORS

Steven A. Shull is University Research Professor of Political Science at the University of New Orleans. He is author of over one hundred publications on American national institutions and public policy. His articles have appeared in *Journal of Politics, Political Research Quarterly, Social Science Quarterly, Legislative Studies Quarterly, Western Political Quarterly, American Politics Quarterly,* and in other journals. His most recent books are *Presidential-Congressional Relations* (1997), *Presidential Policymaking* (1999, edited), and *The President and Congress* (1999).

Thomas C. Shaw is a Survey Specialist at the National Opinion Research Center (NORC) in Chicago. He received his Ph,D. in 1998 from the University of New Orleans. Dr. Shaw's areas of interest are public policy (especially health care), American politics, and comparative politics. He is coauthor of "Vote Controversy" in *Presidential-Congressional Relations* and has several singly and coauthored articles under review at scholarly journals.

CHAPTER 1

Introduction

Ever since George Washington, the interaction between Congress and the president has not only fascinated political observers but usually determined the course of American public policy. No relationship in American politics is more important. Our nation's founders made sure that the two actors would have to engage one another by creating real checks and balances in virtually all of their interactions. But the course of the relationship often has been erratic, navigating obstacles created by the founders to ensure power-sharing between the executive and legislative branches. They may not always work together but they can rarely work apart from each other. Indeed, the enactment (or adoption) of public policy requires constant interaction if changes in government outputs are to occur.

Since the emergence of the modern presidency under Franklin Roosevelt, the presidency has increased its influence in policymaking, presumably at the expense of Congress. Interactions among the first two branches of our national government have indeed become more visible and contentious. The relationship is often viewed as a zero-sum power game, with a clear winner and loser. The scholarly literature typically portrays such a pattern of one institution dominating the other. A problem with such interpretations is that no single pattern characterizes presidential-congressional interactions. Rather, institutional relations are a function of many conditions in the internal and external environments within which presidents and Congress operate in their efforts to adopt public policy.

The purpose of a previous book, *Presidential-Congressional Relations* (Shull 1997), was to describe and better understand relations between these institutions when categorized by policy areas and political time. However, that volume revealed both similarities and differences in such interactions. Some activities were related to one another (e.g., presidents' legislative support and their executive order issuance), while others were more independent (e.g., presidential position taking and legislative vote controversy). The activities were diverse in that some were direct interactions and others were indirect. All four of the above relationships were introduced without attempting to uncover interactions among the presidential-congressional activities themselves or what conditions determine such relations. The present volume systematically

1

examines four direct interactions (government activities) in order to better understand relations between presidents and Congress in the adoption of public policy.

Explaining Congressional-Presidential Relations has several goals apart from demonstrating that such actor relations are multifaceted. The primary thesis is that their behaviors are constrained by environments such that neither presidents nor Congress dominate any of the four types of interaction. As we have asserted, influences on each activity are complex. Accordingly, a tandem institutions perspective (Peterson 1990; LeLoup and Shull 1993; Thurber 1996) has provided the best explanation of support or success to date. However, we seek to explain all four interactions in policy adoption with the same general model. As such, we anticipate that presidential-congressional relations result from a combination of variables from three separable yet interrelated environments (executive, legislative, and exogenous). All three environments should variously influence the four presidential-congressional interactions. We expect that particular elements within the three different environments, such as activities and resources, both facilitate and constrain actor relations. Such exogenous features as the economic health of the nation probably also influence, if less directly, presidential-congressional interactions. Thus, the numerous independent and dependent variables require a multiple perspective as incorporated in this research.

This beginning chapter has several purposes. First, it reviews the extant literature on presidential-congressional relations, illustrating the changing nature of research on this topic. In general, scholarship has moved away from viewing the president as the dominant actor in the relationship, toward one of congressional influence, and ultimately toward emphasizing more equal power sharing between the two institutions. Second, the literature is placed into the context of the four interactions examined in this book: presidential position taking, legislative support, veto propensity, and budget agreement. Third, the broader environments of presidential-congressional interactions are tied in with this research tradition. Fourth, the two controls used in studying presidential-congressional relations (policy areas and political time) are introduced. Fifth, the research explicates how our multiple perspective improves our understanding of presidential-congressional interactions.

RESEARCH ON
PRESIDENTIAL-CONGRESSIONAL INTERACTIONS

The scholarly literature on presidential-congressional relations has grown considerably over the past generation.[1] Much of the early work was descriptive, discussing institutional roles and responsibilities largely in legalistic or constitutional terms (Corwin 1957; Rossiter 1956). This research thought it was most important to see which branch was initiating legislation or formulating policy. Although theories remain in short supply, we now find much more empirical development in the research on the relations between the first two branches of our national government. The emphasis more recently is on adopting public policy rather than on its formulation, often using indicators of presidents' legislative success or support. Although studies relating most directly to decisions that adopt policies are reviewed in this book, just this aspect of presidential-congressional relations alone is broad ranging.

Presidency-Centered Approach

Conflicting interpretations exist about presidential power relations with Congress and the relative discretion that each wields. Alexis de Tocqueville, writing in 1835, saw the president "placed beside the legislature like an inferior and dependent power." Fifty years later, in *Congressional Government* (1885), Woodrow Wilson also viewed Congress as dominant. Yet, later in *Constitutional Government* (1908), Wilson himself, and nearly all twentieth-century writers, saw potential presidential dominance in our governmental system. However, the United States seemingly limits the head of government's programs more than does any other major democracy. Upon investigating presidential-congressional power relationships, one finds that the resources and influence of both presidents and Congress are important.

The post–World War II period obviously saw considerable change in institutional relations. Although some earlier presidents had asserted leadership over Congress, Franklin Roosevelt began a pattern of much greater presidential influence that has persisted to the present time. Among other roles, Clinton Rossiter (1956) saw the president as "chief legislator." Richard Neustadt (1955; 1960) and other writers argued persuasively that the presidential era had arrived and that Congress was ill-equipped to exert policy leadership. Yet Neustadt also realized the limitations of presidential influence. He asserted convincingly that the essence of the president's political leadership over Congress is his ability to persuade. "All presidents wish they could make Congress serve them as a rubber-stamp, converting their agendas into prompt enactments, and most presidents will try to bring that miracle about, whenever and as best they can" (Neustadt 1973, 136).

Neustadt was not alone in viewing presidents as the dominant actor in the relationship. Early studies attempted to discern which branch initiated major legislation, although authors disagreed over the relative percentages. Thomas Schwarz and Earl Shaw contended that presidents initiated less than 50 percent from 1963 to 1972 (1976, 230), but others saw higher figures. Scholars discussing this growing tendency for policy to originate from and even be dominated by the executive include James Robinson (1967) and Samuel Huntington (1961). Of course, who initiates policy may have little importance in the shape policies ultimately take. The "president preeminent" model soon saw a host of challengers.

Congress-Centered Approach

Revisionist writers argued that, despite an increasing reliance on the executive for policy initiation, Congress can still play a major role in the process.[2] A classic early study found that Congress was the dominant partner in twice as many issues from 1880 to 1940, although a trend toward the president during the latter years was observed in the research (Chamberlain 1946). Two writers followed up on Chamberlain's research for the period 1940–67 and found a continued major role for Congress in policy initiation (Moe and Teel 1970). A similar conclusion for the 1950s and 1960s was drawn by James Sundquist (1968). Another observer stated: the "president is often neither the dominant nor the progressive partner in the shaping of domestic policy" (Orfield 1975, 20).

Few writers would go as far as Hugh Gallagher (1977) in asserting that Congress, not the president, is the dominant leader in legislation. Gallagher highlights numerous areas of congressional leadership in domestic policy. Other writers found that Congress was particularly assertive beginning in the late 1960s and into the 1970s (Fisher 1972). At times, Congress has exerted leadership in some social programs that reallocate society's resources from the rich to the poor, such as Medicare and child care. More often than not, however, these earlier authors found policy innovations usually initiated by the executive, determining Congress as less responsive to social rearrangement (Orfield 1975, 262). Innovations by Congress on social policy occur more often when Congress has a liberal (Democratic) cast, particularly following conservative Republican presidents, who show little inclination for such programs. Thus, early research found that Congress plays a more assertive role when presidents are conservative or lack assertiveness (Orfield 1975, 261).[3]

Literature in the 1990s argued diminished presidential influence over Congress, a condition where Congress clearly was not submissive, even in foreign policy (Ripley and Lindsay 1993; Peterson 1994; but see

Hinckley 1994). George Edwards moved away from his 1980 book on *Presidential Influence in Congress* toward presidential constraint in his 1989 volume, *At the Margins*. He found that presidents are not dominant but "are more facilitators than dictators." Jon Bond and Richard Fleisher (1990) using multivariate analysis rather than Edwards's bivariate analysis, observed even less presidential influence than did Edwards. Bond and Fleisher found Congress-centered variables as more important than president-centered variables in explaining legislative support of presidents (see also Brady and Volden 1998).

Tandem Institutions Approach

The early literature suggested that presidents tend to dominate policymaking, particularly the initiation of legislation. Post–World War II presidents were observed to have considerable resources at their disposal. At the same time, the increasingly decentralized and diffused nature of Congress was felt to limit its policymaking role. But the late 1960s and 1970s particularly saw a less submissive Congress with presidential influence perhaps existing only "at the margins." Some have persisted in the view that presidents are more powerful than Congress in the relationship (Mezey 1989; Spitzer 1993), but others see a more equal (or tandem) basis for presidential-congressional relations (Peterson 1990; LeLoup and Shull 1993; Thurber 1996).

Writing in the same year as Bond and Fleisher, Mark Peterson (1990) developed the most elegant model to date of presidential-congressional relations. Like others, he finds limited presidential influence and incorporates a "tandem institutions perspective" based upon the need for cooperation rather than dominance. Instead of using the support score developed by Congressional Quarterly Inc. (CQ), Peterson incorporates a modified and expanded version of the organization's previously available box score measure of success (see chapter 5 in this volume for a discussion of these variables). Peterson then develops an extensive legislative history of the 299 presidential initiatives, offering richer case detail than previously available. He argues that presidents can overcome many barriers to congressional support "by the ways they choose, formulate, and present their policy proposals" (1990, 222).

Multiple Perspectives Approach

We are more persuaded by Peterson's tandem institutions approach (including exogenous influences) than by either a president or Congress-centered approach. Peterson shows that elements from both executive and legislative environments as well as the economy are important for explanation. However, *Explaining Congressional-Presidential Relations* goes beyond even a tandem institutions approach in arguing for an even more encompassing explanation for presidential-congressional interactions.[4] Accordingly, we posit three environments (executive, legislative, and exogenous) as competing determinants of the four presidential-congressional interactions. We expect that none of these environments will dominate *any* of the four government activities but all are important. The three environments encompass both the internal government (structure) and the external (exogenous) environment. This is in keeping with research that documents the importance of both components in understanding policymaking (e.g., Patterson and Caldeira 1988, 118). We consider activities and resources variables within each of the three environmental explanations.

A primary venue for such relations is roll call voting in Congress, including presidential position taking and legislative support of presidents' positions. These indicators collected by Congressional Quarterly, Inc. (CQ), revolve around the adoption of public policy and are widely used in the literature. Also, this book examines two government activities in addition to voting scores (the veto and budgeting). We also seek to understand the interactions among the four activities. In addition to time groupings and policy typologies, three separate environments provide rival explanations of these four direct presidential-congressional interactions. Considerable scholarly literature argues that relations vary across time, in both longer eras and shorter periods; thus political time is an important consideration. Also, if "policy determines politics" (Lowi 1964), grouping the data by issue area may help explain these actors' behavior. Thus, our multiple perspective provides a more encompassing approach to presidential-congressional interactions than the tandem institutions perspective.

PUBLIC POLICY AND POLITICAL TIME APPROACHES

Much of the existing literature offers, consciously or not, a policy content explanation of differences in presidential-congressional relations. Most authors view the president as more important in foreign policy and Congress as more influential in domestic policymaking. Thus, part of the disagreement about relative influence is attributable to policy area differences that constrain the behavior of both branches. A respected body of literature adheres to the notion that the president "proposes" and Congress simply—rather automatically—"disposes."[5] If this early assertion is true, then the foreign policy role of Congress obviously is very different from its substantial power and discretion in domestic policymaking. In addition, interactions have been shown to vary by important time periods and this research incorporates actor behavior differences by certain cycles of time as well as using time series analysis.

Substantive Policy Areas

The policy area approach is based upon the theory that policy content "structure[s] the interests involved and help[s] determine the political arenas in which decisions are contested or made" (Spitzer 1983, xiv). As a result, variations in the content of policies under consideration produce variations in the roles and behaviors of actors. Scholars have suggested that differences in policy content can be substantive (Clausen 1973; Kessel 1974; King and Ragsdale 1988) or functional in nature (Lowi 1964; Froman 1968; Salisbury and Heinz 1970; Edelman 1974). We incorporate a well-known substantive typology in this research, the two presidencies thesis.

Numerous reasons have been offered for why presidents appear to dominate foreign policy (Shull 1979; Fisher 1972). Congress has constitutional powers, but it operates at a clear disadvantage in foreign policy decision making. Writers argue that its diverse and fragmented character makes Congress ill-suited to initiate most foreign policy, often relegating it to reaction rather than initiation (Hargrove 1974, 155; Destler 1974, 85; Donovan 1970). Thus, Congress can exercise negative sanctions by denying support for the president's proposals, but it cannot force him to accept a formal alternative (Hilsman 1968). This view of presidential dominance provides little opportunity for Congress to initiate foreign policy. Indeed, of the twenty-two foreign policy measures Robinson studied, Congress initiated only three, and had an influence greater than the president on only six (1967, 65). Thus, the 1960s writers viewed presidents as having a relatively free hand in foreign policy compared to domestic policy.

This view was advanced by Aaron Wildavsky in a classic 1966 essay. It formed the "two presidencies" thesis utilized in this book as a control for policy content. Researchers after Wildavsky continued to find differences in presidential influence over Congress between domestic and foreign policy but generally not the wide diversity Wildavsky observed (Sperlich 1975; LeLoup and Shull [1979] 1991). If the president has increased his powers somewhat in domestic policy, he has perhaps lost some of his authority vis a vis Congress in the realm of foreign policy (Ripley and Lindsay 1993). In both policy areas, the power of the president in relation to Congress varies over time and issues. Some authors (e.g., LeLoup and Shull [1979] 1991; Manning 1977) feel that budget or economic issues blur the two presidencies thesis. However, the two presidencies scheme has proven effective in differentiating presidential-congressional relations.

Wildavsky ([1966] 1991) used a substantive two-part grouping of policy to establish his two presidencies thesis. He maintained that presidential influence with Congress differs so much in foreign and domestic policy that there are, in effect, two presidencies. During the past thirty years, this thesis has been subject to numerous theoretical and empirical arguments and interpretations. The literature has developed to such an extent that an entire collection of research on the two presidencies appeared (Shull 1991). Up to this point, much of our understanding of presidential-congressional relations in the post–World War II era has been guided by cumulative research on the two presidencies.

Edwards (1980) wrote an important book attempting to explain presidential influence on legislative voting through several variables, including presidential election margins and popularity. Like the studies in the late 1970s, he found less presidential influence, even in foreign policy, than Wildavsky observed. Still, Edwards and others saw opportunities for presidents to have considerable influence. Such influence was found by other writers to exist more in agenda setting and policy formulation (e.g., Light 1982; Shull 1983) rather than later in the policymaking process. The notion of political time may also be useful in understanding presidential-congressional relations.

Using Political Time

In a democracy like the United States, policymaking occurs within a complex internal and external environment. At certain junctures, the political environment is conducive to dramatic policy change, such as the periods following the election of Presidents Franklin Roosevelt, Lyndon Johnson, and Ronald Reagan. Some scholars have attempted to discern broader patterns in public expectations for policy leadership. Arthur Schlesinger Jr. (1986), James David Barber (1980), and James Sundquist (1981) all suggest that American history unfolds in cycles. Schlesinger and Barber argue that public expectations shift from demands for dramatic departures from the past, to a period of consolidation, to a period of reaction and retrenchment. Sundquist emphasizes the existence of particular cycles in presidential-congressional relations. The greater the public desire for consolidation, the greater will be the influence of Congress and the more constraints the president will encounter.

It would be easy to assert that the eighteenth and nineteenth centuries are characterized by congressional dominance and the twentieth century by presidential dominance. Indeed, that is what Sundquist (1981, 21–36) largely does but calls the early period of American history (1789–1860) the era of competition, 1861–1900 the period of congressional ascendancy and, since 1901, the presidential dominance era. Charles Jones has a very different view, admitting that the presidency dominated policymaking in the early portion of the present century, but seeing very little presidential dominance subsequently (1995, 11). Indeed, except for brief periods early in the Johnson and Reagan administrations, Jones believes the post–World War II era is quite balanced, sometimes cooperative, but at other times adversarial. He believes adversity maintains congressional influence (if not dominance).

Stephen Skowronek (1993) views political time differently by tying it in with the notion of presidential leadership. For Skowronek, political time refers to the rise and fall of "regimes," that are led by strong presidents who emerge as leaders after strong election victories. Obviously, most presidents fail to completely crush their election opponents and restructure the politics of the day. Skowronek sees Andrew Jackson and Franklin Roosevelt as playing such political roles in breaking with the past but finds that most other presidents had less lasting effects. Indeed, he presents James Pierce and Jimmy Carter as failing to provide clear courses of action in American politics. Skowronek's main contribution is in showing the necessity of considering individual presidents within the larger political system.

Although some authors refer to long eras in institutional competition (Lewis and Strine 1996), this book explores one mid-range and two short-range cycles of such relations for our extensive forty-seven-year time period (1949–95). The products of policy adoption frequently are measured according to a two-year Congress or a four-or-more-year presidency. However, scholars have observed other cycles of government activities, frequently related to a particular year in presidential term of office (Neustadt 1960; Light 1982; Shull 1983; Nathan 1983; Kessel 1984; Shull and Gleiber 1995; Pfiffner 1996). Hence, important short-term cycles may be reflected in groupings of such years (first, last, reelection) as well as individual presidencies in political time. In addition, we control for two eras of presidential-congressional relations during our time series.

Various groupings of years have been shown by scholars to have theoretical and empirical utility. In this study political time provides valuable controls on the data beyond control for theoretical factors. Dividing these data by early (1949–74) and late (1975–95) should uncover major differences in institutional assertiveness. Literature reveals that previous notions of presidential dominance (Neustadt 1960; Schlesinger 1973) were subsequently challenged by legislative assertiveness in the early 1970s (Barger 1984; Crovitz and Rabkin 1989; LeLoup and Shull 1993, chap. 2). Selected years in the presidential term, while sometimes containing few cases, may also be important to behavior.

Probably the honeymoon year is quite different from other years (Light 1982; Kessel 1984; Shull 1983). James Pfiffner has shown the importance of presidents to "hit the ground running" in their legislative relations. Individual presidents also have been shown to vary in their legislative relations (Beck 1982; Shull and Gleiber 1995) and over time.

Explaining Congressional-Presidential Relations utilizes both analytical devices of aggregation and disaggregation. In our analysis, individual year is the least aggregated, while analyzing all years together is the most aggregated form of analysis. Although incorporating aggregation here as a baseline for comparison, most of the data are analyzed somewhere between these two extremes, including grouping yearly data by early and late eras, by selected year in presidential term of office, and by individual presidents.[6] The utilization of groupings of political time and the two presidencies policy typology help explain the rationale for and the advantages of using both aggregation and disaggregation. These controls provide theoretically meaningful information that goes beyond simple sequence plots.

INTRODUCING FOUR
PRESIDENTIAL-CONGRESSIONAL INTERACTIONS

This volume examines four direct interactions between Congress and the president as they seek to adopt public policy. It considers whether these actors are influenced most by executive, legislative, or external determinants. Several studies analyzing presidential-congressional interactions attempt explanations of one of the CQ measures of presidents' support or success in Congress, occasionally with minor variations thereof. Using multivariate analysis, these authors seek to explain a single dependent variable of vote congruence (Edwards 1989; Bond and Fleisher 1990; Peterson 1990). Although important efforts, CQ indicators of actor preferences based upon congruence on legislative vote positions are limited. Indeed, presidential support in Congress, the most commonly used indicator of presidential-congressional interactions, may not even be the most important one (Shull 1997). In this volume, we include three additional aspects of presidential-congressional relations apart from legislative support: presidential position taking on legislative votes, presidents' propensity to veto legislation, and the level of budget agreement between the two actors.

Presidential Position Taking

The policymaking process is said to occur in sequential steps: agenda setting, formulation, adoption, implementation, and evaluation (Jones

1984; Anderson 1975; Shull 1993; Shull and Gleiber 1994). Certainly during the modern period of American politics, decisions in at least the earliest three stages are shared, and neither actor appears to dominate any portion of the process. Presidents can help further their agenda preferences by taking positions on roll call votes in Congress. Some might consider position taking part of the policy formulation stage (Shull 1983), but it also occurs well into the stage in which policy is adopted. Still, presidential position taking is chronologically the first activity considered here, followed progressively by legislative support. After these vote decisions, presidents decide whether to veto bills passed by Congress, and then budget agreement occurs near the end of the year, often just before congressional adjournment.

Position taking is a discretionary opportunity for presidents to assert leadership in the legislative arena. Presidents cannot introduce legislation in Congress but can express their preferences through this device by responding to roll call votes in Congress. Presidents take positions selectively on recorded votes, so these should be issues they care about, where they feel it is necessary to take a stand, and when the action could help achieve their preferences. Due to the dramatic increase in number of recorded votes during the 1970s and 1980s, most bills cleared from committee come to a roll call vote in one or both chambers. CQ indicates whether the president takes positions on individual votes and we total the number of positions per year. Presidential position taking itself has been examined much less extensively than its related legislative support. Yet position taking on roll call votes is an important avenue for interaction between Congress and the president.

Agenda setting is an early stage in policymaking, but is viewed more often from the presidential than congressional perspective (Light 1982; Shull 1983). These and other authors have examined presidential public documents (e.g., speeches, messages, letters) to ascertain presidential agenda preferences (Cohen 1997). Presidential messages are also the basis for determining CQ's position taking on roll call votes. Such messages occur at the very beginning of the legislative session from presidential state of the union addresses and continue throughout the year. Patterns of policymaking in the post–World War II era depend very much on the nature of both presidential and congressional agendas. Even when their agendas coincide, each branch may have opposing partisan and ideological goals. One characteristic that stands out in policymaking is its incremental nature, making agendas rather stable, despite changes in officials and policy preferences in both branches of government.

The conventional wisdom, then, paints the presidents in a predominant role in agenda setting and policy formulation, particularly during their honeymoon year in office (Neustadt 1960; Light 1982; Shull 1983). In the area of foreign policy particularly, Barbara Hinckley (1994) argues that the congressional role has declined from its assertiveness in the 1970s. Ronald Moe and Steven Teel (1970) were among the earliest challengers of a presidential dominant model in initiating public policy. Yet, other scholars see greater power sharing than Hinckley uncovers. Studies show that while assertive presidents can greatly influence the agenda, Congress plays an important role later, particularly in policy adoption (Baumgartner and Jones 1993; Kingdon 1984; Jones 1994, 164). Presidents who push their agenda preferences with position taking likely have greater success with Congress than do more passive presidents (Fett 1994; Covington et al. 1995; Shull 1997).

Legislative Support

Much literature on presidential-congressional relations examines measures of legislative support or success using indicators collected by CQ. Beginning in 1945, the organization introduced the box score measure in an effort to tap presidential relations with Congress. The box score seemingly measures presidential *success* with Congress by recording whether Congress passed legislation that presidents proposed in their public messages. The reasons for success may be serendipitous or otherwise and sometimes CQ felt that the success scores were misinterpreted. The organization subsequently dropped the box score but contributed to some confusion by developing another measure they call "success," which Lyn Ragsdale (1996, 383) more appropriately labels "congruence" (the percentage of presidential vote positions upheld by Congress). In contrast to success, *support* connotes an alignment with presidential preferences. Support refers to agreement between presidents and individual legislators on various aggregations of roll call votes. Understanding this distinction is useful when analyzing CQ box scores and support scores (Edwards 1985; 1989; Shull 1983). Distinctions among success, support, and other CQ measures, such as key votes, need to be kept in mind (Shull 1997, chapter 6).

Although often used interchangeably, success and support are sometimes confused with broader concepts, such as influence or leadership (see discussions in Pritchard 1983; Edwards 1980). By understanding these different meanings, scholars can more easily clarify what they want to explain. Such definition "is actually a stage at which researchers may easily stumble and undermine the remainder of their efforts" (Edwards 1989, 16). Although success and support have proven useful and reliable (Bond, Fleisher, and Krutz 1996), further progress can be achieved through hard work and ingenuity. Using bivariate and multivariate analyses (e.g., Edwards 1980; Bond and Fleisher 1990; Peterson 1990), success and support variables have helped improve our understanding of presidential-congressional relations. Aaron Wildavsky's ([1966] 1991) two presidencies thesis was an early empirical examination of presidents' legislative success. Subsequent scholars adapted different indicators of success and support in testing this thesis (see selections in Shull 1991). Other scholars have given particular attention to determinants of presidents' legislative success or support (Shull 1983; Bond and Fleisher 1990; Edwards 1980; 1989).

The CQ support score is not a measure of successful presidential initiatives to Congress (the president's agenda), but rather average agreement with his preferences (positions) on votes before Congress, positions that it supports or rejects. Therefore, it is the congressional rather than the presidential agenda that becomes the focus and scholars should not confuse the two. Like the original success measure (the box score), the support score possesses both advantages and disadvantages. Because a support score is assigned to each member of Congress, it is possible to construct a variety of data aggregations. For example, these individual scores can be combined by state, region, party, ideology, and other groupings. As a result, the support score is more versatile than the box score, which is inherently limited by its high level of aggregation. Of course, support scores are a poorer measure of presidential preferences. Critics commonly note three disadvantages: (1) as with the box score, all issues are weighted equally; (2) ambiguities exist in identifying which votes to use; and (3) bias may be introduced by including routine, noncontroversial votes (Bond and Fleisher 1990; Bond, Fleisher, and Krutz 1996; Edwards 1980, 1985; Peterson 1990). Despite problems, legislative support provides an important basis for understanding presidential-congressional interactions.

Veto Propensity

The *veto* is a formal mechanism that makes the president an effective participant in the legislative process. This tool provides presidents the opportunity to shape legislation and guarantees congressional consideration of presidential preferences (Brady and Volden 1998). Robert Spitzer (1988, 25) argues that the presidential veto is his central domestic resource. We believe the veto is a complex power, best understood by theoretically and empirically relating it to the other activities in adopting public policy. Understanding the use of the veto can help us uncover presidential influence over legislation and it is an important manifestation of presidential-congressional interactions. However, the considerable scholarly research on the veto (Watson 1993; Hoff 1991; Rohde and Simon 1985) has considered the device largely in isolation.

Presidential vetoes provide a unique opportunity for examining elite political decision making. The Constitution gives the president only ten days (Sundays excepted) during regular sessions of Congress in which to sign or veto bills. The enrolled bill process (see Wayne et al. 1979) provides the president with advice from relevant agencies through a memorandum from the Office of Management and Budget. Of course, this potentially reduces the time available to consider each bill, further reducing the ability of the president to effectively wield his authority. Unlike most other forms of authoritative allocation of values, the veto power is not granted to a collegial deliberative body, but rather to the unitary executive.

Some observers play down the power of the veto, implying that it is neither strong nor important. For example, until legislation that became effective January 1997, presidents had no item veto, unlike most state governors. Accordingly, they had to accept all of the bill or veto it entirely. In addition, vetoes may be only temporary since Congress may override the veto or revise the legislation only slightly, forcing continued confrontation. Historically, most vetoes have been on relatively unimportant private matters.[7] Major public policy decisions are not always involved as scholarly work has shown (Watson 1988; Ringelstein 1985; McKay 1989; Woolley 1991). Finally, no president has vetoed a significant proportion of legislation passed and, except for Ford, the propensity to veto has declined generally since Truman, even in the presence of divided government. Nonetheless, the veto is a strong presidential tool and an important manifestation of executive-legislative relations. It is a powerful weapon because it is difficult to overturn and seldom reversed by the required two-thirds vote of both houses of Congress. Indeed, only 7 percent of presidential vetoes have been overridden by Congress.[8]

The veto chronologically follows position taking and support and is our most direct activity in the policy adoption stage. However, it is even more controversial and it is used when presidents are weak rather than strong. Presidents use the device or threat thereof to prevent policy adoption rather than attaining their own preferred legislation. If the veto is upheld, then the status quo of public policy remains since no new policy has been adopted. The growing use of omnibus legislation and continuous resolutions have complicated presidential-congressional interactions and have likely lessened the propensity to veto.

Budget Agreement

Budgeting is the fourth and last direct interaction between Congress and the president in the process of adopting public policy. It results from

Congress's decision in 1921 (Budget and Accounting Act) to share the power of the purse by requiring the president to submit an annual budget for legislative consideration. Modern presidents have taken this enhanced power as an opportunity to further their policy preferences (Mowrey 1980; Kamlet 1987). Although research shows striking stability and incrementalism in budgeting (Davis, Dempster, and Wildavsky 1966), it has also proven to be much more contentious since the mid-1970s, perhaps as a result of the Congressional Budget Impoundment and Control Act of 1974 (Kettl 1992; Brady and Volden 1998). Even though the two institutions have very different budget priorities, Congress largely depends on presidents to make necessary budget cuts (Wildavsky 1988). Although deficit politics has heightened political maneuvering and strengthened the president, deadlock increasingly is common in budget decision making.

Like the veto, research on budgeting has a long and noble tradition in the scholarly literature (see Fenno 1966). Since Roosevelt in the 1930s presidents have used the 1921 Budget Act to further their policy preferences by pushing their programmatic requests. Prior to the modern era, the United States had a long tradition of balanced budgets and, despite contentiousness, relatively stable relations between the two branches. Wildavsky (1964) wrote eloquently of institutional agreement over a budget base, around which changes made by Congress usually were small or incremental. However, deficit politics began about the time Wildavsky first wrote, and he subsequently found incrementalism less relevant (1988). Indeed, no formula can substitute for political consensus, which has been much harder to achieve between the two branches. The growing deficit during the 1980s made consensus even more problematic under frequently divided government (Kettl 1989; Cox et al. 1993).

Some writers would like to examine the budget from an economic rather than political orientation. These authors often seek rational models of decision making (ranging from PPBS to MBO to ZZB) but others doubt reforms would affect this budget process (Ippolito 1978, 196–98; Kramer 1979, chapters 3–5).[9] However, most political scientists argue that budgeting is inherently political and it is impossible to remove politics from the process (Kettl 1992, chapter 3; Wildavsky 1988, chapter 6). Budgeting has certainly developed into an institutional power struggle where the agenda has moved more toward presidential control and shifted somewhat away from Congress (Kettl 1992, chapter 6). Congress sought to gain the upper hand in the budget process with the Budget Act of 1974, but found that centralized decision making in Congress is elusive and individual committee decisions remain important. Wildavsky (1988, chapter 4) argues that the act brought more checks and balances but no more congressional control of the process. However, congressional Republicans sought greater influence for party leaders on budgeting after gaining a majority in both chambers in 1995.

Congress did chip away at presidential dominance in budgeting. Howard Shuman (1992, 214) states that the 1974 legislation was designed to discipline both institutions. However, the emerging deficit made discipline even from the conservative Republican 104th and 105th Congresses problematic. They were not able to gain the budget goals that they had sought in challenging President Clinton. Growing frustration helps to explain why Congress felt it necessary to allow presidents to have a modified item veto over funding measures that pass Congress.[10] David Mowrey (1980) suggests that Congress is unable to fill the vacuum in budgeting, even under ineffective presidential management. The 1980s and 1990s brought budget resolutions that were particularly controversial and partisan (Cox et al. 1993). Allen Schick (1986, 8–15) shows how the changed process allowed Congress to influence presidents' budgeting plans but simultaneously gave presidents greater leverage over congressional decisions. Sometimes deadlock occurred while it was avoided on other occasions. Thus, studying budget agreement, defined as the proportion of presidential requests that are appropriated by Congress, should provide insight into increased actor interdependence in policy adoption.

SUMMARY AND CONCLUSION

The final section of the chapter begins by laying out the broad parameters of our research. It reiterates the relevance of both structural and environmental conditions for presidential-congressional interactions. Structural variables encompass internal resources, and activities and such variables as size of executive and legislative staffs are incorporated in this research. Environmental conditions include resources and constraints, both within the two institutions (such as presidents' popular approval and legislative workload), as well as exogenous elements that may also affect their behavior. The final section of the conclusion lays out what we consider to be the five major contributions of our study.

Structure and Environment

The state of the nation, public expectations, and partisan aspects of the two branches are among the many environmental factors that help define parameters for policymaking and shape presidential-congressional relations. The structure of institutions is also important, resulting in differing constituencies, electoral calendars, and public perceptions of the proper role of each actor. Structure includes particular conditions within both institutions, such as norms, tenure, and degree of centralization. Literature about who initiates legislation has been examined and, thus, agenda-setting leadership and followership are important to study to understand final decisions that adopt policy. Contentiousness due to frequently divided government has exacerbated institutional conflict in recent years (Thurber 1996; Shaw and Shull 1996; Edwards, Barrett, and Peake 1997).

The common starting point for studies of presidential-congressional relations is the separation of powers—the division of executive, legislative, and judicial branches in the Constitution. Yet the phrase separation of powers is misleading. The Constitution intermingled powers among three branches of the national government and the states, thereby overlapping responsibility for governing. It is more accurate to think of separation of powers, as Richard Neustadt has characterized it, as "separated institutions sharing powers" (1960, 26). But separated does not mean independent and the primary thesis of this book is that policy adoption requires substantial cooperation. Contentiousness has grown but only ultimate agreement leads to any change in public policy.

The Constitution also proscribes the structure of government, which plays an important role in institutional capacity. The founders' decision to share power through checks and balances would prevent tyranny by blocking the accumulation of power by any one branch. This was accomplished by placing institutions in conflict and competition with each other. James Madison, the principal architect of the Constitution, described in the *Federalist* (no. 51) a system in which "ambition must be made to counter ambition." As the scope of government expanded, and the institutional capacity of both the executive and legislative increased, separation of powers sometimes made governing more difficult.

Contribution of the Research

Explaining Congressional-Presidential Relations enhances the theoretical and empirical development of the existing literature in several ways. First, we seek to understand the multifaceted nature of relations between the first two branches of our national government. The analysis begins by studying four direct interactions between presidents and Congress as they adopt public policy. Although prior research has examined each of these activities extensively, no one has examined them *together,* as interdependent phenomena. Trend analysis will improve our understanding of such relationships over the extended period of our analysis. We are convinced that the legislative support or success that presidents obtain, while important, does not reflect the sum total of such interactions. In this context, we seek a better understanding of whether and how our four presidential-congressional activities are interrelated.

Second, it is important to study whether policy areas help us understand presidential-congressional relations. We expect to observe differences between foreign and domestic policy across our four interactions, thereby confirming the two presidencies as a valid typology of policy content. Policy content may indeed help explain the politics and, perhaps, even the process of policymaking (as envisioned by Ranney 1968; Lowi 1964). And recall that we do envision presidential position taking, legislative support, veto propensity, and budget agreement as occurring within a dynamic, interdependent process. This book will strive to observe the theoretical and empirical utility of policymaking by policy area more definitively (through multivariate analysis in several venues) than has occurred heretofore.

Third, apart from controlling for policy areas, *Explaining Congressional-Presidential Relations* also groups these government activities by political time: overall and by trend, dichotomized by early and late eras, by selected year in presidents' term of office, and by presidents separately (from Harry Truman to Bill Clinton). Research has suggested that each of these time components have explanatory power (Neustadt 1980; Light 1982; Kessel 1984; Shull 1983, 1997; Mayhew 1992; Fiorina 1996; Gibson 1995; Lewis and Strine 1996). Examining the presidents individually (and also chronologically) offers a temporal component to the research as well. Yet we will see that time can be treated theoretically as well as simply empirically.

Fourth, we model the explanatory factors differently than has been attempted heretofore. Three broad environments, containing both activity and resource variables, are first examined to see if they are related. Then we compare their relative explanatory power on each of the four actor relations variables. Intuitively, executive variables should influence "executive" actions (position taking and veto propensity) more, while the legislative environment should better explain "legislative"-oriented variables (legislative support and budget agreement). However, we expect that interactions are more complicated and that components from both environments, as well as exogenous factors, differentially influence the four actor relations variables. External considerations, such as the state of the economy, are seldom incorporated in models seeking to explain presidential-congressional relations (but see Peterson 1990), and we include several.

We cover a lot of ground in *Explaining Congressional-Presidential Relations*, but are also convinced that complexity is the nature of the relationship. These interactions cannot, nor should they be, represented by a single dependent variable as has often occurred. Because the four interactions all tap policy adoption, we expect them to be interrelated. The study also offers a long time series of data over forty-seven years for use by scholars of presidential-congressional relations. At present, research relies on CQ measures for position taking, success, vetoes, and surprisingly elusive budget information from that organization and other sources. Each of these variables suffers from limitations that are not always recognized. None are satisfactory by themselves but, by comparing them directly using a common explanatory framework, theory building on presidential-congressional interactions is enhanced. Thus, assessing several components of policy adoption, comparing the influence of three environments, and controlling for policy areas and political time, provide useful contributions to the literature on the interactions between the first two branches of our national government.

CHAPTER 2

A Multiple Perspectives Approach

INTRODUCTION

In this book we consider the president and Congress as distinct actors who compete to adopt their respective policy preferences. While not explicitly stated as such, this view is consistent with the constitutional establishment of separate executive and legislative branches designed to compete with one another to prevent tyranny. In other words, our founding fathers chose to fragment power between multiple actors who would struggle over their varying preferences with certain institutional checks to prevent any actor from being able to singularly adopt only his or her preferences. While competition between Congress and the president is pervasive, it must ultimately be resolved for public policy to be adopted. We believe that an understanding of the tension between competition and cooperation helps explain presidential-congressional interactions.

The president is often thought of as a single individual, but it would be impossible by virtue of the sheer volume of tasks for any president to act alone. Considerable scholarly literature debates whether to treat the presidency as a singular or plural institution (King and Ragsdale 1988; Neustadt 1960; Lowi 1985; Hager and Sullivan 1994; Rockman 1984; Edwards, Kessel, and Rockman 1993; Ragsdale and Theiss 1997). The president is one person but the presidency today encompasses over a thousand individuals. As such, considerable support staff are available to the president; however, at a certain level of abstraction, this collection of actors can be thought of as one executive actor since they serve at the pleasure of the president. As political appointees, executive staff do not even require Senate confirmation and, thus, it is in their own interests to closely reflect presidential preferences.[1]

Congress presents a slightly more difficult problem in that it is composed of not only two separate chambers but also multiple legislators, parties, and constituencies in both houses.[2] Thus, a problem with considering Congress as a single actor is the fact that it is composed of multiple actors who do not speak with a single voice. No single set of preferences exist that can be ascribed to Congress but, instead, a collection of 535 preferences exist. However, two decision rules allow a singular set of preferences to emerge for Congress. First, bills must pass each house by majority rule, and second, bills must pass in both houses in exactly the same form. Accordingly, one can consider those items that pass in both houses as constituting congressional preferences. Thus, both the president and Congress can be conceptualized as singular actors.

Our analysis is not particularly concerned with the details of the individual preferences held by each actor. It is enough for us to assume that there are two actors with distinct preferences. For our purposes these preferences are expressed through the four interactions that are part of policy adoption. The president expresses his preferences by taking positions on votes on bills in the legislative arena. Congress expresses preferences for or against presidential preferences via its support (or lack thereof) for his positions. The president responds to legislative views through the use of the veto and finally, Congress again expresses its preferences via the purse strings by choosing which programs and to what extent it will appropriate money requested by the president.

Explaining Congressional-Presidential Relations examines these four contemporary relations between Congress and the president. We seek to understand the interactions among these government activities in adopting public policy. The primary thesis of this book is that neither executive nor legislative factors dominate any of the four government activities. We assert that presidential-congressional relations result from separable yet interrelated environments (executive, legislative, and exogenous). All three environments should variously influence these four direct presidential-congressional interactions. We also place policy area and political time controls on these relationships. The dichotomous policy division, domestic versus foreign, is widely examined (Wildavsky 1966; Edwards 1989; Bond and Fleisher 1990; Shull 1991). Aaron Wildavsky's two presidencies thesis appears extensively in the literature and is incorporated here as a control on presidential-congressional interactions. In addition to policy area, we also control for three groupings of political time in these relations: by early/late eras, by selected year in presidential term of office, and by presidents individually.

This chapter lays out in greater detail our multiple perspectives approach to presidential-congressional relations. First, we discuss our research framework using broad brush strokes. We also examine the extant literature, showing its rather diverse nature. Our primary concern is to illustrate the interrelationships among these two actors in adopting public policy. We posit a model where both Congress and presidents use available resources and conduct activities to further their policy preferences. We discuss the singular versus plural nature of the two institutions and how their complicated interactions force us to develop an expanded multiple perspective to better understand the complexity of these government activities.

FRAMEWORK FOR ANALYSIS

We extend previous research by identifying four presidential-congressional interactions that relate to policy adoption. We test the interactions by applying the same general multiple perspectives model to each interaction. Although differences should occur in the way that both the broader environments and the individual component variables affect the different interactions (dependent variables), in general each interaction should be influenced by more than one environment. In addition to the broader environments, we categorize each variable within each environment by whether or not it is a resource or activity variable. We also expect that particular independent variables are potentially important in explaining each of the four interactions.[3] Thus, our analysis in each substantive chapter begins by applying a uniform model of our three environments (executive, legislative, and exogenous) to the particular interaction.

We begin the analysis by examining the trend of each interaction. Then we control for political time with variables for historical era (dichotomous variable for pre- and post-1974), selected years in presidential term, and regime (individual president). Next, we present our general model as an explanation for each of the four presidential-congressional interactions. In this sense, each interaction may have a somewhat unique explanation. However, at the broader level of the three environments, we expect a more generalizable finding: at least two and in some cases all three environments contribute to the explanation of each of the presidential-congressional interactions. Since the analysis is not limited to just institutional variables, we term our approach toward understanding presidential-congressional relations "a multiple perspectives approach." Finally, we control for policy area using the Wildavsky foreign/domestic policy dichotomy.

Environments in Adopting Public Policy

The executive and legislative environments are institutional and for our purposes contain both resource and activity variables. In addition to these environments, we have added a third element, the exogenous environment. Although much of what occurs during policy adoption will be the result of institutional resources and activities, the external environment can and often will affect actors' ideas and preferences in policy adoption. For each environment, we employ three variables to tap the dimension of that environment. Obviously, these three environments (executive, legislative, or exogenous) are broader than just the three component variables. However, one could infinitely add variable after variable to each environment in an attempt to fully capture any of these three environments. Consequently, we focus on three variables for each environment that we feel, taken as a whole: (1) tap the primary domain and breadth of the environment, (2) are well founded both practically and theoretically in previous research, and (3) constitute a solid model in that the variables are theoretically related but not highly correlated empirically with one another.

Executive. A wide range of factors have been identified as related to presidential-congressional relations. Richard Neustadt's (1960) view of presidential power as influence focuses attention on the conjunction of formal authorities and a range of personal skills and relevant political resources. The powerful president uses more than his constitutional authority in the legislative process to increase the congruence between his preferences and public policy adopted into law. Whereas Neustadt argues that popular prestige and professional reputation are the president's primary political resources, the empirical literature has focused on such resources as presidential popularity and the strength of the president's party in Congress (Edwards 1980; Gleiber and Shull 1992; Gleiber, Shull, and Walligora 1998). We believe these factors are theoretically important and influence presidential decision making in policy adoption.

Legislative. The literature on legislative decision making is even more developed. Studies show a wide variety of influences on how legislators make decisions, ranging from personal preferences to political party and constituency influences (Froman 1963; Kingdon 1978; Clausen 1973). Even characteristics of the institution itself, such as leadership and staff resources, are important (Fox and Hammond 1977; Davidson and Oleszek 1996). As for presidents, both activities and resources should influence the decisions of legislators, individually and collectively. Dennis Gleiber and Steven Shull (1992) used several of these activities and resources to predict presidential-congressional relations and so a range of variables should be important in our analysis.

Exogenous. These anticipated relationships also are likely influenced by exogenous factors, which we expect have an impact over time. This expectation is in keeping with the view that political actors are influenced by forces outside their institutions, a view derived from systems theory (Easton 1965). The size of government and state of the economy, for example, should increasingly influence presidential-congressional relations (Peterson 1990). These external factors constrain government programs. We expect that particular elements within the three different environments both facilitate and constrain presidential-congressional relations. Thus, circumstances entirely outside government are not ignored in our design. Such external features probably also influence, if less directly, presidential-congressional relations. In addition, the exogenous environment contains the most directly related process (interaction) variable occurring alongside each activity.

Assessment. The process variable is expected to be another influence on the particular interaction we are examining. For example, we use presidential position taking as our process variable when explaining legislative support. Since we are using year as the unit of analysis, it is not possible to posit a specific chronological process from position taking to support to veto propensity to budget agreement. This is due to the fact that we are considering all phenomena for each interaction at one time by using annual data; yet we know that not all positions are taken before all measures of support, and support shifts from bill to bill even while vetoes may be occurring. However, if one considers individual pieces of legislation, it should be clear that such a temporal process exists. That is, a bill exists and the president either takes a position or does not. This decision then influences the support given to the bill by Congress and, subsequently, whether or not it is vetoed and funds appropriated.

Although we do not posit such a specific process when using year as the unit of analysis, we do anticipate that certain of the dependent variables are more likely to influence other dependent variables. Again using position taking and support as an example, it is clear that not all positions are taken prior to all indicators of support. However, since support levels are typically adjusted in response to whether or not the president takes a position on a bill, we can say that support is generally reactive to position taking. Therefore, even though we cannot specify a chronological sequence, we should expect certain of the dependent variables to be influenced by others. In the case of the example above, even aggregated to the annual level, we expect position taking to influence levels of support. Similarly support should affect veto usage but not the reverse.

Presidential-Congressional Interactions

We have argued that explaining presidential-congressional interactions requires considering the executive environment, the legislative environment, and those exogenous influences from outside government. Such interactions likely vary over time. Recall too that considerable literature examines policy as occurring sequentially in stages, typically from agenda setting to evaluation (Jones 1984; Anderson 1975). Shull and Gleiber (1994) test for such a process but use a single indicator to reflect each stage in the process. In our analysis, we view even the single adoption stage as relatively complex and identify at least four direct interactions occurring between Congress and the president: presidential position taking, legislative support, veto propensity, and budget agreement. This next section reviews existing findings regarding the four government activities and suggests how they relate to the adoption of public policy.

Presidential Position Taking. Presumably position taking reflects presidential preferences, but such floor vote positions are based on matters regarding Congress', not necessarily the president's agenda. While such position taking is used to express presidents' preferences in the legislative arena, the extent to which Congress actually supports presidential positions reveals Congress's own assertiveness, deference to presidential preferences, and, in part, executive-legislative policy congruence. During the legislative process, some of these votes and positions are actually changed as Congress modifies bills from introduction to final floor voting. Although Congressional Quarterly (CQ) monitors these changes, they are difficult to discern. Accordingly, support and related aggregate measures are not perfect indicators of presidents' legislative preferences, perhaps even at the time of the vote (see chapter 5). Still, presidents are unlikely to take positive stands on legislation they oppose (Peterson 1990). While many of these roll call votes on which position taking is based deal with measures initiated by the executive, they are now in the legislative arena, frequently in revised form.

Chapter 1 revealed that little systematic research exists on presidential position taking. In a prior study (Shull 1997, chapter 4), presidential position taking was compared on all legislative votes and on important legislative votes only (Mayhew 1992). One of the particular differences observed between all and important legislation is the much greater frequency of position taking on the latter—twice the rate as on all other legislation. Also, important legislation revealed more variation by presidential party than did all legislation, especially on foreign policy position taking. Additionally, the number of roll call votes cast relates to the level of presidential position taking. Certainly it occurred *relatively* less frequently in the 1980s and 1990s as the number of roll call votes increased than during the 1960s when fewer occurred (Shull 1997, chapter 4).

More specific findings can also be summarized by policy areas and by political time. As expected, position taking increased over time and was greater after 1974 than before. Also, it was greater on domestic than foreign policy. Position taking occurred least often during the first year of the presidential term, contrary to expectation. However, when controlling for the number of roll call votes taken, position taking is actually least during reelection years, a time when presidents may have less time to devote to more mundane (as opposed to important) legislative matters (Shull 1997, chapter 4). Reelection years also revealed the least differences by policy area with much less attention to domestic policy then.

Among individual presidents, Johnson and Kennedy were the most assertive presidents, as anticipated, and Eisenhower and Reagan were least assertive in taking vote positions. This latter finding was not exactly as expected, because Ford, who had been so nonassertive in civil rights position taking (Shull 1993), was actually twice as assertive as Reagan in frequency of position taking (but equal on position taking as a percentage of roll call votes). Eisenhower took the highest percentage of his positions on foreign policy while Johnson took the fewest percentage there. Although most positions presumably reflect presidential preferences, sometimes presidents appear to take them just to be on the winning side (Shull 1983). All in all, examining presidential position taking descriptively by political time and policy areas (Shull 1997, chapter 4), proved a worthwhile enterprise.

Legislative Support. Congressional Quarterly, Inc. collected both success and support measures for a considerable period of time and, despite problems, they have been widely used in the literature of presidential-congressional relations. Variations on an earlier available success measure have appeared (Light 1982; Peterson 1990; Shull 1997, chapter 6). Here, we present findings on the CQ support measure across the substantive typology of public policy and the groupings of political time. One advantage of CQ's support score over its earlier box score is that it is available overall and for individual legislators. Scholars and journalists alike have relied on this indicator to reflect legislative-executive attitude congruence. With the success (box score) measure, similar content analysis judgments of presidential preferences are required and some margin of error may also exist. The support score offers a broad spectrum of presidential-congressional interactions (more so than the box score; Bond, Fleisher, and Krutz 1996, 110), encompassing both routine and controversial matters. Do the various CQ indicators measure presidential influence or power in Congress?

Robert Dahl defines power (or influence) as "A influences B to the extent that he gets B to do something that he would otherwise not do" (1963, 40). This definition of influence (or an analogue of it) is widely accepted by members of the scholarly community (Edwards 1991; Mouw and MacKuen 1992; Pritchard 1983; Sullivan 1991b). From this perspective, influence in Congress is observed only when members deviate from the way they would normally vote (Mouw and MacKuen 1992, 581). This more stringent definition undercuts past efforts to measure presidential influence using box scores and support scores (Bond and Fleisher 1980; Edwards 1980). Anita Pritchard argues that "support scores indicate only how often congressional members vote as the president would have liked them to vote, which does not mean the president influenced the voting decision" (Pritchard 1986, 481). Thus, support scores reflect assertiveness or policy congruence, but not necessarily influence. Understanding the measurement controversies better prepares the reader to assess the CQ support score used here and other alternatives. Researchers generally have found that presidential party margin is more important than public approval in influencing presidents' legislative support (Edwards 1989; Bond and Fleisher 1990; Peterson 1990; Brace and Hinckley 1992; Rivers and Rose 1985; Collier and Sullivan 1995; Ostrom and Simon 1985).

Shull (1997, chapter 6) observed important policy area and political time differences in legislative support. Overall, support has declined somewhat over time and, while a mere one percentage point differentiates the foreign and domestic support of Democratic presidents, a more identifiable 6.5 percentage points difference was found for Republicans. This finding confirms the greater two presidencies finding for Republicans than Democrats that Bond and Fleisher (1990) observed. Johnson's and Nixon's support was almost imperceptible by policy area, while domestic and foreign support diverged ten or greater percentage points for Ford and Reagan. Year-in-presidential-term differences were not very significant for legislative support, with only first years differing from other years by significantly higher levels. Also, it was only during first years that major differences occurred by policy areas, with presidents' foreign policy vote positions being supported nearly six percentage points more often than their domestic positions.

Veto Propensity. Our four diverse government activities help reveal the president's and Congress's understanding of the nature and functions of their offices. The propensity of presidents to use their veto power is the subject of much prior research. The congressional override of vetoes has also received some scholarly attention but that is beyond the scope of this study.[4] Some scholars find that Democrats are more assertive than Republicans and, thus, will use the veto more (Lee 1975). The statistical result may simply be a reflection of the partisan nature of divided government during this particular historical era. Indeed, other scholars find presidential party, which, of course, is related to ideology, less predictive of veto use (Copeland 1983; Simonton 1987; Shull, Gleiber, and Ringelstein 1992). Rather than presidential party, we consider whether presidential popularity and other resources and activities also influence veto propensity.

Research has examined veto propensity over long time periods, and its usage has varied greatly. Lewis and Strine (1996, 102) observe increased use of the veto during reelection years in the modern era. Another control for political time is individual president. Some presidents, like Richard Nixon and Gerald Ford, used the veto to reorder congressional priorities (Spitzer 1988, 84). Ironically, Ford, who was relatively passive in position taking (Shull 1997, chapter 4), was not so in veto propensity. Clearly, this was one area of high assertiveness for him compared to other presidents. However, he was more politically vulnerable than most presidents, who realize that the veto is essentially a negative weapon of last resort, once all other presidential tools have been employed. Modern presidents treat the veto as a scarce resource and use it infrequently because its use reveals political weakness rather than strength.

In deciding to veto, the president does more than examine his political resources. He also examines his likelihood of success. Prior successful use of the veto should increase his willingness to use it again. On the other hand, prior overrides should reduce veto use as some scholars observe (Copeland 1983; Rohde and Simon 1985). Thus, the greater the net positive experience with the veto, the greater its use, while less prior success should result in greater presidential caution. However, prior legislative decisions may account for less of the veto decision than do other factors. This is because such specific decisions are dependent upon presidential interactions with politically relevant others. Literature already shows many of these components, such as the presidents' party margin in Congress, to be influential in their legislative success (Edwards 1989; Bond and Fleisher 1990; Rivers and Rose 1985). However, rather than using variables as individual influences, we place them in the context of a broader multiple perspectives approach. The existing research does not delve very deeply into examining the veto by political time or policy area (but see Ringelstein 1985; Lewis and Strine 1996). Therefore, we develop these notions more fully in this volume.

Budget Agreement. The dominant concept in traditional research on budgeting is that, unlike the veto, budgeting is not very controversial between Congress and the president. This notion relates to Aaron Wildavsky's (1964) assertion of incrementalism, or small change from prior decisions. However, a number of writers questioned the theory of incrementalism before Wildavsky (1988) himself recanted it. Some scholars argue that the concept is ambiguous; that an incremental process does not necessarily produce an incremental result (Bailey and O'Connor 1975; Berry 1990) . Lance LeLoup (1980) also contends that the concept is "detrimental to understanding the dynamics and process of budgeting." Paul Schulman (1975) and others show that budgets of certain agencies, such as early in the NASA space program, may not exhibit incremental tendencies at all. Authors also disagree over the magnitude of incrementalism, using figures ranging from 5 to 20 percent change in congressional appropriations from presidential budget requests (Shull and Franklin 1978).

Research shows that individual presidents have different budget goals and vary in their use of this budget tool. David Mowrey (1980) examined three administrations (Eisenhower through Johnson), finding that presidential preferences are paramount. He found that such goals were more important than either staff structure or personality in presidents' budget preferences. Ironically, the deficit grew the most under the most conservative president of the post–World War II era, Ronald Reagan. Mark Kamlet (1987) observes that Reagan was able to influence the defense budget but was not able to cut the domestic budget as much as he had hoped. The deficit increase was due largely to Reagan's tax cut, which also reduced budget options of both presidents and Congress.

Individual presidents see the budget process differently and exhibit varying degrees of involvement. LeLoup (1980, 144–46) shows that Gerald Ford, who most would consider a nonassertive president, was actually a budget "enthusiast" as was Harry Truman. Both presidents brought an interest in the topic with them from their years in Congress. On the other hand, LeLoup calls Dwight Eisenhower and Richard Nixon budget "reluctants." Since LeLoup's book, we know that Ronald Reagan, Jimmy Carter, and Bill Clinton were much more involved in the details of budgeting than was George Bush, who expressed his boredom with the topic (Rockman 1991). These differences among individual presidents suggest that examining presidents separately will be a useful control toward understanding budget preferences and activities.

Apart from individual presidents, another political time variable is divided government, which Cox and coauthors (1993) argue increases conflict over the allocation of resources. However, Donald Kettl (1992) and David Brady and Craig Volden (1998) observe that unified government does not necessarily solve budgeting problems. As mentioned earlier, we use political party in a different way, as part of the legislative environment rather than as a control for political time (see Shull 1997). Certainly presidential party differences emerge where, at least in the modern era, Democratic presidents have been more willing to commit greater total funding than have Republicans (Cox et al. 1993, 99). Little research has examined budgeting by our third control for political time, year in presidential term of office. A notable exception is James Pfiffner's work (1996, 94), which shows the necessity of different budget strategies during the president's first year compared to the last (lameduck) year.

At least some differences in budget priorities by policy areas have been observed. Democrats request greater funding for domestic social programs and Republicans have supported greater defense spending (McCubbins 1991). Another important policy difference is that domestic matters have become more important components of the federal budget than has defense. This is largely due to the expansion of entitlements, which by law are tied to inflation and cannot be altered without changing legislation. Thus, they are called "uncontrollables." Defense, on the other hand, remains somewhat more controllable, and thus, a ready candidate for cuts during tough economic times (Kettl 1992).

PRELIMINARY EXPECTATIONS

Political time and policy areas provide important controls in examining actor relations. Overall, the expectation is for greater position taking and veto propensity over time but less legislative support and budget agreement. These expectations reflect growing assertiveness by both actors. The extent to which presidents choose to be active in policy making is a crucial consideration. Also important is whether they desire expansion or contraction of government programs (LeLoup and Shull 1999, chapter 3). Either of these preferences implies a change in policy from the status quo. Decision-makers seldom offer totally new or innovative ideas; most policy adoption builds heavily from existing programs (Wildavsky 1979, 65; Jones 1984). To the extent that policy innovation does mean altering the nation's agenda, however, innovative policies (that is, vigorous actions to expand or contract), frequently occur with partisan or ideological changes in government, or both. Substantive policy areas and divisions of political time should contribute to the understanding our four presidential-congressional interactions.

Expectations by Policy Areas

The two presidencies thesis has long been used in studying presidential-congressional relations. Despite being only a dichotomy, considerable research finds variation in domestic and foreign policy areas (Wildavsky [1966] 1991; LeLoup and Shull [1979] 1991; Fleisher and Bond 1990; Renka and Jones 1991; Sullivan 1991). Other scholars, and even its originator (Oldfield and Wildavsky [1989] 1991), have questioned its appearance in more recent years (Sigelman [1979] 1991; Edwards [1987] 1991). Nevertheless, the two presidencies formulation continues to be widely used (Shull 1991; 1994; Lindsay and Steger 1993). The two presidencies typology discriminated well in a previous study (Shull 1997) and is used in this research as a separate control for the four inter-actions. We were able to compile all these government activities by the domestic and foreign policy distinctions. Presidential position taking is greater in domestic policy while legislative support is greater in foreign policy. Also, few foreign policy vetoes occur and presidents seem to obtain more of their budget preferences in that policy sphere but research is sparse. Overall, the executive environment probably is more determinant of foreign policy interactions while the legislative environment likely influences domestic interactions more.

Expectations by Political Time

Numerous authors argue that presidential-congressional relations vary across time, in both longer eras and shorter periods; thus our notion of political time is an important consideration in policy adoption. Broader time periods should matter, with executive variables being more impor-tant earlier in the study during the era of a "heroic or imperial presi-dency" (Schlesinger 1973) and the legislative environment being more pervasive since the mid-1970s under a more "imperiled or impossible presidency" (Barger 1984; Crovitz and Rabkin 1989). Also, the grow-ing deficit should make exogenous factors important during the more recent period. Within more specific time frames, executive variables probably are more important during the 1960s and 1980s while legisla-tive variables likely are more influential during the 1950s, 1970s, and 1990s. Research has shown considerable variation in behavior by each of the aggregations of data: early/late eras, year in presidential term of office, and presidents individually. For example, presidents appear to fare better earlier rather than later in their terms of office. Congress appears less deferential in later years when presidents may be more vul-nerable politically.

We have already hinted at expectations by our mid-range control for political time: early (1949–74) versus late (1975–95) time periods. Earlier we referred to the many different divisions and conceputaliza-tions of eras in presidential-congressional relations. Some such divisions cover our entire nation's history (e.g., Schlesinger 1986; Sundquist 1981) or nearly one hundred years (Lewis and Strine 1996). Our shorter time frame still provides the opportunity to examine a mid-level era dis-tinction of twenty-six and twenty-one years respectively in duration.

Although we present the time plots in the substantive chapters, we have already hinted at some of the results. First, we expect an increase in presidential position taking but a decline in legislative support over time. The two different eras should highlight the differences in these two government actions even more than looking at a straight time line. We expect that veto propensity will be less differentiated by early and late periods but should be somewhat greater later than earlier. Finally, although budget agreement is rather stable over our time frame, the growing incidence of divided government and partisan conflict should reveal somewhat less agreement in the more recent period.

Presidents are expected to be more assertive during their first and last years in office and less so during re-election years (Light 1982, 41; Kessel 1975, 9; Shull 1983; Pfiffner 1996). Not only are they less assertive during reelection but they also receive less support from Congress at that time (Wayne 1978, 130; Shull 1997, chapter 6). Thus, there should be less congressional acquiescence during presidential reelection years. The reasons for these expectations are simple. Although the first year requires organizing and gaining experience in office, presidents realize they must make their mark early while the honeymoon lasts. Thus, they should be most aggressive then and also when they are lame ducks. During this last year, they have greater freedom of action and presumably wish to leave a historical legacy. Reelection years differ because the heightened political climate may give presidents caution (i.e., less assertiveness). Congress, then, will be more assertive during presidents' last and reelection years.

Although presidents differ by party, the individuals themselves are also unique. Indeed, Nathaniel Beck (1982) and Samuel Kernell (1986, 223) believe that policy agendas vary more by administration than by party. We know that Kennedy and Johnson were quite legislatively assertive (position taking) and Eisenhower and Ford were not. Congress became more contentious during the 1970s and greater partisanship and vote splitting occurred under Nixon and Ford. This trend has continued to the present. Legislative support is also highly partisan with Kennedy and Johnson faring best and Ford and Bush faring worst (Shull 1997). Thus, presidential-congressional interactions vary greatly among individual presidents, which should be the most distinguishing element of political time. However, all three elements of political time should have discriminating power.

Expectations for Government Activities

Presidential Position Taking. Presidents take positions frequently on roll call votes in Congress but even more often on votes on important legislation (Shull 1997, chapter 4). This finding relates to Gary King and Lyn Ragsdale's argument that presidents do not take positions on trivial issues (1988, 49).[5] Position taking likely has increased over time as presidents increasingly have pursued their policies in the legislative arena. However, position taking as a function of the total number of roll call votes has declined (Shull 1997, 58). Indeed, position taking as a percent of all votes increased from Eisenhower through Johnson, but then decreased beginning with Nixon as Congress began requiring that most decisions be based on roll call votes. Since the number of roll calls began declining again by the 1980s (Rohde 1994), the proportion of position taking relative to all votes should begin increasing again up through the Clinton administration. The controversial 1995 first session of the 104th Congress produced a record number of roll call votes, with Clinton taking twice as many positions during the second as during the first half of the year (*CQ Weekly Reports*, January 27, 1996, 198).

Position taking may also vary by policy area, with presidents likely taking positions relatively more often in domestic than in foreign policy, partly because more votes occur in the former area. Still, position taking probably has increased in foreign policy, but the once greater deference to presidents in international affairs likely has diminished since the congressional reassertion of the 1970s. Because domestic matters probably are more controversial, presidents may feel greater need to assert their preferences by taking positions on such roll call votes more frequently than on foreign policy votes.

Position taking probably varies considerably by the political time groupings used in the analysis. Perhaps the most dramatic difference should be by eras, where position taking has increased dramatically in the modern era due to presidents increasingly "going public" in this period of divided government (Shull 1997, chapter 4). Presidents (especially assertive ones) presumably take positions at a higher rate during their first (honeymoon) year than during last or reelection years. Of course, such position taking by selected year likely also varies by policy areas, where greater attention should be given to foreign policy during last and reelection than during first years. Domestic issues should get more attention during presidents' first years. Individual presidents probably vary considerably in position taking on legislative votes. From past research, Kennedy and Johnson probably are among our most assertive presidents and Eisenhower and Ford likely are among the least assertive legislatively (LeLoup and Shull 1993, chapter 3). Johnson and Ford emphasized domestic position taking while Kennedy and Bush focused on foreign policy.

Legislative Support.   Roll call analysis provides significant benefits but also some problems for studying presidential-congressional relations.

One problem concerns ambiguity in what is being measured. Differences of opinion occur about what the indicators drawn from roll call votes mean. Authors allude to the following diverse concepts: "power" (Wildavsky [1966] 1991; Peppers [1975] 1991; Sigelman [1979] 1991); "success" (Bond and Fleisher 1990; Edwards 1985; Hammond and Fraser 1984a; 1984b); "support" (Covington 1987; Edwards 1985; Fleisher and Bond 1983); "influence" (Bond and Fleisher 1980; Edwards 1980; Sigelman, [1979] 1991; Mouw and MacKuen 1992; Pritchard 1983; Sullivan 1991b); still others refer generally to presidential relations with Congress (LeLoup and Shull [1979] 1991). At least ostensibly, concepts like success and support may appear somewhat analogous; however, they are fundamentally different (see chapters 1 and 5).

Previous literature has shown that presidents generally fare well, obtaining about 57 percent legislative support of their vote positions from Congress. Obviously, differences in presidents' legislative support should occur across political time and policy areas. Certainly, presidents' legislative support should be greater in foreign than in domestic policy (see various studies in Shull 1991). Congress appears to defer to presidents in foreign policy but less so in controversial domestic matters (Shull 1997). It should be obvious by now that support has decreased over time and, particularly in more recent years within the time frame analyzed, due to increases in both position taking and divided government. Also, presidents should be supported at higher levels during their first (honeymoon year in office) than during reelection or last (lame-duck) year. Finally, examining individual presidents reveals Johnson's support to be greatest and Reagan's least among their post–World War II contemporaries (Shull 1997, chapter 6). Overall, we have greater prior evidence for our expectations in legislative support than for other interactions, particularly budget agreement.

Veto Propensity. We observed earlier that presidents increasingly are turning to prerogative powers like the veto as a device to assert their policy preferences in the legislative arena. In addition to increasing assertiveness on the part of presidents, the growing independence of Congress has prompted greater veto usage. Thus, we expect somewhat greater veto propensity in the more recent era (post-1974 than previously). That means presidents since Nixon are more likely to use the device, which likely occurs more often during last and reelection years than during the first year in office. Research suggests presidents more frequently veto legislation sponsored or passed by the opposition party, especially when the opposition party has simple majority control of Congress (Lee 1975, 542; Copeland 1983; Rohde and Simon 1985; Simonton 1987; Hoff 1991). Thus, the greater the size of the opposition party in Congress, the greater the president's perceived need to veto. Of course this is not a simple monotonic relationship since the size of the opposition is an indicator of the potential for overriding a veto. Presidents know that overrides are rare but still must consider this possibility and its potential effects on their political leadership.

Apart from preferences and activities, resources should also be important in the decision to veto. Resources have two distinct effects in the process of presidential influence. Political resources may be converted directly into political success or may condition the conversion of preferences and the president's persuasive skills (Shull, Gleiber, and Ringelstein 1992). The particular mixture of congressional and presidential power resources and the degree of institutional conflict affect the president's decision to veto. A popular president may have less need to veto legislation (see Lee 1975; Rohde and Simon 1985; Woolley 1991). Paul Light (1992) suggests that presidents are less likely to veto when they are politically vulnerable. Thus, variables such as the vote margin and party cohesion on final passage of bills also could be important in veto propensity (Hoff 1991). Presidents today are probably challenged more often in foreign policy and so likely will use the device more in that policy realm than previously.

Budget Agreement. Budgets are a primary battleground of presidential-congressional relations because they are obligatory decisions that occur each year. The fact that what presidents request from Congress may differ from what Congress actually appropriates shows a diversity of preferences. Protracted controversy occurred particularly under Nixon but has worsened since about 1981 when the deficit grew dramatically (Schick 1986). The 1974 Budget Act created more central decision making in Congress and subsequent reforms required that cuts in revenue had to balance cuts in spending, which likely increased institutional conflict even further. Accordingly, the deficit is a constraining influence on decisions made by these two actors, particularly since, until fiscal 1999, a deficit occurred every year since fiscal 1969. Apart from the deficit and prior outlays, general economic conditions, such as taxing and spending decisions, may also affect budget agreement.

Scholars see the climate for budgeting changing over time (Kettl 1989; Cox et al. 1993). Since Congress is a more capable and independent body since the 1970s, an interesting comparison can be made between the two time periods in our study, prior to reform (1949–74) and since the 1974 Budget Act (1975–95). Although the president may set the budget agenda (Shuman 1992, 16), presidential involvement in the details of budgeting is very limited. The Office of Management and Budget (OMB), located within the Executive Office of the President

(EOP), is responsible for squaring agency requests with presidential preferences. The role of the OMB became more political beginning with the Nixon administration (LeLoup 1980). When presidents are enthusiasts rather than reluctants, however, the roles of the OMB and other agencies will be more limited. Because presidents lack authority to do more than submit a budget proposal, they must rely heavily on persuasion. We have already asserted that when their activities and resources are greater, presidents should receive appropriations from Congress closer to their original requests than should presidents who make less effort and are resource poor. Also, budget agreement is likely greater in foreign than in domestic policy. This discussion suggests that budget agreement will be affected by all three environments, particularly the exogenous one, and will also be influenced by political time and policy area considerations.

Assessment. Table 2.1 provides a way of summarizing our multiple perspectives approach. First, we lay out the four interactions, that is the phenomena we seek to explain. The interrelationships among the four dependent variables are examined in chapter 3 before ascertaining the degree to which they are influenced by the environments and controls utilized in chapters 4–7. Many of the components of the model will be quite familiar to students of presidential-congressional relations. However, apart from the standard predictors (such as presidents' popular support or margin of their partisans in Congress), other variables are included that heretofore have not been used in studying congressional-presidential relations. Including both resources and activities helps expand the dimensions of our three broader environments: executive, legislative, and exogenous. The table shows how in studying each presidential-congressional interaction, we consider the most directly related process variable as part of the exogenous environment. Table 2.1 provides the parameters of the study, previewing the theoretical and anticipated relationships we explore.

SUMMARY AND CONCLUSION

This chapter has examined the extant research on each of our four government activities, direct presidential-congressional interactions in the adoption of public policy. More systematic research exists on legislative support than on the other three presidential-congressional interactions, but none has been ignored in the scholarly literature. Part of the problem with the existing research on these actor relations, however, is that each of these interactions has been examined in isolation and sometimes the analyses are not driven by theory. We argue here that they are interrelated as part of the temporal process of policy adoption. In addition, except for the veto, most research covers rather limited time periods, which frequently does not allow for the inclusion of short-range cycles, let alone even longer eras of presidential-congressional relations. Although presidents are often considered individually, few examinations have used year in presidential term of office as a control for political time (Brace and Hinckley 1992; Shull 1997). However, almost no research has examined mid-range political eras, our before-after 1974 dichotomy. In addition, little attention, at least in studying the veto and budgeting, has been given to policy areas as a control in the analyses.

The main purpose of this chapter was to develop the framework for *Explaining Congressional-Presidential Relations*. We examine political decisions within the context of a multiple perspectives model that

TABLE 2.1
Scope of Coverage of Explaining Congressional-Presidential Relations

Dependent Variables	
Actor Relations Variables	*Likely Explanatory Variables*
Presidential Position-Taking	Budgeting/presidential/exogenous
Legislative Support	Position taking/congressional
Veto Propensity	Legislative Support/presidential
Budget Agreement	Veto/Support/congressional/exogenous

Control Variables
Policy Typology
The Two-Presidencies Thesis (domestic versus foreign)
Aggregations of Time
Trend Analysis (overall)
Political Time (historical era, selected years in term and individual presidents)

Independent Variables
Executive Environment
Resources: President's Public Support, Size of the Executive Office. Activity: Speechmaking.
Legislative Enivronment
Resources: Size of Committee Staff, Party Margin in Congress. Activity: Volume of Legislation.
Exogenous Environment
Resources: Deficit/Spending Index, Size of Government.

encompasses necessary activities and resources as being important to subsequent relations between Congress and presidents. We argue that presidents and Congress, both individually and collectively, as a result of their larger institutional environments, have competing preferences, but it is in the interests of both to compromise such preferences in order to adopt public policy. Both entities also have resources and engage in activities to further their own preferences but they also must operate within broader internal and external environmental contexts.

Although each actor possesses distinct preferences that he or she would like to see put into effect, institutional and individual[6] characteristics influence how each actor expresses his or her preferences via the interactions that we are examining. Our multiple perspectives approach uses measures of both resources and activities from each environment (executive, legislative, and exogenous) to help explain all four interactions. We feel that this more encompassing model produces a better understanding of how resources and activities across environments affect presidential-congressional interactions. Thus, no single environment should completely account for any of the four interactions examined herein; rather, they are influenced variously by elements of each.

Government activities, then, result from the preferences, activities, and resources of both Congress and presidents and also from factors outside their own institutions (the exogenous environment). These external considerations, in addition to related activities from the process model that we incorporate into the exogenous environment, lead us to propose that the best explanation of presidential-congressional interactions is more encompassing even than the tandem institutions perspective. We call this broader explanatory model a multiple perspectives approach because it offers a more comprehensive explanation than considered previously. The measurement of all of the concepts and more specific variables are provided in the following measurement chapter as is our process model of presidential-congressional interactions.

CHAPTER 3

Measurement Strategies

This chapter begins by laying out the operationalization of the four dependent variables measuring presidential-congressional interactions in policy adoption: presidential position taking, legislative support, veto propensity, and budget agreement. Chapter 1 posited that these four government activities probably are not independent of one another and we consider how they are interrelated overall as well as when lagged across four-year time intervals. We expect the four interactions to reflect a temporal process between the two institutions. For example, presidential position taking should influence legislative support while veto propensity should relate most directly to budget agreement. In short, we posit a process occurring where subsequent activities are influenced by those that precede them temporally. This chapter reveals the complexity of multiple presidential-congressional relations as they adopt policy.

Next, we explicate exactly how we use political time and policy areas as controls in the analysis. Political time refers here to both long- and short-term variables: our long-term eras (pre/post-1974) were selected because many observers consider congressional resurgence to have occurred by then. The two short-term periods included are selected year within presidential term of office and individual presidents. Another aspect of political time is the trend analysis, which shows both short- and long-term effects of time. All of these elements and the data and analysis techniques are discussed in the methodological appendix. These controls for political time are analyzed separately. Policy area refers to our incorporation of the foreign-domestic issue area distinction in the analysis. In this control, the four dependent variables are divided according to the domestic-foreign counterparts and compared with the overall values as a baseline.

We also discuss the nine independent variables (three each within each of the three environments), encompassing both activities and resources. These include *executive* (speech making, popular support, and executive staff size); *legislative* (number of public laws, presidential party margin, and committee staff size; and *exogenous* (an index for economic health of the nation, the size of government, and the related process variable, for example, position taking in explaining support). We already have shown how all three environments contain both activities and resources in order to include several elements from the institutional and exogenous influences. As mentioned in chapter 2, we expected each environment to influence the four government activities (presidential-congressional interactions). Thus, such interactions in policy adoption require a multiple perspective to enhance understanding. Finally, a summary and conclusion serves as a prelude to the data analysis of the presidential-congressional activities examined in chapters 4–7.

OPERATIONALIZING PRESIDENTIAL-CONGRESSIONAL INTERACTIONS (DEPENDENT VARIABLES)

This section discusses the nature and measurement of the four dependent variables, which are direct presidential-congressional interactions. We have suggested that other such direct relations may occur, such as the nomination-confirmation process, but each of the four public interactions incorporated here deals with some component of policy adoption. At the same time, we expect them to occur temporally and, thus, discuss them in order: presidential position taking, legislative support, veto propensity, and budget agreement. At the level of the individual bill, we posit this chronological process but our data are aggregated by year, which does not allow us to fully incorporate a temporal process. All four variables have received attention in the scholarly literature but no prior research has examined them *together*, as part of an interdependent process or system of policymaking.

Two of our presidential-congressional interactions are based directly on floor voting in Congress. Although roll call votes contain some pitfalls, they are public, tangible measures of legislative action and appear representative of other behavior (Hammond and Fraser 1984a). Of course, recorded votes are more prevalent in later years than earlier years of the study. One reason is that legislative reforms in the 1970s required recorded votes for most issues, although the number of recorded votes declined beginning in the 1980s. Second, decision making has become more contentious in Congress, breaking down unanimity thereby lessening the opportunity for uncontested voice votes (see Shull 1997, chapter 5). Scholars disagree over weighting and statistical techniques for analyzing roll call votes (Anderson et al. 1966; MacRae 1970), but they encompass valuable information unobtainable elsewhere.[1]

The data for position taking and support are based on the House of Representatives because only lower chamber data are compiled by Ragsdale (1996) across issue areas.[2] The other two variables are a bit more complicated to analyze by chamber. Veto propensity is a presidential response to laws, passage of which requires action by both chambers. Further analysis (beyond the scope of this project) could examine the subsequent action by each chamber separately as Congress responds to the presidential decision. The final dependent variable, budget agreement, is also a function of both chambers agreeing upon a final dollar figure. Unfortunately, budget data by chamber are not readily available for our time series. We now discuss the operationalization of each of the four dependent variables.

Presidential Position Taking

Due to the dramatic increase in number of recorded votes, at least during the 1970s, most significant legislation does come to a roll call vote. Congressional Quarterly determines whether the president takes positions on particular votes, "by examining statements by the president or his authorized spokesmen" (*Congressional Quarterly Weekly Reports*, January 27, 1996, 239). Position taking and subsequent support are appropriate measures for time-series analysis (Bond, Fleisher, and Kurtz 1996, 109). Beyond its role in ascertaining presidents' legislative support or success (see this distinction in chapter 5), presidential position taking itself has not been examined extensively (Shull 1997; Shull and Gleiber 1994). Yet presidential position taking on legislation is an important avenue for interaction between Congress and the president.

Position taking is the number of times each year CQ records the president as taking a clear public stance on legislative roll calls at some point prior to the vote (*Congressional Quarterly Almanac* 1956, 92). Because it is based on every floor vote on which the president takes a stand, multiple counting may occur on a single piece of legislation. Although some scholars do not like this coding convention, it is quite possible that the number of roll calls may indicate the importance of the issue (e.g., over a hundred votes on the 1964 Civil Rights Act alone). Numerous votes on a particular piece of legislation may also reveal amendment frequency as an indicator of controversy (see Shull 1997, chapter 5) or attempts at log rolling by diverse coalitions. Comparisons can be made on the propensity of presidents to take positions on legislation overall as well as by the two issue areas of public policy.[3]

We found a novel way to expand our position taking and support measures back to 1949 using the box score indicator of requests, rather than position taking as the denominator and then using the same numerator for support (average percentage voting with the president in the House). Thus, we have combined one element each from the box score (success) and the support measure for those years. Although we realize that bias could occur in such a procedure, we examined these earlier data as well as support from 1953 to 1956, since Ragsdale (1996, 382) argues that position taking in those years may not be comparable to later ones. In addition, CQ did not code them into readily identifiable policy areas then, so Ragsdale's data begin in 1957. Gomez and Shull (1995) use a jackknifing technique in collecting these position taking data and no bias was revealed for the earlier years (1949–56) through this procedure.[4]

Legislative Support

Although a measure of the president's legislative initiatives (the box score collected by Congressional Quarterly) was once available, scholars now are largely relegated to examining legislative support or success on votes on which presidents take public positions.[5] Despite the increase in recorded voting in committee decisions, scholars have been unable to identify a clear presidential role at the committee stage (see Shull 1997, chapter 1). Certainly many bills die before reaching a roll call vote, but at least in recent years, most laws pass with a recorded rather than a voice vote, so a clear public record exists. Of course, a roll call vote need not signify final passage; indeed, it may merely amend legislation. Most of the increase in roll call votes are amendments to legislation, which are often quite controversial (Rohde 1994, 118; Shull and Klemm 1987).

The presidents' legislative support reflects the mean percentage of members of the House who vote yea on a measure the president favors or nay on one he opposes.[6] It is not the commonly used individual member support score. Legislative success (both indicators) and support of the president and the conditions that seem to influence them have been examined extensively in the literature. Indeed, considerable, often multivariate, analysis has been conducted using these variables or variations of them (Cohen 1980; Rivers and Rose 1985; Edwards 1989; Bond and Fleisher 1990). The legislative support score utilized here is for all roll call votes, and is the average percent of the House in agreement with presidents' positions overall and as categorized by Ragsdale's (1996) policy areas. Despite problems with the support score documented earlier, its wide use in the literature necessitates a thorough analysis here.[7]

In measuring support, Congressional Quarterly Inc. uses all public messages to determine the president's position on roll call votes (see chapter 4). CQ includes procedural votes only if they reflect a substantive issue while votes on appropriations "generally" are not included. (For an example of coding rules, see Congressional Roll Call 1986, 23-C.) Only members who cast a yea or nay are counted in calculating the scores. Thus, scores for individual members may be based on different numbers of roll call votes. As with success, one can calculate a percentage combining House and Senate support for the president or keep the chambers separate. Again, the organization makes judgments as to whether particular votes approximate a president's stated policy preference.

Veto Propensity

The veto is the only presidential-congressional interaction utilized in this research that has been tabulated for the entire time period of our nation's history. Perhaps as a result, it has a long tradition in scholarly research as revealed in chapters 1 and 2. Several types of vetoes exist. In this analysis we use a frequency count of the number of public bills vetoed per year, as found in the *Congressional Quarterly Almanac*.[8] Sufficient reason exists to believe that the politics of the United States in the post–World War II era is sufficiently different to justify separate analysis of modern pocket and regular vetoes. Regular vetoes are more indicative of presidential-congressional interactions because they can be overridden by Congress. In contrast, no recourse is possible by Congress for pocket vetoes. Thus, only presidential activities and resources come more into play on pocket vetoes, not those of Congress (Shull, Gleiber, and Ringelstein 1992).

Problems arise when attempting to examine vetoes by policy areas. An example occurs with King and Ragsdale's (1988) categorization of presidential vetoes. Few vetoes are issued in some policy areas (e.g., none for foreign aid from 1957 to 1984). Obviously it would be difficult for scholars to compare veto issuance across their seven policy categories, let alone the even more infrequent veto challenges or overrides. Fewer problems occur when examining only foreign and domestic vetoes, but some individual year Ns for the former are limited. Indeed, we will see that no vetoes at all were issued during five of the years analyzed. Accordingly, caution is warranted in examining veto propensity.

Several other components of the veto can be analyzed, such as the mere threat of rather than the actual veto of legislation. Robert Spitzer (1988, 1997) discusses this interesting variable but it is difficult to identify and somewhat subjective. The veto, of course, is a presidential response to Congress, but further congressional action is also possible. One interesting variable is override attempts, which is a vote, successful or not, in either chamber to override a presidential veto. Such decisions are, of course, even less frequent than vetoes and, along with the extremely rare successful congressional overrides, are difficult to incorporate into quantitative research. The item veto, which became legal briefly in 1997 until it was struck down by the Supreme Court, would have complicated subsequent analysis of this prerogative power.

Budget Agreement

Chapters 1–2 suggested that budgeting has increasingly been an area of presidential-congressional disagreement. This has been especially true since the Budget Act of 1974 (Wildavsky 1988). With growing presidential responsibility in budgeting, Congress has not always maintained its own leadership, increasingly relying on presidents to set the stage, but often being unable or unwilling to make difficult modifications of such requests. Such occurred even on "dead on arrival" budgets during the Bush years. Certainly budget resolutions in Congress became increasingly difficult to enact and internal partisanship and institutional rivalries have persisted. We know that the annual appropriations process now governs significantly less of the budget since much of the budget is largely uncontrollable and dominated by entitlements (Kettl 1989; Wildavsky 1988). Entitlement reform is now a serious agenda item and Republicans in Congress started chipping away at it beginning in 1995. Until fiscal 1999, deficit politics increasingly dominated budgeting, reducing discretion on actors' decisions. Discretion exists on the remaining controllable 25 percent where deals are struck and, thus, budgeting continues to be an important interaction between Congress and presidents (Wildavsky 1988).

Although presidential budget requests and congressional appropriations have long been incorporated in scholarly literature, little research uses them over a long time series. A reason for this situation may be that definitions of such terms changed over time and presumably no consistent time series was available. Ornstein and coauthors in *Vital Statistics on Congress* (1996, 186) provide differences in requests and appropriations values from 1968 to 1994 only. Kiewiet and McCubbins (1988) consider presidential budget requests as a good measure of presidents' budget preferences but their usefulness could be questioned. The presidents' requests come from the annual budget they submit, while appropriations include all regular budget authority funds for each year (*Budget of the United States Government*). The final figure we use is the percent of the president's annual budget request that is appropriated by Congress (e.g., requests divided by appropriations).

We are aware of some potential for aggregation bias but believe our control for defense/nondefense budget agreement over a long time period provides the best available comparison of presidential and congressional foreign-domestic preferences. Some confusion at first arises in the data over exactly what is being measured. First, our measure does not account for tax expenditures. Second, according to Norman Ornstein and his colleagues (1996, 186) the values are for calendar, not fiscal years: "The amounts shown are for budget authority provided in appropriations acts and do not include permanent appropriations or budget authority provided in legislative acts." However, two years overlap in both sources and because those concurrent years have the exact same values, we believe that we have uncovered a consistent and reliable indicator of budget agreement over forty-seven calendar years.

Process Model of Interactions

A large body of literature discusses policymaking as a temporal process (Shull and Gleiber 1994; Peters 1996; Jones 1984; but see Sabatier and Jenkins-Smith 1993). These studies examine the evolution of policymaking from an early idea stage (e.g., agenda settting) across a sequence of behaviors in which a policy is formally initiated, adopted into law, implemented by the bureaucracy, and evaluated by the public or experts. Because all four of our government activities focus on policy adoption, our concerns are different from other writers. Although we expect presidential position taking, legislative support, veto propensity, and budget agreement to be related to one another, we anticipate that they will be uncorrelated enough so that they can also be studied separately.

Accordingly, we seek to understand how each of these activities might influence the others. In order to test these relationships, we examine the degree to which they are correlated at any one time and over a four year time period. Matthew McCubbins (1991) argues that since the veto occurs late in policymaking, it should be influenced by preceding decisions. We have posited a general temporal sequence in the order presented, where each activity relates most closely to the activity that proceeds it: presidential position taking, legislative support, veto propensity, budget agreement. The latter should relate most directly to position taking, therein continuing the "process" anew sequentially. Therein lies a process model of policy adoption through presidential-congressional interactions.

Our four dependent variables are moderately correlated. Even though related, we believe that they reflect four quite different activities in presidential-congressional relations. Table 3.1 shows that the highest correlation is between presidential position taking and legislative support, unsurprisingly since the numerator of the latter is the same variable as the former. The significant correlation ($r = -.50$) suggests that presidents taking fewer positions on votes in the House are more likely to be supported by that body (see Brace and Hinckley 1992). The next correlation is between support and veto propensity ($r = -.31$), where presidents are more likely to be supported in the House on their vote positions when they issue fewer vetoes. The correlation between the veto and budget agreement is almost nonexistent and insignificant ($r = .23$).

Finally, we observe another modest (r = .33) relationship between budget agreement and position taking, so the former encourages the latter. A common result we observed is that legislative support relates significantly to each of the other three executive-legislative interactions.

Despite only moderate correlations among these four government activities, we believe that they may reflect a temporal process in presidential-congressional relations. Indeed, the coefficients reported above suggest that actors respond to previous actions, sometimes positively, sometimes negatively. We test for such a process by examining one- to four-year time lags through regression analysis. For presidential position taking, the best fit variables are one- and three-year lagged budget agreement scores (see table 3.2) and we choose the former. We have already shown that position taking and support are negatively related but a one- to four-year time lag does not improve the basic relationship; none of the lagged variables are significant. Thus, congressional support is an immediate response to presidential position taking. The next relationship appears to take a short time to percolate. Only a one-year lag provides a better fit than same-year between support and the veto. Also, no significant lags occur for veto propensity and budget agreement. Finally, time lags do improve the relationship between budget agreement and position taking. A three-year lag is significant and a one-year lag nearly so in this relationship. We use the one-year lag due to its greater theoretical significance.

The above procedures suggest that our four dependent variables are interrelated and influence one another over at least the short term. Therefore, in the subsequent chapters, we have decided to include these process variables in the models to help explain each presidential-congressional interaction. In that sense, we include the most directly related

TABLE 3.1
Correlation Matrix of Dependent Variables

	Position Taking	Support	Veto	Budget Agreement
Presidential Position Taking	1.00	−.504 (.000)	−.002 (.990)	.330 (.025)
Legislative Support		1.00	−.306 (.036)	−.456 (.001)
Veto Propensity			1.00	.232 (.120)
Budget Agreement				1.00

"process" variable as part of the exogenous environment. Since these variables are most often related in the same years, we incorporate a one-year time lag only when using budget agreement to influence position taking. This macro process (encompassing from one to four years) should not be confused with the micro policy adoption process hypothesized to occur within a single year.

OPERATIONALIZING THREE ENVIRONMENTS (INDEPENDENT VARIABLES)

We posit that three environments will differentially influence the four actor interactions (government activities). They include aspects of the executive, legislative, and influences outside both institutions. Presumably, executive conditions are more important for some interactions

TABLE 3.2
Lagged Regressions of Dependent Variables in Process Model

	Regression Coefficient	Sig T
Budget Agreement Predicting Position Taking		
Budget Agreement, Current Year	1.33	.338
Budget Agreement, 1 Year Lag	2.64	.053
Budget Agreement, 2 Year Lag	1.19	.348
Budget Agreement, 3 Year Lag	2.87	.036*
Position Taking Predicting Legislative Support		
Position Taking, Current Year	−.05	.254
Position Taking, 1 Year Lag	.00	.951
Position Taking, 2 Year Lag	−.05	.270
Position Taking, 3 Year Lag	−.02	.641
Support Predicting Veto Propensity		
Support, Current Year	−.30	.034*
Support, 1 Year Lag	−.30	.065
Support, 2 Year Lag	.04	.793
Support, 3 Year Lag	.04	.799
Veto Predicting Budget Agreement		
Veto, Current Year	.07	.432
Veto, 1 Year Lag	.12	.229
Veto, 2 Year Lag	.03	.804
Veto, 3 Year Lag	−.12	.256

* Significant at .05 or 95% confidence interval.

than others, while the opposite circumstances may occur for legislative variables. Because we doubt that any one actor dominates, we expect that variables from each environment are differentially important. Such findings would confirm the posited multiple perspectives approach. That is, executive variables should have greater influence on position taking and veto propensity than on legislative support or budget agreement. That is because the former two are prompted from presidential responses while the latter two are more under Congress's control. In addition, the notion that exogenous factors also influence policymaking is important in our research. Certainly we expect characteristics of the economy or the broader government itself to be important in presidential-congressional interactions.

Executive

In both the executive and legislative environments, we include measures of activities and resources. We will presently show that both aspects are important influences on actors' behavior and they are not highly correlated with one another. Thus, they probably represent different dimensions of these two environments. The executive environment incorporates two resources: Neustadt's (1980) notion of popular prestige and size of the executive office. It also encompasses an indicator of presidents' public speeches as a measure of presidential activity or assertiveness. As others have done, we use popular support in Gallup polls as our measure of public prestige (Edwards 1989, chapter 6; Bond and Fleisher 1990, chapter 7). It is the average score per year on the familiar question: "In general, how is [president's name] handling his job as president?" Neustadt criticizes the Gallup support score as personal popularity and not a complete measure of prestige (1980, 65; Rivers and Rose 1985, 184). However, as a general measure of popular prestige it contains all of the conceptual components of mass approval of presidents. Empirical studies using popular support find it related to legislative success (Rivers and Rose 1985; Zeidenstein 1983) and thus, in part, construct and content valid. However, other research questions the influence of popular approval on legislative support (Bond and Fleisher, 1990; Edwards, 1989).[9] Our indicator is the mean percent approval score per year.[10]

The second indicator in the executive environment is one that focuses on staff resources. We use the size of the Executive Office of the President, called "Total Executive Office" by Harold Stanley and Richard Neimi (1995, 247). Obviously, this variable has deviated from a very low figure under Truman (about 1,200 employees) to its highest level under Nixon (over 5,700 in 1972). Size of the Executive Office has gradually decreased to about 1,550 under Clinton, its lowest level since 1986 (Stanley and Neimi 1995, 248–49). Staff resources should allow greater presidential capacity to gather information and act in their congressional relations. Obviously, this declining resource must be husbanded carefully by presidents.

The third executive indicator is an activity variable of presidential rhetoric. The president communicates to persuade citizens, political elites, and public servants. Even with an extensive repertoire of persuasive techniques, modern presidents may become isolated in the White House. The result is that presidential persuasion has come to rely heavily on going public (Kernell 1986). Public messages, such as Jimmy Carter's fireside chats, are used to further their policy preferences. They seem a useful surrogate of Neustadt's concept of persuasion. Ragsdale has done some interesting research on presidential speechmaking (1984) and we are indebted to her once again for these data, which also appear in her 1996 edition of *Vital Statistics on the Presidency*. Our indicator of presidential activity is the number of minor speeches made by the president annually. The number of major speeches are few (often less than four per year) and relatively constant but the number of minor speeches varies considerably. Thus, presidents use this resource of "going public" quite differently in their congressional relations. Ragsdale defines minor speeches as "substantive remarks made to a specific group or in a certain forum . . . usually as specific . . . as major addresses, but they are shorter and not nationally broadcast" (1996, 150).

Legislative

Similar to the executive environment, the legislative environment consists of one activity and two resource variables. Congress-centered variables have been considered by Bond and Fleisher (1990) to be more important than president-centered ones in explaining presidents' legislative success. Of course, they consider the president's party margin to be a congressional rather than a presidential variable and its placement is crucial because of its perceived prominence in explaining all four interactions. Given that both electoral politics and government institutions in the United States are organized by the two major political parties, partisan strength in Congress is a relevant elite-based political resource for both actors. However, it is a characteristic largely outside presidents' direct control and, thus, considered here as part of the legislative environment. To measure party margin in Congress, we utilize the percentage of the president's partisans in the House only for position taking and support and in both chambers of Congress averaged for veto propensity and budget agreement.

The second legislative resource variable is change in the size of House committee staff, which was very difficult to obtain for the entire time series. We used a table (in Ornstein et al. 1996, 137) that contained intermittent values prior to 1970. The authors cited numerous references for these data so we expected no trouble in replicating their measure for the earlier period. However, all the earlier sources (e.g., Hammond and Fox 1976) provided the same raw table as Ornstein and coauthors, consisting of a very spotty listing of observations for the earlier years. These authors alluded to a study of committee staff but the annual data did not exist on the pages they provided. Therefore, we used the total staff (combined statutory and investigative) of House standing committees from 1946–70, which appears on page 537 of the document they cite. Thus, a House committee staff variable, which we convert to a change variable, does indeed exist for the entire data series.[11] The resource House staff size facilitates the role of Congress in policy adoption.

The third congressional variable is activity- rather than resource-based. It is the number of public laws enacted annually by Congress. Unlike the previous variable, this indicator obviously is the product of both chambers. We are quite aware that more laws pass in the second year (session) of a two-year Congress since the first year normally consists of bill introduction and committee activity. However, we are interested in the changing output of Congress over time and do not think this variation within single Congresses should affect our results. Some scholars have found a relationship between legislative activity (number of bills introduced) and veto usage (Hoff 1991; Kallenbach 1966). Thus, we expect that our output measure of activity (number of public laws) also relates to veto propensity. Patterson and Caldeira (1988) find bills and resolution passed (a slightly different variable from ours) to be important in predicting controversy of congressional voting. Despite some limitations, our measure of activity (or workload) as found in *Congressional Quarterly Almanac* is a useful indicator of presidential-congressional interaction. We are aware that the growth of omnibus legislation could undermine the validity of this variable, but the Patterson and Caldeira variable suffers from the same potential problem.

Exogenous

Like the two institutional environments, the exogenous environment contains three variables. As with the above two environments, one exogenous variable deals with institutional resources (number of civilian employees) in the federal government. These data come from the *Economic Report of the President* (1996, table B-31) and are reported in thousands of persons sixteen years or older in the federal civilian labor force. This source provides other variables that could be used across our time series. We wanted to include an activity variable and initially focused on the number of pages in the *Federal Register* but, because it was so highly correlated with other variables in the analysis, it had to be dropped. We think the size of government may tap public perceptions of "big government" and is a useful exogenous resource to further policy-making preferences. Caution is warranted since contracting out and other activities over time could affect the ability of government size to influence government activities.

The second variable in the exogenous environment is an index that deals with the economic health of the nation. It was utilized by David Mayhew (1992), where he called it "budget situation," as an influence on the passage of important legislation. We prefer to think of this variable as a broader economic indicator and call it "economic situation." The variable is operationalized as the nation's deficit or surplus divided by federal outlays (expenditures). This index provides a good indicator of discretion that institutions have to develop public policy and may even be viewed as a resource variable. Even though the raw variables alone would be highly correlated, our indicators are indexes or percentages (e.g., requests divided by appropriations and deficit or surplus divided by outlays). As calculated, we find the resulting measures (budget agreement and economic situation) not highly related.

The third exogenous variable is the process variable as an influence on government activities. As was demonstrated earlier in this chapter, a process of policymaking occurs where each subsequent activity is, in part, a function of the activity that precedes it theoretically if not necessarily empirically. Sometimes these influences reflect a one-year lag and at other times they appear to occur within the same calendar year as the subsequent variable. In any event, they are more "global" interactions not directly tied to either of the executive or legislative environments. Accordingly, these temporal process variables round out our exogenous environments.

Relationship among Environments

In this section, we discussed the relationships among the independent variables of the research, consisting of indicators of the executive, legislative, and external environments. The bivariate correlations among these component variables appear in table 3.3. There it may be observed that most of the variables are not highly correlated; thus, they measure different components of three different environments. Within the executive environment, the highest (but still rather low) correlation is between

TABLE 3.3
Correlation Matrix of Independent Variables

	Executive Environment			Legislative Environment			Exogenous Environment	
	Minor Speeches	EOP	Popular Approval	House Staff	Party Margin	Workload	Econ. Situation	Size of Govt.
Exec.								
Minor Speeches	1.00							
EOP Size	-.132 (.382)	1.00						
Popular Approval	-.378 (.010)	-.161 (.281)	1.00					
Legis.								
House Staff	.380 (.009)	.097 (.514)	.032 (.831)	1.00				
Party Margin	.124 (.411)	-.044 (.771)	-.003 (.985)	-.122 (.413)	1.00			
Workload	-.344 (.019)	.032 (.833)	.191 (.205)	-.163 (.279)	.060 (.690)	1.00		
Exog.								
Econ. Situation	-.353 (.016)	.101 (.501)	.057 (.703)	.046 (.760)	.305 (.037)	.294 (.047)	1.00	
Size of Govt.	.196 (.191)	.183 (.219)	-.235 (.112)	-.006 (.967)	-.273 (.064)	-.397 (.006)	-.631 (.000)	1.00

presidential speechmaking and popular approval ($r = -.38$). This finding, consistent with Brace and Hinckley (1992), suggests that giving minor speeches is negatively related to a president's popular prestige. The three variables within the legislative environment are even less related, such as the relationship ($r = -.12$) between presidential party margin and House committee staff size. The two exogenous variables are more highly correlated at ($r = -.63$), suggesting that as the size of government increases the budgetary situation worsens. The prior government activity (e.g., position taking in examining support) is also part of this exogenous environment. All in all, we feel confident in asserting the utility of our three environments in explaining presidential-congressional interactions.

OPERATIONALIZING APPROACHES
(CONTROL VARIABLES)

In this study, two different approaches are used to control the relationships between the dependent and independent variables. The first is policy area, dichotomizing the data into domestic and foreign, which has a long tradition in research on presidential-congressional relations. Many authors have observed differences by domestic and foreign policy areas but questions have also arisen about appropriate measurement. The second control variable is political time, consisting of divisions into (1) early/late periods, (2) selected year in presidential term of office (first, last, and reelection years), and (3) individual presidents. Two of these three distinctions proved useful in the earlier volume (Shull 1997) in accounting for presidential-congressional relations.

Policy Areas

Many studies have analyzed presidential success and support using Aaron Wildavsky's ([1966] 1991) domestic and foreign dimensions (LeLoup and Shull [1979] 1991; Cohen [1982] 1991; Bond and Fleisher 1990; Edwards 1980; 1989). A policy approach is both valid and valuable since considerable research has shown that presidential support varies by the type of policy (Pritchard 1983; Gibson 1995; Shull 1983; 1997). Given the advantages of the policy approach, Anita Pritchard calls the cumulative data of CQ support scores "a relatively crude measurement of congressional voting decisions" (1986, 481). This book accepts her position that votes should be studied by policy area. Probably it is time to move beyond general measures of support to ones that are more refined, thus allowing scholars to test hypotheses of greater depth and sophistication. A policy approach advances such insight and understanding. Certainly conceptual difficulties and problems with coding exist, but they should not be deterrents.

The operationalization of the substantive typology of public policy is discussed here. The brief one sentence description of each roll call vote provided by Congressional Quarterly can be used to categorize the data. For a time, CQ differentiated issues into domestic and foreign in the annual editions of its annual *Almanac* or *Congressional Roll Call* publications. Authors disagree about how particular issues should be classified and also about the more recent decision by CQ to include a separate budget or economic category. In any event, categorizing issues into the substantive groupings is possible once clear decision rules are established.

Because of changes in categorization by CQ over the years, their designation of foreign and domestic is not used. Rather, votes from Ragsdale's (1996) disaggregated seven issue areas are grouped into domestic and foreign. Specifically, foreign aid, foreign trade, and defense become the *foreign* category, and government, social welfare, resources, and agriculture become the *domestic* category. The specific issues that are included in each of these two typologies, the broader two presidencies and the narrower King and Ragsdale categorization, appear in Shull (1997, appendix A, table A-1). As shown there, intercoder reliability was well within acceptable levels and, thus, domestic issues can be differentiated from foreign issues. The great advantage of the Ragsdale data is that she categorizes position taking, support (House only), and vetoes by her seven issue areas and we can then aggregate them by policy areas. However, we made our own designation for budget agreement, consisting of a defense-nondefense designation.[12]

Political Time

Using political time in this volume goes beyond standard examinations of chronology or presidents as units of analysis. Aggregating by years allows for differing levels of generality, ranging from the most to the least aggregated. The first is looking at each activity across the entire forty-seven-year time period. Such aggregation permits examination for general patterns. Overall patterns of position taking, legislative support, veto propensity, and budget agreement are provided. Gross differences across policy areas over the entire time period can be observed. In addition, we incorporate trend analysis and a time lag of the annual data. Thus, the data are examined overall and then by three aggregations of political time.

The first of these groupings of time is a dichotomy splitting the study into two time periods (early and late). We have already demonstrated that scholars generally see presidential-congressional relations from the 1940s to the 1970s quite differently than they view the more current period of interactions. We know that many efforts were made by Congress during those transition years (1969–74) to reassert its influence over what many considered to be an imperial presidency (Schlesinger 1973; LeLoup and Shull 1993, chap. 2). Some of these reform efforts proved more effective than others but they did bring forth a renewed vitality to Congress in its relations with the executive. As such, writers subsequently spoke of an imperiled or impossible presidency rather than an imperial one (Barger 1984; Crovitz and Rabkin 1989). Congress has been more willing to challenge presidents in each of our interactions and we separate our data out to control for these two eras: *early* (1949–74; n = 26 years) and *late* (1975–95; n = 21 years).

Comparisons of selected years in presidential term of office are also useful. Although fewer data points may appear for each, scholars have found variation in presidential-congressional relations by such years (Light 1982; Kessel 1984; Lewis and Strine 1996; Shull 1997). Of particular interest are *first*, *last*, and *reelection* years within each administration.[13] Such groupings are useful but can be re-aggregated, thereby retaining all data points. Shull and Dennis Gleiber (1995) found that year in term effects on government activities in civil rights are less than when aggregating by individual presidents.

Individual presidents are compared to see if the thrust of policy adoption has altered over time, both within one administration and across presidential terms. Data for Truman at the beginning of his term and Clinton at the end of his are incomplete but we are able to explore the entire administrations of Eisenhower through Bush. Previous research finds distinctions for individual presidents in presidential-congressional relations (Shull 1997; Peterson 1990). All in all, these three political time aggregations are important in this analysis and controlled separately in the regression equations rather than simply as percentage of observations used previously (Shull 1997).

SUMMARY AND CONCLUSION

This chapter divulges the sources of our data and explains how we operationalize our variables. It began with the four dependent variables: presidential position taking, legislative support, veto propensity, and budget agreement. We observed that these four government activities are interrelated both conceptually and temporally. Indeed, we introduced a process model wherein each interaction was a function of the most logically related process variable. The data and analysis techniques for this research appear in the Methodological Appendix.

The research also utilizes the two presidencies typology and offers several controls for political time, particularly by early/late eras, by individual presidential administrations, and by selected year within presidential term of office. The control for policy area splits each of the four dependent variables into its foreign and domestic components and compares regressions on each with the general models. Separate regressions using each of the aggregations of political time provide controls on the overall relationships. In addition, we provide a one-year lag and a count variable as further controls for time.

Most importantly, the analysis seeks to explain these four interactions as a function of three environments. The analysis in the following chapters should tell us which environments help us understand complex interactions between Congress and the president. We expect the executive environment to be more influential for position taking and veto propensity while the legislative environment should provide greater explanatory power for legislative support and budget agreement. However, that explanation is too simple because we expect that both institutional environments as well as the exogenous (external) environment will make some contribution to the explanation of all four government activities in adopting public policy.

Considerable debate has arisen over the advantages of various measures of presidential-congressional relations. Certainly there are difficulties with all such indicators, as scholars have documented (Edwards 1980, 50–53; LeLoup and Shull [1979] 1991, 39; Peppers [1975] 1991; Ripley 1972; 1979, 69; Shull 1979, 1981, 1997; Sigelman [1979] 191; Bond, Fleisher and Krutz 1996; Wayne 1978, 168–71). No single quantitative measure of presidential-congressional relations is perfect. Qualitative indicators could be just as important, but they are difficult to obtain. The meaning of measures is not always clear; for example, we have already shown that success and support are often confused. Environmental circumstances also intervene, such as the following: To what extent do relations between presidents and Congress vary over time? At what stage is the president in his term of office? Do individual presidents matter more than other aggregations of the data? Do activities or resources provide the best explanation of actor relations? Do interactions vary by policy area? These questions are frequently addressed but seldom resolved in the scholarly literature. We will show that the multiple perspective does an excellent job of answering these questions and of explaining four different presidential-congressional interactions in the adoption of public policy.

CHAPTER 4

Presidential Position Taking

NATURE OF POSITION TAKING

Every president begins with his own agenda, the items that he would like to see considered and passed by Congress. If presidents had their way, the list of agenda items would probably be quite long indeed. Even conservative presidents, such as George Bush, are assertive, albeit to reduce rather than expand government. However, time and available resources constrain all presidents' agendas. One of the ways presidents advance their agendas is by taking positions on legislation before Congress. Position taking is the expression of a particular preference on bills facing congressional roll call votes, but unlimited position taking is not possible. In the first place, the president requires ample staff to research the particular bills that are making their way through Congress. Second, position taking implies a certain degree of commitment to a piece of legislation. Consequently, resources are also necessary to both track the legislation and to lobby needed support when legislation comes to a roll call vote. Therefore position taking makes use of political capital and cannot be entered into frivolously.

Examining presidential position taking proves a worthwhile enterprise because it reflects the expenditure of political capital in efforts to align the president's agenda with bills already in Congress. Position taking is not an obligatory action, but is anticipated by Congress and reveals presidential policy assertiveness and policy preferences on matters before Congress. In addition, a president may take positions on popular bills just to increase his success ratios, which might also enhance his image.[1] Since such position taking is intimately connected with Congress's agenda, it is an agenda the president cannot control but will seek to influence. As such, position taking should relate considerably to other aspects of presidential-congressional relations. For example, literature has revealed a negative relationship between the volume of presidential position taking and legislative support (Shull 1997).

Research has examined Congressional Quarterly (CQ) measures of presidential position taking but largely as it relates to either support or success scores (see Shull 1997, chap. 6). Some research suggests that votes upon which these CQ indicators are based appear fairly representative of all roll call votes (Hammond and Fraser 1980, 42). In chapter 1, we saw that presidents' positions on legislative votes may not even be on issues on the president's agenda, unlike his requests for legislation. Thus, positions and requests are not the same thing, and ambiguity may occur in identifying actual legislative proposals by the president (King and Ragsdale 1988; Bond, Fleisher, and Krutz 1996; Shull 1983). Requests are derived from presidents' speeches but sometimes come from remarks by other "top officials."

Paul Light (1982) shows that many of the president's legislative requests subsequently are repeated. Requests for legislation as measured by CQ are either adopted or not, sometimes without a roll call vote identified. Thus, scores are not available for individual legislators (Edwards 1980; 1985; Peterson 1990; Shull 1983), making only aggregate rather than individual legislator analysis possible (Bond, Fleisher, and Krutz 1996). Finally, the equal weighting of all requests (Edwards 1980; Shull 1983) does not distinguish the important from the trivial. Many of these concerns about presidents' legislative requests have led scholars to focus instead on presidential position taking. This latter indicator of presidential-congressional relations has been incorporated widely and position taking has largely supplanted requests in the scholarly literature.

In this chapter, as in the following three chapters, we follow a standard outline in terms of presenting our expectations and results. First, we present our expectations for the political time control variables (historical era, year in presidential term, and individual presidents). Second, we discuss our expectations for the three environments (executive, legislative, and exogenous) and the process model and posit influences overall and by the policy areas (foreign and domestic). Third, we present the sequence plot of position taking and examine the nature of the time series. Fourth, we present the results for the political time control variables followed by the results for the general and policy models. Finally, we summarize these findings and develop conclusions about this important aspect of presidential-congressional relations.

EXPECTATIONS

Trend

The expectations for position taking are very much dependent upon how the variable is aggregated. First we consider the overall trend in the variable. One could examine position taking as a percentage of roll call votes, which over time has declined. This decline, however, is due not to presidents taking fewer positions but, rather, to the fact that a dramatic increase occurred in the number of recorded roll call votes during the 1970s and 1980s. As a result, position taking has declined in relation to such votes because the latter half of the time series became flooded with roll call votes. Accordingly, rather than looking at position taking as a percentage of roll call votes, we consider the actual number of positions that presidents take. Although number of available roll call votes are important, many are amendments to legislation or routine matters. As such, little reason exists to control for position taking as a percentage of such votes, particularly when such a control forces the variable to decline over time.

We anticipate that position taking is increasing in absolute terms over time, from 1949 to 1995. Although presidents are not taking as many positions in relation to the total number of votes, position taking today is greater overall than in the past. Indeed, contemporary presidents tend to "go public" with their preferences (Kernell 1986). In fact, the public expectation since Franklin Roosevelt has been for more active presidents (LeLoup and Shull 1993). Although Eisenhower might prove an exception,[2] whether they are for or against "big government," the general trend should be for presidents to take more active roles in national policymaking. Consequently, we expect to see position taking increase as presidents, even if only symbolically, take a more active stance on problems facing the nation.

Political Time

We introduce three political time controls: historical era, year in term of presidential office, and individual presidents. We have already referred to our expectation that position taking is increasing, thus there will be more positions taken per year after 1974 than before. We think this has occurred despite assertive presidents (e.g., Kennedy and Johnson) in the earlier time period. We also recognize that some recent Republicans appear relatively nonassertive. Shull (1993) observed Ford taking no positions at all on civil rights policy during two and one half years in office. Thus, position taking is only partly related to the number of roll call votes in Congress.

In looking at the second aspect of political time, we anticipate that the year in term of the president has an effect on position taking. We expect that presidential position taking should be greater during the first (honeymoon) year. We anticipate this increase in position taking because the honeymoon is when the president's political capital should be at its zenith (Light 1982; Pfiffner 1996; Shull 1997). Presumably, the president's political capital will deteriorate steadily from this point.

Although Light (1982) argues that the president can replenish his political capital through the "cycle of increasing effectiveness," it is doubtful that the president ever again sees the kind of capital he possesses in the first year.

However, during last (lame duck) years, we expect position taking to be even higher than in first or reelection years (Shull 1997, 51). During this last year, presidents have an incentive to take positions in order to make a name for themselves in history. If the president can attach himself to important legislation, he may be able to boost both short- and long-term popularity. In contrast, during reelections, the president may or may not opt to take many positions, depending upon his approval ratings. If approval is high and the president's campaign is going strong, the president may opt to take fewer positions in order to reduce the chance of being associated with a controversial and thereby potentially disruptive piece of legislation. If approval is low, however, the president may attempt to change public opinion by engaging in an active campaign of position taking. Research suggests that presidents may be too preoccupied with campaigning to be assertive legislatively during reelection years (Tenpas 1997). Accordingly, reelection years should have fewer positions than either first or last years.

The final control for political time is individual presidents and we expect to find that presidents reveal considerable variation in position taking. While the presidency can be studied in a broader institutional context, the individual president is at the center of such institutional resources (King and Ragsdale 1988; Neustadt 1960; Hager and Sullivan 1994). Therefore, individual preferences flow through the institutional components of the executive office. In particular, we expect higher position taking for Johnson and Nixon and lower position taking for Ford and Reagan. Additionally, because of our expectation for the overall increasing trend in position taking, we reiterate that more contemporary presidents (e.g., Bush and Clinton) take more positions than their earlier counterparts (e.g., Truman and Eisenhower). According to James Pfiffner (1996), some presidents (e.g., Carter) will take more positions in a scatter shot (shotgun) approach than others (e.g., Reagan) using a more strategic and parsimonious (rifle) approach.

Environmental Influences

We anticipate that all three of the environments (executive, legislative, and exogenous) will influence presidential position taking. Since the president is rooted in the executive branch, we expect to find both executive activities and resources influencing whether or not the president decides to take a position on legislation. Additionally, the president is either working with or against Congress depending on the partisan composition of Congress and the president's ideological preferences.[3] As such, Congress is in a position to either facilitate or obstruct the president's preferences. Since position taking expends political capital (Light 1982), the president must take into consideration a number of factors regarding the legislative environment and whether or not he feels his own legislative agenda can pass Congress. However, not taking a position may also alienate groups that supported the president for election. Consequently, the legislative environment should also play an important role in determining presidential position taking. No doubt presidents will consider the partisan make up and their probability of success in their decision calculus. Finally, we expect that the exogenous environment should also influence presidential position taking. One of the prime aspects of the exogenous environment is the economic health of the government. Economic considerations should be influential in that available resources or their lack thereof either help or hinder the success of legislation. Again, as long as position taking expends political capital, the president should take into account economic considerations before deciding to make particular decisions.

We have outlined above our general expectations for the three broad environments. We expect all three environments along with the budget request/appropriation interaction (process variable) to have some influence on presidential position taking. As such, position taking is a prime example of the guiding focus of this work, that a multiple perspective is necessary to fully understand and explain presidential-congressional interactions. We now proceed to specify the expectations for the independent variables in the three-environment model.

Executive. We incorporate three executive environment variables: minor presidential speeches, number of employees in the Executive Office of the President (EOP), and presidential popular support. The activity level of the president should be relevant as a determinant of position taking, but increased activity might reduce position taking since a highly active speaking schedule would reduce the time needed to assess the legislative agenda. That is, position taking requires staff and time both to initially evaluate legislation to determine if a position is to be taken and to follow up on eliciting support for the position. Therefore, we expect either no effect or a positive effect from the speech making activity variable.

The number of employees in the EOP should also influence presidential position taking. The number of employees in the EOP, especially in the Office of Legislative Liaison, equates to staff resources that can be used by the president to further his preferences. Consequently, we hypothesize that as the number of employees in the EOP increases, presidential position taking will also increase. Presidential popular support is another resource variable that the president can use to further his legislative agenda in Congress. Thus, even though popular support is not a resource the president can control (Brace and Hinckley 1992), it is a resource he can employ. Presumably a president will be more likely to engage in increased position taking when his popular support is low as Brace and Hinckley observe.[4]

Legislative. The legislative environment also contains three variables: (1) number of public laws, (2) difference in (gain/loss) House congressional staff, and (3) presidents' party margin in Congress. Number of public laws conceptually represents the workload of Congress (Davidson 1996). While workload may certainly affect the ability of Congress to address and adequately deal with the legislative agenda items on which the president has taken a position, workload should have little impact on presidential position taking. However, if Congress is in the mood to pass lots of legislation, presidents may take positions to go along for the ride. Yet it is unlikely presidents know how busy the legislative agenda will be; that is, the intensity of the workload is only known in the past tense. As such, it is doubtful that the president's decision to take positions on legislative items is determined by a phenomenon that is not completely known. Similarly, change in House staff size should not be influential in presidential position taking. As a resource variable the change in size of House congressional staff is of greater interest to legislators than the president.

In contrast, the president's party margin in Congress should be quite influential for presidential position taking. This variable represents a sort of baseline of likely support or opposition (depending on the size of the margin) that the president can expect from Congress. Unlike congressional workload, presidential party margin is known at any time during a president's term. Consequently, the president knows when he decides whether to take a position what his base level of support is in Congress. It is reasonable to expect the president to take a more aggressive stance on the legislative agenda when his party margin in Congress is high because more political capital is available and Congress is more likely to support presidential initiatives. Therefore, we hypothesize that as the president's party margin in Congress increases, the president will take more positions.

Exogenous. We incorporate two variables in the exogenous environment: economic situation (surplus or deficit/outlays) and size of government (number of civilian federal government employees). The former represents a direct economic constraint on legislative action via expenditures and the deficit and was developed by David Mayhew (1992, 1996). As the economic situation variable worsens (that is the deficit increases), less resources are available since both the deficit and interest payment on the deficit are increasing. A worsened economic situation should be followed by popular criticism that may spawn a negative attitude toward new legislation and policy initiatives among the public at large. In contrast, as the economic situation improves, there should be more available resources and less public scrutiny of new policies and government spending. Again, presidents are concerned with their political capital and so should take the economy into account when deciding whether or not to expend political capital by taking a position. We propose then that as the economic situation variable increases (worsens), the president will take fewer positions. By and large, a president should take fewer positions when economic constraints exist because he cannot afford to waste too much political capital fighting unwinnable conflicts.[5]

We expect that size of government should have little to no effect on presidential position taking. While a contemporary popular antigovernment mood exists, it seems doubtful that this phenomenon would necessarily discourage the president from taking positions on roll call votes. In fact, increased size of government seems likely to result in presidents being active position takers on legislation to reduce big government. Alternatively, reductions in the size of government might increase presidential position taking on policies that would increase government size. Across the three environments then, only some variables should have much of an effect.[6] However, we expect influences from more than one environment to influence presidential position taking. This underscores our belief that a multiple perspectives approach is necessary when studying presidential-congressional interactions.

Process

In addition to the three environments discussed above, the process among the dependent variables (four government interactions) should also play a part in determining presidential position taking. The percentage of the president's requested budget that is approved by Congress provides a clear indication of Congress's willingness to work with and support the president. Budget agreement goes beyond the success or failure of a single bill in that it represents the president's overall plan on government spending. Consequently, the percentage of budget agreement (presidential requests/congressional appropriations) should be a major indicator for whether the president views Congress as friendly or hostile to his policy concerns. We assert then that position taking is influenced by the previous year's budget agreement.[7] We use a one-year lag of the budget agreement variable because of the typical length of time it takes to resolve and pass the budget (see chapter 3, table 3.2).

The president is taking positions on legislation throughout the time that Congress is in the process of approving the budget; consequently, the current year requests and appropriations are still in a state of flux. The result is that the only budgetary cue available to the president is the degree of budget agreement from the previous year.

We therefore expect that the one-year lag of budget agreement will influence presidential position taking. Obviously, incremental tendencies and a reduction in discretionary funds dampen the accuracy of this measure; however, it should be noted that differences of only a few percentage points can mean millions of dollars and the effective survival of affected policies. Thus, we hypothesize that as the one-year lag of budget agreement increases, the president is more likely to take positions since he perceives a supportive Congress.

Policy Effects

Having introduced the general model, we now turn to examining the effects of the three environments by policy area. Our expectation in looking at position taking by domestic policy is that both the legislative and executive environments will still be important in determining presidential position taking. However, congressional variables should play a larger role since the president will be engaging and compromising with Congress for the passage of domestic legislation, on which Congress pays great heed. Executive resources should play some role in determining the president's decision on whether to take a position or not, but size of the president's partisan margin and workload could be important in domestic position taking.

We expect to find that the executive environment is most important in determining presidential position taking on foreign policy legislation due to greater legislative deference in these programs. It should be kept in mind though that because position taking is concerned with presidential preferences on bills already in Congress, fewer pieces of legislation will occur in foreign policy since it is doubtful that Congress will initiate as much foreign as domestic policy votes. Thus, we expect to find that legislative variables have less effect on position taking on foreign policy, while executive variables should be more influential in this policy domain.

RESULTS

Trend Analysis

As expected, the trend in position taking over time is in fact increasing. Figure 4.1 shows that over time the number of positions taken yearly by presidents has gone from in the twenties to well into the eighty to one hundred range. Regressing a monotonically increasing count variable against position taking reveals a statistically significant relationship in a positive direction. The regression coefficient indicates that for every year increase in the count variable, position taking increases by 1.64. In contrast, regressing a one-year lag of position taking against itself does not indicate a statistically significant relationship. This indicates that while position taking is consistently increasing over time, its increases are not necessarily related to the previous year's values. At a certain level, one would expect this increase to eventually level off since a single individual can only do so much and the president's time is already at a premium. However, from an institutional perspective, as long as adequate staff resources are available to take the lead on a particular piece of legislation once the president takes a position, then it is possible that increases in positions taken can continue.

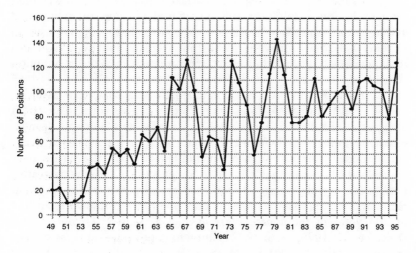

FIGURE 4.1
Presidential Position Taking, 1949–1995

Note: Position taking refers to CQ compilation of the number of times per year that the presidents take a stand on roll call votes in the House.

Trend Analysis

	B	Sig T	
Count	1.64	.000	Adj. R^2 = .48
One-Year Lag	–.99	.650	Adj. R^2 = .31

The plot in figure 4.1 reveals at least two extreme observations. Although the political climate and rhetoric of 1979 indicated a continued strong antigovernment sentiment, the end result of 1979 was a major increase in the scope of government. This was also true for position taking. President Carter in 1979 took more positions than any other president for which we possess data. In particular in 1979, Carter took positions on bills regarding the energy mobilization board that would authorize a board to facilitate priority energy projects through the bureaucracy, on hospital cost containment, and, finally, on the authorization of loans to the Chrysler corporation.

The year 1972 marked the fewest positions taken by a president since the 1950s. Although there were years with fewer positions (1951 possessed the absolute fewest number of positions), 1972 is an interesting outlier since it occurs during a period of greatly increased position taking. In particular, Nixon took positions on bills that year dealing with the Strategic Arms Limitations Treaty (SALT) agreement that prevented treaties from limiting U.S. nuclear forces to levels lower than those of the Soviet Union. As well, Nixon took positions on military aid authorizations amending legislation that would have originally set an October 1 deadline for withdrawal from Vietnam. Finally, Nixon also took positions against Labor-HEW appropriations and water pollution control.

Recently, Bill Clinton has continued to be a somewhat assertive president in terms of position taking on legislative votes. The 104th Congress (1995–96) tried very hard to assert its own domestic agenda, especially in the House with its "Contract for America" against a weakened President Clinton. As mentioned in Shull (1997), the Senate actually helped Clinton in that it failed to adopt most of those conservative Republican agenda items. Clinton then actually reduced his position taking in 1996, taking positions on only 69 of 867 House votes and 59 of 306 votes in the Senate ("Presidential Support," *AllPolitics*.com, December 27, 1996, 2). In 1997 Clinton took positions on items such as the Fiscal 1998 Labor HHS Appropriations/National Education Testing bill that would prohibit the use of federal funds to develop new national student tests in reading and math, and the Fiscal 1998 Commerce, Justice, State Appropriations/Legal Expenses bill allowing defendants who prevail in federal trials to recover legal expenses.

Political Time

The results in table 4.1 show that our broadest conceptualization of political time, historical era, has had a major impact on position taking. This model possesses an adjusted R^2 of .49 and shows that a strong increase in the number of positions taken occurred after 1974. The unstandardized coefficient, which is statistically significant, is 30.28. Compared to the constant of 61.35, this coefficient shows an increase of 49 percent in the number of positions taken after 1974. The most likely explanation for this increase in positions is the increase in the number of items that actually come to a roll call vote after 1974 and, therefore, more openness of the legislative process, which allows greater opportunities for presidents to express policy preferences.

We expected that in looking at select years in presidents' terms, an increase would occur in positions taken during the last year of the presidency. In table 4.1, we see that the relationship is statistically significant and positions go down (−15.39) in the first year relative to the constant value (79.75) and in comparison to last years. While presidents might take advantage of the political capital afforded them in the first year, it

TABLE 4.1
Position Taking and Political Time Controls

	Unstandardized Coefficient	Adjusted R^2
Historical Era		
Political Era, Post-1974	30.28*	.49
constant (1974 and before)	61.35***	
Select Year in Presidential Term		
First Year	−15.39*	.52
Last Year	−6.52	
Reelection Year	−15.90	
constant	79.75***	
Individual President		
Harry Truman (constant)	15.98	.63
Dwight Eisenhower	24.43	
John Kennedy	49.98**	
Lyndon Johnson	82.45***	
Richard Nixon	57.42***	
Gerald Ford	53.08**	
Jimmy Carter	95.77***	
Ronald Reagan	73.34***	
George Bush	86.25***	
Bill Clinton	85.60***	

*   Significant at the .05 level
**   Significant at the .01 level
***   Significant at the .001 level

may be that Light (1982) is correct that presidents have spent so much time and resources getting elected that they do not have a clear idea of what their policy agenda is in the first year and, therefore, are not taking many positions. This finding may also be the result of just plain shock at being elected president. Although most presidential candidates have experience in political office, probably little really prepares a person for being president of the United States. As such, presidents may experience a period of stunned incapacity during their first year, which they overcome as they become used to being president. Other than the constant, none of the other years in presidential term had a statistically significant effect on position taking.

In looking at the individual presidents, we first see that the individual president matters quite a bit, explaining 63 percent of the variation in position taking. Obviously, individual presidents influence position taking as variation in position taking occurs despite the general upward trend. Two factors may be working here, personal characteristics of the individual and external events. First, each president is obviously different and, regardless of the trend in position taking, he will use his own best judgment in deciding whether or not to take a position. It is likely that characteristics akin to Barber's (1992) personality types may have some effect on how different presidents act in terms of position taking. One could easily imagine an active-positive president taking more positions than a passive-negative one. In any event, some of the variation in position taking is likely due to personal characteristics.

Second, external events should also have an effect on an individual president's decisions to take positions. As much as dummy variables capture information regarding the particular president, they also capture information about the particular time period during which the president serves. Consequently, if events occur that require increased legislation, the president may well find himself reacting to such events with increased position taking.

In fact, President Clinton found just the opposite in working with the new Republican Congress in 1995. Coattails not being what they used to be, Clinton ultimately could not control the events that led to the new Republican 104th Congress. However, such events dictated certain reactions from the President. Although 1995 was one of Clinton's most assertive years in terms of position taking, his overall amount of position taking decreased during the first part of the year while the Republicans were pushing their Contract with America. Another strategy was to select Republican-sponsored legislation that he also favored. Looking at just domestic policy issues, Clinton took eighty-four positions in the House and reacted to the Republicans by focusing most of those eighty-four positions on Republican initiatives with which he agreed. Some of the bills that Clinton took positions on included a bill that would allow Alaskan North Slope oil to be exported, as well as bills on speed limits and welfare (*CQ Almanac* 1995).

What we see in this Clinton situation is the president reacting strategically to events over which he has little control. First, Clinton moderated his position taking during the first part of 1995 in response to the new enthusiastic and active Republican majority that was pushing its own agenda. Even though he moderated his position taking early in the year, Clinton was still able to assert himself later after the Republican enthusiasm had cooled and 1995 was ultimately his most assertive year to date. Secondly, Clinton focused on selecting Republican initiatives that were acceptable to him instead of taking positions on Democratically sponsored bills that were likely dead on arrival. Although Clinton continued to face the Republican dominated 104th Congress in 1996, the spirit of compromise had greatly increased since the government shutdowns of 1995 over the budget. The result was that Clinton took a number of important positions during 1996 and 1997, including stands on minimum wage increases, welfare reform, and health insurance portability.

General and Policy Models

The multivariate analysis that follows examines position taking as a function of three variables from each of the three broad environments. Examining the results of the general model in table 4.2, one sees the first indication of the success of our multiple perspectives approach.

Variables from each of the three environments are statistically significant: popular approval (executive), party margin (legislative), and size of federal government (exogenous). In addition, the model possesses a robust adjusted R^2 of .60. Overall then, the model does a good job of explaining this presidential-congressional interaction. Although not completely consistent with our propositions, it is noteworthy that at least one variable from each environment is influential in determining position taking.

We had anticipated that popular approval would possess a negative correlation with position taking. The unstandardized coefficient indicates that for a one unit increase in popular approval, position taking decreases by –.65. Thus, as Brace and Hinckley (1992) found, unpopular presidents are more likely to engage in greater position taking. One possible explanation for the negative relationship is that aggregate popular approval scores have been declining over time. Since we know that presidents have been consistently more active position takers over the last half century, it appears that presidents are having to take positions despite lower approval ratings. This is an important finding revealing that presidents are reacting to lower popular approval. Perhaps this phenomenon results from increasing pressure for presidents to "solve" the problems facing the nation or merely a reaction to more active legislative agendas in recent years.

As expected, the president's party margin in Congress is both statistically significant and possesses the predicted positive direction. The unstandardized coefficient indicates that a one percent increase in party margin leads to a .82 increase in position taking. The expectation here was that as the margin of the president's party increased, the president would feel more assured of congressional support for his preferences and therefore would take more positions. Our findings indicate that this expectation is supported; presidents are more assertive position takers when their party expands their control of the House (see table 4.2).

Finally, as the size of the federal government increases so does presidential position taking. We did not originally expect much of a relationship between government size and position taking; however, the .25

TABLE 4.2
General and Policy Models for Position Taking

	General Model	Domestic Model	Foreign Model
Executive Environment			
Popular Approval	−.65*	−.33	−.31*
Employees in EOP	.21	.41	−.17
Minor Speeches	−.54	.12	−.19
Legislative Environment			
Committee Staff	−.46	−.40*	−.32
Party Margin	.82*	.43	.38*
Workload	−.34	−.22	−.12
Exogenous Environment			
Economic Situation	−100.16	−47.28	−59.40*
Size of Federal Govt.	.25*	.16	.81
One-year. Lag of Budget Agreement	.34	−.18	.42***
constant	−.311	−2.39	−.40
Adj. R^2	.60	.51	.65
LaGrange Multiplier	1.02	.43	3.17

*   Significant at the .05 level
**   Significant at the .01 level
*** Significant at the .001 level

regression coefficient indicates a significant and positive relationship between these two variables. In retrospect, the size of the federal government represents the scope of government. As the scope of government increases, it seems likely that the overall amount of legislation would increase. This overall inflation of legislation would necessitate additional activity by the president. One form of this additional activity would be increased position taking on new legislation. From this finding, we can conclude that as government continues to expand, presidents will find themselves facing more and more legislation and will likely increase their activity level in response.

Our next step is to split position taking into the domestic and foreign policy issue areas. In the domestic policy model, the number of positions taken on domestic matters becomes the dependent variable. Although the model possesses an adjusted R^2 of .51, there is little that one can say regarding the model since only one variable attains statistical significance (see table 4.2). In fact, that significant variable is not one that we expected to have a serious influence on domestic position taking. We saw little reason to expect that House committee staff should influence the president's decision to take more or less positions on items in the legislative agenda. Although it is possible that fewer staff equates with fewer items on the legislative agenda, this line of reasoning does not follow since workload also has little effect.

In contrast, the foreign policy model not only possesses a healthy adjusted R^2 of .65 but, similar to the general model, supports the multiple perspectives approach. Again, variables from all three environments contribute to explaining positions taken on foreign policy matters. Since the president is typically seen as the leader in foreign policy, it is almost inconceivable that the president would fail to take a position on a legislative agenda item that dealt with foreign policy. Again, popular approval and party margin prove statistically significant (see Table 4.2). It is likely that the same effect is occurring regarding position taking on foreign policy votes as is occurring in the general model. Certainly, the logic behind party margin as seen in the general model also applies here. However, we also see some differences from the general model; both economic situation and the one-year lag of budget agreement attain significance in foreign policy position taking.

Looking first at economic situation, we see that as it increases, the number of foreign positions taken goes down, −59.40. The point to keep in mind is that an increase in economic situation is actually an increase in the deficit which equates to an economic decline; that is, the economy is getting worse. Often one of the first areas of spending to be cut during such economic circumstances is military spending. The findings indicate that presidents are aware of such moods and, accordingly, take fewer positions on foreign policy items during such periods.

In terms of the one-year lag of budget agreement, the unstandard-ized regression coefficient .42, indicates that as the level of budget agreement increases, the propensity to take positions on foreign policy votes also increases. According to our framework, 100 percent budget agreement represents an almost perfect symmetry between presidential requests and congressional appropriations, and presidents prefer more budget agreement to less. Thus, as budget agreement approaches perfect symmetry, presidents are likely to feel that Congress is working with them or at least that their respective preferences are congruent. Consequently, presidents are more likely to take positions on foreign policy legislation with the expectation that Congress will support their positions as they have supported them in other interactions, namely budget agreement.

Ultimately, we expected and find that all three environments have an effect on the general and policy models. These expectations were realized in two of the models but not for the domestic policy model. However, the success of the general and foreign policy models provide strong evidence that multiple environments are necessary to understand the presidential-congressional interaction of position taking. In both cases, variables from the executive, legislative and exogenous environments attain statistical significance and contribute to the explanation of position taking. In particular, popular approval and party margin proved important in both models. Exogenous variables were important in both models but the particular variables were mixed from the general to foreign policy model. Size of federal government was significant in the general model and economic situation and the one-year lag of budget agreement was significant in the foreign policy model.

SUMMARY AND CONCLUSION

Our trend analysis reveals that position taking is increasing steadily over time. The count variable exerts an effect on position taking; however there is no effect for the lagged variable. The number of positions taken in the current year are not necessarily a function of the number of positions taken in the previous year. The effect from the count variable is most likely due to the consistent increase in the scope of government throughout the time period that we examine. It seems likely that such increases in the scope of government will continue to increase despite Republican attempts to the contrary. The reason for this is that once in place, programs tend to perpetuate themselves. Also, with the world becoming a far more complex place to live, government will continue to be prevailed upon to intervene into private matters. Thus, it also appears likely that presidential position taking will continue to increase. The interesting question then becomes, is there an upper limit to the number of positions that can be taken during a year? Certainly, this is somewhat a function of staff resources in the sense that the president must rely on others to assist in position taking as in other matters. However, at a certain point, will an upper limit be reached beyond which it becomes counterproductive for the president and his staff to issue positions?

The political time controls used herein show that a number of factors affect position taking outside of our multiple perspectives model. First, the historical era of pre- and post-1974 indicates a sizable increase in the number of positions taken in the post-1974 period. Secondly, select years in presidential term reveal that presidents are less likely to take positions in their first (honeymoon) year than in other years. This reluctance to take positions may stem from the fact that the president and his advisors have been focusing on winning a presidential election and not preparing a legislative agenda (of which positions on bills facing Congress are a subset). Finally, individual presidents and the unique characteristics surrounding their particular term(s) in office are quite important in understanding position taking. Certainly, it is the president's prerogative to take a position or not. Thus, personal characteristics regarding assertiveness, style, and preferences have an impact on decisions to take positions. Events that occur during a particular president's term may also influence the amount of positions presidents decide to take.

The president uses position taking to assert his preference on items in the legislative arena. By taking positions he alerts legislators to his agenda preferences and, in doing so, attempts to influence legislators' voting behavior. Although popular approval possessed a negative relationship with position taking, it could be said that this resource actually supports the argument that the president is using position taking to attempt to enact his preferences. One would expect people to increase their preference-seeking activity when their popularity is high, but presidents' increasing their position taking activity even when their popularity is low, shows how important such preference-seeking activity has become.

As expected, presidents' party margin in Congress had a strong positive effect in both the general and foreign policy models. Clearly, position taking is an expenditure of political capital and the president does not want to waste any such capital since it is doubtful that he will get it back. As such, it makes sense that one of the biggest cues for the president in terms of whether or not to take a position would be his party margin. Ideology of both presidents and members of Congress could also be important (Brady and Volden 1998).

As stated earlier, contemporary presidents are expected to take an active role in addressing the nation's problems. In attempting to address these problems, the president and Congress add human resources to the federal government. Whether by establishing a new committee or agency to address a particular problem or by reorganizing an existing agency or department to meet either contemporary or future demands (Light 1995), the president and Congress are engaged in expanding the size of the federal government in an effort to adopt public policy. As government expands, more legislation is required to address the duties and functions of government itself, and as legislation increases, presidents will take more positions.

Overall, our foray into presidential position taking produced a number of interesting findings. The explanatory power of all three models (general, domestic, and foreign) were strong, indicating that while we may not have completely tapped the domain of potential explanans, we have certainly uncovered a number of important ones. Certainly, not all of our expectations were confirmed in the results; however, the expectations for each individual variable are somewhat less important to us than the bigger picture. In the bigger picture, we see that our multiple perspectives approach aids in understanding presidential-congressional relations. Discounting the domestic model, we see that in both the general and foreign policy models, variables from each of the three environments attained significance in explaining the dependent variable (position taking). Thus, in order to understand the phenomenon of position taking, one needs to account for not only both institutional environments (executive and legislative), but also the exogenous environment.

In conclusion, position taking is an effective and presumably cheap means to define the presidential agenda. The president does not have to formulate legislation but merely have his staff review existing legislation and take an appropriate position. Our evidence suggests that positions are an important presidential tool, especially when popular approval is low. However, when the presidents' margin of partisans increases, they take more positions in the hope that more of their agenda preferences will be adopted. Although these two institutional variables as well as the exogenous size of government variable influence presidential position taking, position taking is also a personal choice left up to the president. Finally, as we see in our political time controls, the individual president is important in whether or not they decide to take a position on roll call votes in Congress.

CHAPTER 5

Legislative Support

NATURE OF SUPPORT

Many concepts have been used to describe presidential-congressional relations.[1] Success, support, concurrence, leadership, and influence all appear in the scholarly literature (Edwards 1980, 1989; Shull 1983; Bond and Fleisher 1990; Peterson 1990) and sometimes are used interchangeably. Ironically, this diverse terminology usually refers to one single relationship between the first two branches of our national government, that is, congruence of preferences. The most commonly examined indicator in recent years is the extent to which Congress supports the president's positions on roll call votes before the legislative body. This important measure, collected by Congressional Quarterly (CQ) for over forty years, is often confused with other indicators of presidential-congressional interactions.

This chapter begins with conceptual and measurement questions about this support component of executive-legislative relations. It considers related concepts identified by CQ: success, support, and then ideas used by other authors. Utilization of the organization's key votes measure may be seen in Shull (1997, chapter 6) and is not covered here. CQ has collected both success and support measures for a considerable period of time and, despite problems, they have been widely used in the literature of presidential-congressional relations. Scholars also use variations on an earlier available success measure (Light 1982; Peterson 1990). This chapter assesses these alternative indicators, but utilizes legislative support of presidents' positions on roll call votes on legislation before Congress.

At one time, CQ measured legislative *success* through its box score indicator. CQ included in this measurement only the specific legislative requests contained in the president's public statements and whether or not Congress enacted such measures within the same calendar year. Although CQ did not specify which statements they used, Shull (1983) and others have included all public remarks (taken from *Public Papers of the Presidents*) as opposed to just the State of the Union addresses used by some scholars (e.g., Light 1982; Cohen 1980). Policies emanating from the executive branch that are endorsed by the president but not specifically requested by him are excluded. When such requests or proposals were substantially changed or amended by Congress, CQ made a judgment (without supplying specific coding rules) about whether the legislation conformed to the president's original request. (For an example of coding rules, see *Congressional Quarterly Almanac* 1963, 86.)

Success is a tangible measure of presidential preferences that provides numerous advantages to scholars (Hammond and Fraser 1984a; Shull 1983; Rivers and Rose 1985; Spitzer 1983; Covington et al. 1995). Unfortunately, the disadvantages of the indicator are just as pronounced, leading CQ to abandon the box score measure after 1975.[2] Congressional Quarterly made judgments about success with which they are no longer comfortable. The organization's principal apprehension about its box score was that writers were quoting aggregate figures of presidential success without adequately considering the substance of the initiatives themselves or other qualitative or quantitative factors that may influence the results.

Problems associated with the box score have been discussed by many scholars. Its most widely recognized drawbacks include the following: first is insensitivity to legislation that takes more than one year to pass (Bond and Fleisher 1990; Cohen 1980, 4; Edwards 1980; Peterson 1990; Shull 1983, 195–99). This is because calendar year is the unit of analysis. Paul Light (1982) and others show that many of the president's legislative requests are repeated subsequently. A second problem is ambiguity in identifying actual legislative proposals by the president (King and Ragsdale 1988; Shull 1983). They are derived from presidents' speeches but sometimes come from other "top officials." Third is the lack of scores for individual legislators (Edwards 1980; 1985; Peterson 1990; Shull 1983), making only aggregate rather than individual level analysis possible (Bond, Fleisher and Krutz 1996). Finally, the equal weighting of all requests (Edwards 1980; Shull 1983) does not distinguish the important from the trivial.[3]

Despite these acknowledged problems, some scholars still consider box scores a potentially valuable data base (Spitzer 1983; Hammond and Fraser 1984b; Shull 1983). CQ box scores are far from perfect, but they do provide a conceptually valid measure of presidential success (on *their* preferences) in Congress. Improvements can be made by modifying the coding rules and expanding the presentation of the data (Shull 1983). Mark Peterson (1990) used a form of the box score in his analysis and rekindled interest in similar measures. These changes in part address some of the empirical problems that led to the demise of the box score indicator of success.[4] In recent years, CQ has used success in a different way, analogous to what Lyn Ragsdale (1996, 383) calls "concurrence." Now success connotes the proportion of presidential vote positions that are upheld by Congress. Thus, it is no longer an indicator of presidents' agenda success but of legislative agreement (both chambers) with their vote positions. The formula for CQ's newer success score is the number of times Congress upholds presidents' vote positions divided by number of positions taken per year. Unlike the earlier success measure, CQ's current one is more closely related to their support score; both now use number of presidential positions as the denominator, with vote as the unit of analysis.

The second, now more common CQ measure is the *support* score, available overall and for individual legislators, the latter being the unit of analysis. Support refers to the percentage of members voting in accordance with the president's vote positions. Scholars and journalists alike have relied on this indicator, collected continually since 1957.[5] Like the original success measure (the box score), the support score possesses both advantages and disadvantages. Because a support score is assigned to each member of Congress, it is possible to construct a variety of data aggregations. For example, these individual scores can be combined by state, region, party, ideology, and so on. As a result, the support score is more versatile than the box score, which is inherently limited by its high level of aggregation. Of course, support scores are a poorer measure of presidential preferences. Critics commonly note two disadvantages: first, as with the box score, all issues are weighted equally (Bond and Fleisher 1990; Edwards 1980, 1985; Peterson 1990). Second, ambiguities exist in identifying which votes to use; bias is introduced by including routine, noncontroversial votes (Bond and Fleisher 1990; Edwards 1985). Obviously, such decisions affect the results and all roll call votes are included here.

Students of presidential-congressional relations need to keep in mind the very different nature of CQ's presidential legislative success (both indicators) and legislative support. Steven Shull (1983) found that presidents from 1953 to 1975 averaged only 44 percent (old box score) success, but their overall support (CQ's current success measure) from Congress on votes was much higher (73 percent). Why should every president fare better on CQs support than on its original success score? A proposal by the president must pass both houses to be approved. His position on a roll call, however, often refers to any recorded vote in either chamber. Obviously, since the early 1970s, support is based more on amendments, due largely to the substantial increase in the number of roll call votes. In addition, while final passage of legislation usually constitutes a roll call, many votes are not on final passage, especially in the Senate.

Scholars have sought other measurement strategies to develop indicators of presidential-congressional interactions. Thomas Hammond and Jane Fraser analyzed success (box score)[6] by creating baseline models that reflect statistical chance (1984a, 1984b). Each baseline model is designed to embody certain assumptions about the voting behavior of members of Congress, the importance of party, and the existence of factions. The authors concede that they "are trying to judge presidential performances, not explain them" (1992, 644). There is no attempt to discern which model best reflects the actual conditions that affect success. As a result, this baseline approach provides interesting results, but it does not directly explain success.

Terry Sullivan offers a measurement strategy that relies on presidential administration head counts used to determine the initial positions of members of Congress. The aggregated difference between initial positions and final votes is Sullivan's approximation of influence, which he calls "sway" (1991b, 693). This strategy is appealing because change is measured directly; it is not based on a subjective construct. Of course, Sullivan's approach is vulnerable to criticism. In particular, Edwards (1991) questions his understanding of influence and the reliability of head counts. Because head counts are ascertained by the administration itself, they may serve political purposes more than methodological ones. In addition, they are available for only a few administrations.

Nevertheless, Sullivan addresses Edwards' concerns, stating that "change is central to the definition of influence" (1991c, 732). Given this perspective, future research on influence should move toward a more direct measure of influence. Sullivan is on the right track; conceptually, the change in initial positions and final votes seems like the most appropriate measure of influence. The key obstacle to this approach is in the identification of initial legislator positions and whether such head counts are comparable across administrations; indeed, they are not available for all modern presidencies. Despite these limitations, head counts reduce the president's information and time costs since he has no need to influence a member already in agreement with his position.

This discussion has covered success, support, and influence as three distinct concepts. By observing these distinctions, scholars can more easily clarify what they seek to explain. Presidential-congressional relations have been observed empirically for over forty years through the above CQ measures of presidents' legislative interactions, and their extensive utilization by scholars has prompted debate about what they actually measure. Understanding the measurement controversies better prepares the reader to assess the CQ support score used here as well as other alternatives. Recall that neither CQ's current success nor support scores necessarily reflect the passage of legislation. We chose support because it is widely used in the literature and also because it is readily categorized by policy area while none of the alternatives are so coded in the

Ragsdale (1996) data set. Support is also the indicator with the longest time series after modification by Brad Gomez and Shull (1995).

This chapter now continues the examination of legislative support for the president as did the discussion for position taking. First, we lay out some general and more specific expectations for presidents' legislative support overall and when controlling for trend and political time. Then we consider explanations of such support and why we think certain environmental variables should be influential. In this context, we provide a model of our three environments predicting support overall and then when controlling for policy area. Then we summarize the findings and draw some conclusions toward seeking greater understanding of legislative support of presidents' positions on roll call votes.

EXPECTATIONS

Trend

Due to the considerable prior research on presidents' legislative support, it is easier to hypothesize what variables should be important than for our other three interactions. In chapter 4, we observed gradually increasing presidential position-taking over the course of this study. But since we also observed position taking and support to be negatively related, it makes sense that support will reveal a downward trend over time. We attribute this decline in part to frequently divided government and growing partisanship in legislative roll call voting (Shull 1997; Shaw and Shull 1996).[7] Increased contentiousness from these conditions as well as growing legislative assertiveness likely have dampened presidents' abilities to obtain their policy preferences. Congress may react to assertive presidential position taking with lower support, thereby increasing its independence as a coequal in policymaking. Thus, we expect to see some diminution in legislative support for presidents' vote positions since the early 1970s as Congress seems more and more willing to challenge presidents.

Political Time

Previous literature has shown that presidents generally fare well, obtaining about 57 percent legislative support of their vote positions from Congress (Shull 1997, chapter 6). Obviously, such support in the House should vary considerably according to groupings of the data by the three time periods used as controls in this analysis.[8] They range from most aggregated (political era, with two periods) to least aggregated (individual presidents, with ten individuals), with year in presidential term in the middle (with four groupings). It should be obvious by now that presidential support should be greater in the earlier period (before 1975) than after, at least within the time frame analyzed. Despite being only a dichotomy, historical era should be a useful control on presidents' legislative support and also for this time period, somewhat reflects divided versus unified government.

One might think that presidents would be supported by Congress at higher levels during their first (honeymoon year in office) than during reelection year. Although presidential experience is greater later in their terms, their political capital has also diminished by then (Light 1982). Indeed, research has shown that presidents actually obtain greater support during first year than during any other designated year in term (Shull 1997, 90). That finding is not a result of presidents taking more positions during first year because they actually take slightly more positions during their last year in office. Both position taking and support are less during reelection years. Accordingly, we have some basis to expect some variation in support by year in term of office.

Not all earlier presidents should fare well in legislative support (e.g., Dwight Eisenhower), nor should all later presidents do poorly (e.g., Jimmy Carter; see Shull 1997, chapter 6). Researchers have observed that legislative support was much greater for John Kennedy and Lyndon Johnson than it was for Gerald Ford and Ronald Reagan. Thus, individual presidents should reveal great differences in legislative support. Bill Clinton had quite a lot of support in his first two years, but it dropped dramatically in 1995 before increasing somewhat in 1996 and 1997 (LeLoup and Shull 1999, 83). Among three aggregations for political time, Shull (1997, 90) revealed that individual president had the greatest discriminating value for legislative support. This is due, in part, to the fact that the individual president variable contains more categories (ten presidents). Nevertheless, we also expect political era to be a useful control, more so than year in term, for tapping presidents' legislative support.

Environmental Influences

We now turn to the three environments as rival explanations for legislative support of presidents' positions on roll call votes. We think that all three environments (executive, legislative, and exogenous) could contribute to presidential support in the House. To reiterate the general expectation from chapter 2, we anticipate that legislative variables, particularly activities more than resources, will be especially important for such support. As mentioned there, the decision is in the legislative arena, with the votes on which support is based representing Congress' but not necessarily presidents' agendas. Thus, legislative factors should predominate. As mentioned in chapter 4, presidents expend political capital by expressing positions on legislative votes and they must consider the risk in such an action; that is, Congress may seek greater independence to challenge presidents' very act of expressing a preference. But characteristics of the president, particularly his available staff resources (more than his popularity or other resources) may also be important from the executive environment. Even exogenous factors (like the state of the economy) may have an impact on this important executive-legislative interaction. Thus, we expect that while the legislative environment is more important for support than the other two environments, all three contribute to our understanding of legislative support of the president. If that finding emerges, then our multiple perspective will obtain some face validity. Next, we lay out more specific expectations for the variables within each of these environments.

Executive. Despite occurring in the legislature itself, we expect variables within the executive environment to have some influence on legislative support for presidents' vote positions. We have already discussed the controversy in the literature over the impact of presidents' popularity (Rivers and Rose 1985; Zeidenstein 1983), but we doubt based upon research from other scholars that it will have much effect (Brace and Hinckley 1992; Collier and Sullivan 1995; Bond and Fleisher 1980, 1984, 1990). Thus, the influence of popular approval should be small and possibly even negative. Still, the role of popularity could vary by policy area, as we shall see shortly. The other presidential resource, Executive Office staff, might facilitate legislative liaison efforts, which would be beneficial to the level of support presidents obtain. The last executive environment variable is the activity of making discretionary minor speeches. We hypothesize that minor speeches will have a negative effect on the legislative support presidents receive. Paul Brace and Barbara Hinckley (1992) observe this effect compared to the positive effect of major speeches on presidents' legislative relations. We consider their finding of a reciprocal relationship with popularity in the methodological appendix.

Legislative. Because legislative support is tapping a congressional response to presidential actions, we expect legislative variables to be more important but still not exclusive or totally dominant in explaining support. We doubt that workload activity (number of public laws) has much to do with legislative support. It is possible that if Congress is enacting many laws, that it would not have time to give presidents' vote positions much scrutiny. However, these are matters on which legislators must decide anyway and little deference to presidents occurs even when Congress is busy. Legislative committee staff, on the other hand, could provide legislators with more time to research and follow up with the White House on presidential vote positions, so its effects should be positive. The third legislative environment variable, the presidents' party margin in the House, should be the dominant legislative variable in explaining support. We hypothesize that the greater the president's party margin in the House the greater his legislative support.[9] Obviously, this circumstance favors Democratic presidents who always (except Clinton in 1995) had partisan majorities and, thus, unified party government during the forty seven years of this study.[10] Indeed, presidential party margin within the legislative environment should be crucial. Much previous research documents the pervasiveness of party affiliation in roll call voting in Congress in general (Turner 1951; Froman 1963; Clausen 1973) and for support and success in particular (Edwards 1989; Bond and Fleisher 1990).

Exogenous. We use two variables within the external environment: number of federal civilian employees and economic situation. The former measure is, of course, a resource not unlike those human resources included in both the executive and legislative environments. It seems to us to measure scope of government. We do not have an exogenous activity variable per se, but the economic situation may approximate it because it encompasses elements of both the state of the economy in terms of the deficit or surplus and government spending. Presumably, variables in the external environment should have less direct influence than the institutional variables on presidents' legislative support, but they should have some effect.

The state of the economy should be more important than size of the federal government in explaining presidents' legislative support. Under scarce resources or difficult economic times, Congress may exhibit less support for presidential positions that would expand the role of the federal government, a big portion of which is government employees. Certainly other environmental variables not tapped here could influence presidents' legislative support, and some authors discuss the concept of skill. Brad Lockerbie and Stephen Borrelli (1989) find a modest relationship between skill and legislative success but Dennis Gleiber, Shull, and Colleen Waligora (1998) think their measure of editorial support for presidents better taps Neustadt's (1960) notion of professional reputation than does skill (see also Bond and Fleisher 1990, chapter 8 and Edwards 1989, chapters 9–10 on skill). Of course, how a president is viewed by interest groups and the "Washington community" should influence legislative support for his preferences but these influences are difficult to gauge. Despite our expectations for legislative support, we still anticipate some influence from the other two environments on legislative support for presidents.

Process

As we have asserted throughout this book, our four interactions between the president and Congress are expected to be related, sometimes with time lags and other times within the same calendar year. Prior interactions, either lagged one or more years or current decisions, are also part of the environments in which these two actors operate. In some sense, these prior actions are also thought of as the external (or perhaps past) environment. Position taking in the same year should be closely but inversely related to presidential support. Because one is a direct response to the other, no time lags are required as discussed in chapter 3 (see table 3.2). CQ records vote positions and support annually but, of course, some of the legislation upon which the votes are based may carry over the entire two-year Congress.

Another reason exists for our expected relationship between presidential position taking on House roll call votes and average member support thereof. The reader will recall that support is composed in part of position taking and, thus, they are automatically related. However, Shull (1997, chapter 6) observed that this type of assertiveness hurts presidents' subsequent legislative support. Obviously, the propensity for presidents to take positions should have a lot to do with whether those positions are supported and, as anticipated earlier, we expect the relationship to be negative. Still, the relationship between these two variables may be reciprocal, an issue we discuss in the appendix.

Policy Effects

Considerable previous research has examined differences in presidents' legislative success and support when differentiated by foreign and domestic policy areas. Most authors find such support to be somewhat greater in foreign than in domestic policy (see various studies in Shull 1991). Literature suggests presidents are deferred to in foreign policy but not when they take benefits from one group and give them to another (i.e., redistributive policy; Shull 1983, 1997). However, Shull 1997 did not observe large differences in support between domestic and foreign policy areas, so we think that such a division might not be very discriminating for legislative support. Indeed, the previous study found a two-presidencies effect for Republican presidents only, similar to what Bond and Fleisher (1990) have observed. Nevertheless, we anticipate at least somewhat greater legislative support for presidents' positions in foreign policy and it provides a useful control in the analyses that follow.

Further expectations are that the executive environment will be more influential for foreign support and the legislative environment will be more important for domestic support. This expectation relates to the considerable literature cited in chapter 1 suggesting relative policy emphases by these two crucial actors. We suspect that difficult economic times as reflected in the exogenous environment could dampen legislative support for presidents in both policy areas, but especially domestic. Foreign policy support should be less variable (more stable) than domestic support and, thus, less explainable by resources and activity variables from the three environments. Still, presidential popular support (executive environment) should influence foreign support more, while the more partisan nature of domestic policy should make party margin (legislative environment) more important in that policy realm.

RESULTS

Trend Analysis

Figure 5.1 reports the data points for legislative support in the House for presidents' vote positions from 1949 to 1995. We can see that a gradual

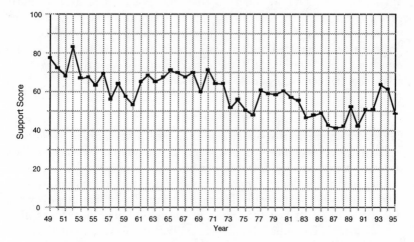

FIGURE 5.1
Legislative Support, 1949–1995

Note: Legislative support refers to the percentage of House members siding with the presidents' positions on roll call votes.

Trend Analysis

	B	Sig T	
Count	.62	.000	Adj. R² = .58
One-Year Lag	.27	.012	Adj. R² = .37

decrease in such support has occurred, averaging about 70 percent support in the 1950s but below 50 percent in the mid-1980s. The overall average legislative support for presidents' vote positions during this time series is 57.4 percent. Since both the count and lag analyses are significant, the downward trend predicted is confirmed. Certainly, spikes occur in legislative support, with the highest levels in 1952 and 1970 and the lowest levels in 1976 and 1987. We now discuss some of the highs and lows of legislative support over our forty-seven-year period.

An early high period, 1952 is not discussed due to the slightly different calculation mentioned in chapter 3. Many would be surprised to see high levels of support for Richard Nixon in 1970, but Shull (1997, chapter 5) observed that partisan voting was very low and the volume of important legislation was at quite high levels then. Except for Eisenhower, Nixon's legislative success (average percent concurrence on his positions in both the House and Senate as opposed to individual legislator scores) was higher than for any Republican except Reagan in 1981 (*CQ Weekly Reports*, January 27, 1996, 239). Indeed, it was a feat that even Johnson could equal in only a single year (see figure 5.1). The only other levels of support approaching these values were for Bill Clinton in 1993 and 1994. In the latter year, Clinton obtained victories in pushing for the death penalty in crime legislation, his "goals 2000" program in education, and in achieving his GATT program in trade. His relatively few defeats were on a bill to encourage telephone and cable competition, overhauling laws regarding superfund hazardous wastes sites, and campaign finance reform (*Congressional Roll Call* 1995, 4–C).

Although Clinton's legislative support was very high in 1993 and 1994, it dropped dramatically in 1995 before returning to moderate levels in 1996 and 1997. Even though his support was low in 1995, such domestic positions as job training and eliminating the Interstate Commerce Commission were upheld by Congress. As mentioned earlier, Clinton's legislative support increased considerably during 1996–97 from the 1995 low value. Although CQ's most recent success and support scores are both based upon presidential position taking, the results can be quite different. For example, Clinton's overall success in 1994 was 87.4% while his overall support in the House was just 61.2%. They were more comparable in 1995 at 26.3% and 36.2% respectively. His success varied by issue area (30% in defense and foreign policy, 28% in domestic policy, and 13% in economic policy and trade; *CQ Weekly Reports*, January 27, 1996, 237). Clinton's 1996 House success was 51% in domestic and 56% in foreign policy (*AllPolitics*.com, "Presidential Support," December 27, 1996, 7). In 1977, Clinton was supported on a treaty upholding U.S. trademark regulations but not supported on a bill he favored allowing federal funds for a Teamsters Union election.

Very low support is evident in figure 5.1 for Ronald Reagan during 1986–88. Certainly, Reagan's support with both the public and Congress slipped partly as a result of the Iran-Contra scandal. The year 1987 was the lowest CQ "success" (concurrence) score to that date and stemmed largely from widespread defections from formerly loyal Republican legislators. Recall that Reagan had lost his Republican majority in the Senate during the previous election. Reagan did obtain support for a revision of deficit reduction and trade provisions, but was defeated in his plan to accelerate the strategic defense ("Star Wars") initiative, his interpretation of an antimissile treaty and, of course, confirmation of his Supreme Court nominee Robert Bork. George Bush nearly reached Reagan's lowest support in 1990, only one year after his honeymoon (first) year in office.

In addition to examining these individual outliers, we test for trend in the model by using two variables. The first is a count variable, and the final parameters show an adjusted R^2 of .58 after controlling for auto-correlation. The second iteration is a lag, where the final parameter was an adjusted R^2 of .37 after correcting for autocorrelation with a Prais-Winsten transformation. These values also appear in figure 5.1. Since both of these tests were significant, a clear downward trend in support is observed for this time series (1949–95) on presidents' legislative support in the House.

Political Time

The next analysis examines legislative support of the president when controlling for the three aspects of political time: political era, year in presidential term, and individual president. The results of these regressions appear in table 5.1, and all three required corrections for auto-correlation. The first control is early-late era, the final parameter of which explains 58 percent of the variance in support. We observe that support averages nearly 66 percent in the early period but almost fourteen percentage points lower in the period since 1974. Both coefficients are significant at the .001 level.

The second control for political time is by selected year in presidential term of office, with an adjusted R^2 of .48. However, it may be seen in table 5.1 that none of the years (first, last or reelection) explain any of the variance in legislative support of the president in the House nor are any remotely close to statistical significance. None of these selected year designations differed from the constant and, while significant, that variable is the theoretically uninteresting residual category "other" years. As expected, presidents were supported slightly less during reelection and honeymoon (first) years in office. The very small Bs (unstandardized coefficients), however, give us very little confidence in this control for presidents' legislative support.

The final control in table 5.1 is for individual president. This time cycle is much more powerful than either of the other two, explaining 71 percent of the variance in presidential support. As the trend suggested, support dropped subsequent to Truman, who serves as the constant. Every subsequent president had less legislative support, although Kennedy and Johnson not significantly less. Ford, Reagan, and Bush received 26–28 percentage points lower support on average than did Truman. As mentioned previously, the number of data points are few for Ford and Clinton, because of limited years, so caution is urged in interpreting these individual president comparisons. Despite this limitation, the controls for political time were useful in our estimations of presidents' legislative support in the House.

TABLE 5.1
Legislative Support and Political Time Controls

	Unstandardized Coefficient	Adj. R^2
Historical Era		
Political Era, Post-1974	−13.67***	.58
constant (1974 and before)	65.77***	
Select Year in Presidential Term		
First Year	1.58	.48
Last Year	3.20	
Reelection Year	1.10	
constant	59.21***	
Individual President		
Harry Truman (constant)	75.89***	.71
Dwight Eisenhower	−13.57**	
John Kennedy	−8.79	
Lyndon Johnson	−6.32	
Richard Nixon	−14.72***	
Gerald Ford	−26.09***	
Jimmy Carter	−16.20***	
Ronald Reagan	−27.94***	
George Bush	−26.51***	
Bill Clinton	−18.05***	

* Significant at the .05 level
** Significant at the .01 level
*** Significant at the .001 level

General and Policy Models

The results of the regression analysis in the general model of legislative support can be seen in table 5.2. The overall explanatory power of the nine variables in the general model is very high, with an adjusted R^2 of .84. Clearly, the three environments explain legislative support much better than they do position taking in chapter 4. The overall model is, of course, significant, as are three of the predictor variables at the .001 level of significance, and two others at lower levels. A correction for autocorrelation was necessary. Employees in the EOP (executive environment) and presidential party margin (legislative environment) are important predictors of their support in the House and in the predicted directions. One possible if not probable explanation why the former is significant is that presidential staff resources provide greater opportunity to lobby Congress in support of presidential policy preferences. Another possibility is its curvilinear nature. That is, staff size increased through the Nixon administration but dropped subsequently.

TABLE 5.2
General and Policy Models for Legislative Support

	General Model	Domestic Model	Foreign Model
Executive Environment			
Popular Approval	.29	.38	−.32
Employees in EOP	.24***	.28**	.23***
Minor Speeches	.10	.16	.36**
Legislative Environment			
Committee Staff	−.24	−.29	−.37
Party Margin	.69***	.58***	.37***
Workload	.13	.11	.57***
Exogenous Environment			
Economic Situation	28.10*	25.69	42.58*
Size of Federal Govt.	.78**	.84*	.10**
Presidential Position Taking	−.18***	−.12*	−.16***
constant	6.61	2.69	2.19
Adj. R^2	.84	.68	.72
LaGrange Multiplier	.29	6.30	2.55

*   Significant at the .05 level
**   Significant at the .01 level
*** Significant at the .001 level

Most surprising of all is the high level of explanatory power from all three variables in the exogenous environment. While the importance of the process variable (position taking) is predictable, economic situation and size of the executive branch are also statistically significant. What we are left with, then, is a single significant predictor from each of the two institutional environments and all three from the exogenous environment as important influences on presidents' legislative support on their roll call vote positions.

No other predictor approaches significance, including presidential popular support, a finding congruent with much of the scholarly literature (e.g., Bond and Fleisher 1990; Collier and Sullivan 1995; Peterson 1990; Brace and Hinckley 1992). Several variables from the institutional environments washed out of the general model and had no effects on legislative support for presidents' positions on House roll calls. Apart from popular support, these include speeches within the executive environment, and House committee staff and number of public laws within the legislative environment. Obviously then, these findings for legislative support of the presidents' vote positions provide strong validation of our overarching multiple perspectives approach.

We now examine the models of presidential support in the House when controlling for policy area (domestic versus foreign dichotomy). These results also appear in table 5.2 and both analyses also required corrections for autocorrelation. The domestic model is significant and explains 68 percent of the variance (adjusted R^2); substantial but a considerably lower level than for the general model. Employees in the EOP, party margin, size of the federal government, and position taking are all significant. Of these four variables, party margin and position taking decrease some in the domestic sphere and the resource variables, employees in the EOP (executive) and size of federal government (exogenous), actually increase somewhat over the general model. The process interaction, position taking, was a significant exogenous factor in all three models (the general and the two policy areas). It is also apparent in table 5.2 that legislative support for presidents' positions on all votes was better explained than was support for either policy position votes.

Our three environmental components explain foreign policy support somewhat better than they do domestic support (adjusted $R^2 = .72$). The foreign policy model still is significant and fully seven of nine component variables attained statistical significance at the .05 level or higher. Minor speeches (executive) and workload (legislative) emerge significant in the foreign model when they were not important for either general or domestic support. Only presidential popular approval and congressional staff size fail to attain statistical significance and, thus, our model explains this phenomenon well.

In summary, we believe the control for policy area is worthwhile despite the similarity in their explanation. Several variables were significant in the foreign policy area that were not in the domestic realm (see table 5.2). The observant reader will note also that explanatory power was lower for both policy models (especially domestic) than for the general (non–policy designated) model of legislative support of presidents' vote positions. All three environments help explain support in general and both policy areas, but there were some changes across issue domains. Contrary to expectation, popular approval was no different for domestic than for foreign policy support, yet several other variables differed dramatically by policy area. Despite very good explanatory power for all three models of legislative support, the domestic model was least well explained by our three environments (executive, legislative, and exogenous).

SUMMARY AND CONCLUSION

This chapter began with the reminder that legislative success and support are quite different concepts. Although both are collected by Congressional Quarterly, they have sometimes been used interchangeably and some confusion exists in the scholarly literature. Here we study legislative support of presidents' roll call vote positions in the House overall and by issue area (Ragsdale 1996). We agree with the views of some authors that high support taps congruence of preferences with the president but not necessarily his influence or leadership over Congress. Empirical testing has been more elusive for the latter concepts.

Legislative support demonstrates a downward pattern from its high levels in the early 1950s. The lag and a count variables reveal a monotonically decreasing trend in legislative support. Controls for political time itself also provided useful demarcations of legislative support for presidents' vote positions. Obviously presidents since 1974 fared much worse than their predecessors. Yet, Democratic presidents Truman, Kennedy, Johnson, and Clinton received much higher levels of support from Congress than did Republicans Ford, Reagan, and Bush.[11] Thus, political era and, especially, individual president, provided useful controls on the relationships observed. This was less true of selected year in presidential term because, while some modest differences were observed, none were statistically significant. Thus, among the time aggregations, individual presidents had better ability to differentiate support for presidents' vote positions than did either political era or, especially, selected year in presidential term of office.

All in all, the general model consisting of three variables each from all three different environments, did an excellent job of explaining legislative support of presidents' roll call vote positions. The results were generally as predicted, with the prior presidential-congressional interaction (position taking) significantly influencing presidents' legislative support in the House in both general and policy-specific models. Yet, the other two variables in the exogenous environment were also important. Two other variables stand out as contributors to overall support: presidential party margin in the House and number of employees in the Executive Office of the President. The former is clearly necessary but we speculated that the latter also provides resources that help presidents lobby congressional support. The important implication of these findings is that, in addition to the exogenous related behavior (e.g., position taking), variables from both legislative and executive environments are necessary for a full understanding of overall support. Such a finding for legislative support of the president confirms research arguing for a multiple perspectives approach.

When dividing the support data by policy area, differences in domestic and foreign support were observed. As others have found, foreign policy is supported at slightly higher levels, but this two presidencies effect appears only for Republican, not Democratic presidents (Shull 1997, chapter 6). The best explanatory power of all appeared for the general model, although foreign policy also had a high percentage of the variance explained. Only slight differences in variable explanation appeared in the general and domestic models. However, two additional variables (minor presidential speeches and legislative workload) were useful in foreign policy but not in domestic or general policy.

Both the political time and the policy aggregations were useful in this analysis. Indeed, we achieved greater explanatory power with these combinations of environments, variables, and controls than any prior researchers. Legislative support for presidents' vote positions was well explained by our three environments in general and when controlling for domestic and foreign policy. Our primary conclusion is that the complex nature of presidents' legislative support requires variables from all three environments but is subject to substantial explanation.

The Congressional Quarterly organization provides numerous measures of presidential relations with Congress. Key votes, success (both new and old), support, and the information accompanying these votes yield important data for scholars. But in failing to recognize the quite different nature of the indicators, authors have frequently used them incorrectly. Success originally was based on initiatives to Congress that come from presidents themselves. Support is derived from legislative roll calls on which the president takes a position; thus, they are sponsored by Congress. Therefore, the support measure reflects member responses not to presidential policy but merely to their positions on particular issues before Congress. Scholars must keep in mind the conceptual and measurement differences, and also strengths and weaknesses, among these indicators in studying presidential-congressional interactions.

CHAPTER 6

Veto Propensity

NATURE OF THE VETO

The use of vetoes helps reveal the president's understanding of the nature and functions of his office. The founders' deep antipathy to the abuses of the veto in the hands of colonial governors was moderated by the failure of the Articles of Confederation, which provided virtually no executive power. The framers of the Constitution realized this limitation and responded by creating an executive with both a qualified (regular) and absolute (pocket) veto for self-protection from legislative intrusion (Spitzer 1988, 8–17). Presidential use of the veto has varied widely, presumably due more to particulars of the political situation rather than to the formal authority available. This authority derives from the Constitution and law, which together are basically constant across time and presidents. Accordingly, variation in its use must be explained by the internal and external circumstances presidents face in their legislative interactions. Variations in resources and activities employed to attain their preferences should help further our understanding of this "vital tool for shaping presidential-congressional relations" (Spitzer 1997, 1). Samuel Kernell (1991, 101) argues that "the veto is easily the most powerful weapon a president has to frustrate the designs of an opposition Congress."

Scholars have used fairly sophisticated multivariate techniques to study regular veto use and several studies incorporate long time periods in their analyses (e.g., Hoff 1991; Lee 1975). Although the device seems simple upon cursory examination, the veto is a complex form of political power. This tool of nullification is best understood, not simply by identifying empirical correlates, but by developing and testing theoretical explanations, such as those incorporated in this research. The empirical literature on presidential vetoes focuses attention on correlates as determinants and explanation. A wide range of factors have been identified as hypothetically or empirically related to veto propensity, such as presidential popularity or party margin in Congress. While not ignoring past findings, we believe that a better understanding of the veto will result from our encompassing multiple perspectives approach. Neustadt's (1960) view of presidential power as influence focuses attention on the conjunction of formal authorities and a range of personal skills and relevant political resources. Readers will recognize many of Neustadt's notions in this volume, but in addition to his focus on individual characteristics, we also include broader institutional and environmental explanations.

Presidential veto propensity, like position taking on legislative votes, is based on a frequency count. However, unlike position taking, which we have observed occurs frequently (as many as 140 per year), the public bill veto is a much rarer occurrence. As a result, this often visible and dramatic event, since it must be accompanied by a message, is potentially more costly to presidents' political capital than position taking and, thus, used more cautiously. Recall too, that many positions taken are on legislation that may not pass. But in vetoing, presidents have challenged final legislative decisions, which would actually adopt policy were the president to sign such legislation. Indeed, even though all four of our interactions occur in the policy adoption stage, the veto meets a strict definition of adoption most closely. Their infrequency may not qualify the veto as the president's "central domestic resource" Spitzer (1988, 25) or the "most important check and balance" (Sundquist 1986, 1). However, we believe that this activity, the only one of our four spanning our nation's entire history, deserves attention from students and scholars.

In January 1997, President Clinton obtained a power available to three fourths of the nation's governors but to none of the forty-one previous presidents—the item-veto. Although long advocated by presidents, budget deficits during the 1980s and 1990s led Republicans in the House to push such legislation in their "Contract with America" when they took control of the body in 1995. They used legislation rather than a much more difficult to enact constitutional amendment, leading some to doubt whether this modified item-veto was constitutional. The law allowed the president to rescind within five days individual items in appropriations bills not exempted by Congress. These cuts take effect immediately unless Congress passes a disapproval bill within thirty days which, if vetoed by the president, Congress may override with a two thirds vote in both houses as with the traditional veto. President Clinton first used the line-item veto on August 11, 1997, to eliminate three tax or spending breaks from the fiscal 1998 budget. Although nearly eighty measures in the 1998 budget could have been item-vetoed by Clinton, he used the device sparingly, perhaps because of its precarious position constitutionally. Legal challenges followed quickly and the Supreme Court declared the device unconstitutional by a 6-3 vote June 1988. Thus, balance was restored to executive-legislative relations.

Now that we have introduced the veto, the remainder of this chapter lays out our expectations and results for presidents' use of the regular veto. We present a time line which, like support but unlike position taking and budget agreement, is widely available elsewhere. However, even though we examine the veto for a shorter period than do some studies, we observe it with more determinants and through time series analysis. We examine veto propensity using a lag, trend, and when controlling for our three elements of political time: political era (early versus late), year in presidential term (first, last, reelection), and by presidents individually (Truman to Clinton). We then test the relative influence of the three environments on veto propensity, positing that while the executive environment may be important, the other two are not without influence. Then we summarize these findings and draw conclusions about this third presidential-congressional interaction. Although we join a long line of scholars studying the veto (Mason 1890; Towle 1937; Hoff 1991; Spitzer 1988; Copeland 1983; Rohde and Simon 1985), we provide a sufficiently different (multiple) perspective and, in addition, unlike all our predecessors, compare the veto to other presidential-congressional interactions.

EXPECTATIONS

Trend

In examining presidents' propensity to veto legislation, which is commonly presented in American government textbooks, the initial impression might be that modern presidents are utilizing this device less frequently than their earlier counterparts. Part of the discrepancy depends upon the type of veto one is considering. We limit our empirical analysis to the set of regular, public vetoes since 1949 using year as the unit of analysis. Few would argue with the decision to exclude the vetoes of private bills, which are unlikely to be part of the political struggles between institutions over public policy. In addition, private legislation has declined dramatically during the twentieth century.

The regular-pocket veto distinction is also important. Sufficient reason exists to believe that the politics of the United States in the post–World War II era is sufficiently different to justify separate analysis of modern pocket and regular vetoes (Hoff 1991, 312–13). The pocket veto is a unique form of executive decision making in that presidents act with little or no accountability to Congress. As such, the pocket veto provides the president with nearly complete discretion and absolute power where it applies at the end of a two-year Congress. Obviously, both devices of regular and pocket vetoes help further the president's role as "chief legislator" (Rossiter 1956).

Accordingly, when examined, public, regular bill vetoes should reveal an increase in issuance over the period of our analysis. This is because divided government is more prevalent in the more recent rather than the earlier years of our study. We have already discussed the growing contentiousness between the two branches beginning in the late 1960s and continuing to the present time. We have provided evidence that presidents do not dominate Congress and, as Edwards (1989) states, may exert influence only "at the margins." However, we think that increased public expectations of presidential assertiveness, and perhaps frustration over their inability to control policy outputs, will lead presidents to take this action to further their policy preferences. As presidents more and more find themselves in hostile political environments, they will assert this and other prerogative powers. In short, we anticipate gradual increases in veto usage over time.

Political Time

As with all four of our interaction variables, we control for three aspects of political time: political (or historical) era, year in presidential term of office, and individual president. Conventional wisdom and research might suggest that Democratic presidents often are more assertive and reveal greater proclivities to exercise the veto (Lee 1975). Yet other literature finds little basis for presidential party to predict veto propensity (Copeland, 1983; Simonton, 1987). We do think that Republican presidents, by virtue of always experiencing divided government during this entire time period, will resort to the veto more often than Democratic presidents. Although ideology may predict the propensity to veto specific legislation, we do not anticipate liberals or conservatives to be more likely to use the veto power. Besides, presidential party margin in Congress correlates so highly with ideology that the latter is not included in our analysis.[1] It is strength of political preferences and their congruence with the substantive content of specific legislation that should result in the application of the veto authority. Historical era could have some effect because of the frequency of divided government and the growing contentiousness of voting in Congress. Thus, veto propensity should be greater since 1974 than in earlier years.

Year in presidential term should be a better predictor of veto propensity than it is for some of our interactions. Again, this is due to the veto's considerable visibility and "last resort" character. Vetoes seem unlikely during presidential honeymoon years, which should be negatively related to veto propensity, but the more contentious last and reelection years should be positively related to veto use. Samuel Hoff (1991, 318) finds that lateness in the presidential term is significantly related to veto usage. In an earlier chapter, we mentioned the veto threat, which is probably a more potent device when the president still has political capital, earlier rather than later during his term of office (Kessel 1984; Light 1982; Shull 1983). Thus, veto propensity should increase across a president's term of office.

The final control for political time is individual presidents, where we expect substantial variation in veto propensity. Although we could be charged with eyeballing the data, it is easy to predict that Republicans Eisenhower, Ford, and Bush will use the veto much more often than will any of the Democratic presidents. The exception is Clinton, who faced divided government after 1995. Spitzer (1997, 12) argues that veto threats and actual vetoes were central powers under Bush; indeed, he used such threats three times more often than his nearest competitor. Again, this expectation is due more to the divided government phenomena, which during the period of this research at least, correlates almost exactly to presidential party. Although we do not make much of the post–1994 exception to unified government for Democrats, it is reasonable to assume that Clinton used the device more during his third year than in his first two years during which he enjoyed Democratic majorities in both chambers of Congress.

Environmental Influences

As with the other presidential-congressional interactions, we expect that all three environments will have something to do with presidential veto propensity. We have posited that the executive environment should be important because it taps both presidential resources and activities. Like position taking, vetoing seems to be expected of assertive presidents, who will use this device to further their policy preferences. Obviously, the veto takes place in a legislative environment, which has grown increasingly hostile to presidents. The particular mixture of congressional and presidential power resources and the degree of institutional conflict between the actors affect the president's decision to veto.

It is possible that forces outside of either of the executive or legislative environments could also influence presidential veto usage. We doubt that economic situation will have much affect for regular, public bill vetoes because presidents must veto all of the legislation rather than being able to eliminate a particular component (except for the brief existence of the item veto in 1997–98).[2] However, the previous legislative support presidents receive, the process variable from the exogenous environment, should influence their willingness to use the veto (Watson 1993, 32). We now lay out expectations for each of the three environments.

Executive. Whereas Neustadt argues that popular prestige and professional reputation are the president's primary political resources, the empirical literature on the veto has focused on the political resources of presidential popularity and the strength of the president's party in Congress as predictors of the veto (Lee 1975; Copeland 1983; Rohde and Simon 1985; Simonton 1987; Wooley 1991). Our minor speeches variable may reflect Neustadt's theoretical concept persuasion, which could influence our four presidential-congressional interactions. We believe these individual factors are particularly important in influencing presidential decision making in this important venue of legislative adoption. These executive variables along with our other factors should help predict presidential propensity to veto.

The literature is mixed over whether popular presidents have greater legislative success (Edwards, 1989 and Rivers and Rose, 1985; but see Bond and Fleisher, 1990; Collier and Sullivan 1995 for the alternative view). Both success and veto propensity relate to influence and George Edwards (1980) considers popular approval an important source of influence. Thus, a popular president may have less need to veto legislation (see Lee, 1975; Rohde and Simon, 1985; Woolley, 1991) because the resource popular prestige has a ubiquitous effect for the president in policymaking (Gleiber and Shull 1992). Despite this anticipated relationship, Paul Light (1982) suggests that presidents are less likely to use vetoes when they are not able to use them successfully.

We have argued that, apart from popular support, EOP staff provides presidents with a valuable resource. Staff size likely facilitates presidents' knowledge of the intricacies of a particular piece of legislation as it weaves its way through Congress. Richard Watson (1993, chapter 3) provides a fascinating discussion of the role of the OMB in presidential veto decisions. We expect that greater number of employees in the Executive Office of the President (the largest unit of which is the OMB) should relate positively to veto usage. We agree with Neustadt (1973) that staff cannot substitute for presidential knowledge and "only the president can be the expert" but, as we argued earlier, staff resources can contribute to the notion of skill, which should relate very much to the presidents' perceived need to exercise this prerogative power. Staff give the president more time to fully consider all implications of the legislation since just ten days provided for consideration by the Constitution would be quite limiting without other sets of eyes examining congressional actions.

By Neustadt's (1960) account, the most important component of conceptualization of presidential power is persuasion. Persuasion for Neustadt is the ability to change the perceptions of others in the political process so that they see their preferences in congruence with the president's preferences. Persuasive presidents, who are both frequent and consistent in their pronouncements and actions, may enhance the probability of their message being received, accepted, and reinforced. While personal and private communications, like calling a congressman to the White House, are clearly important, they are less amenable to observation and record and must be consistent with public statements and actions to be effective. Minor speeches may also tap the concept of going public (Kernell 1986). Presidents making more public statements are assumed to be more actively engaged in persuasion, such that this public aspect of the process is an indicator of the effort, if not the skill, of its authors (Kerbel 1991). More public messages (in this case, minor speeches), are expected to be positively related with greater use the of veto, while presidents who are less active in announcing their preferences and positions publicly are expected to use the veto less often.

Legislative. Another presidential resource identified by Neustadt is professional reputation. To date there is no generally accepted indicator of this critical theoretical concept. The strength of the president's party in the Congress may provide some information about the president's reputation.[3] And, party margin influences the potential for successful leadership in final policy adoption, especially at the veto override stage. Research suggests the president is more likely to veto legislation sponsored or passed by the opposition party, especially when the opposition party has a simple majority control of Congress (Lee 1975, 542; Copeland 1983; Rohde and Simon 1985; Simonton 1987; Hoff 1991; Watson 1993). Thus, the greater the size of the opposition party in Congress, the greater the president's perceived need to veto. Of course this is not a simple monotonic relationship since the size of the opposition is an indicator of the potential of override with its attendant reduction in perceptions of presidential power, potentials for future political leadership, and success (Shull, Gleiber, and Ringelstein 1992).

Although presidents' party margin in Congress should be the most important influence on veto propensity in the legislative environment, another legislative resource is change in size of its committee staff.[4] We do not think this variable will be as important to presidents' decisions because they depend little on legislative staff. Yet, larger legislative staff could caution such actions by presidents because it allows greater legislative scrutiny. Also, it is possible that the staffs of the two branches will interact, but we have no way to tap this aspect of presidential-congressional relations. Thus, change in the relationship between legislative committee staff size and veto propensity should be limited.

The last legislative environment variable is our workload variable, number of public laws. Although we had limited expectations for this variable for our other presidential-congressional interactions, it is quite possible that the number of total laws enacted will work to increase the likelihood of a veto. Indeed, the more laws that pass simply increase the probability that the president will find more legislation objectionable and thus resort to more vetoes. Hoff (1991, 317) finds a significant relationship between number of public laws and veto usage. Also, much legislation passes during the waning moments of a Congress and we think that presidents will especially scrutinize such legislation.

Exogenous. As with the two institutional environments, the exogenous environment consists of three variables. We have already alluded to the notion that the economic situation (deficit or surplus as a function of federal spending) should not have much to do with veto propensity. Hoff (1991, 315) argues without much theoretical justification that greater unemployment relates to increased veto frequency. Bad economic times could lead to conservative (e.g., Republican) presidents vetoing new programs. We also doubt that the size of the government, our second exogenous variable, will relate to veto use. However, to the extent that larger numbers of employees represent growth in government, it too could serve as a dampening effect on new legislation for conservative presidents. The main reason, however, that we do not expect as much effect from the exogenous environment is due to the highly political and public nature of the veto. All in all, then, we expect relatively little influence from the exogenous environment on presidential veto propensity. Indeed, exogenous influences should be greater for more routine functions of government, like presidential position taking and budget agreement. However, finding any relationships with variables from all three environments will provide further support for our multiple perspectives model.

Process

For veto propensity, legislative support of the presidents' vote positions is the process variable of concern (see chapters 2–3). Of course, legislative support is not exactly an exogenous influence but is part of the interactions between Congress and presidents. A president who gets his way with Congress should have little need to veto; hence the relationship between these two variables should be negative. Watson (1993, 52) found legislative support to be the best single predictor of veto propensity. Indeed, we reported a Pearson's product moment correlation of $r = -.306$ in our table 3.1 of chapter 3. We have suggested that support relates to other interactions (position taking and budget agreement) and its perceived association with veto propensity is no exception. Also, table 3.2 reports that no time lag is necessary in examining the relationship between legislative support and veto propensity; only current year among the four possibilities is statistically significant. Thus, we include legislative support in the current year as an exogenous (process) predictor of veto propensity.

Policy Effects

To this point, we have given our expectations for the full model explaining veto propensity without considering any differences by policy areas. The existing literature finds mixed policy area influence. Albert Ringelstein (1985) and Richard Watson (1993) divide vetoes according to substantive policy areas similar to categorizations by Aage Clausen (1973) and John Kessel (1974). Both Ringelstein and Watson find few vetoes in some areas (especially in foreign policy), but mixed propensity in the other domestic issue areas. Spitzer (1988, 67) focuses on the Theodore Lowi (1964) typology and observes propensity greatest in domestic distributive policy (especially pork barrel measures). Regrettably, we think the few vetoes that occur do not easily divide into domestic sub-issue areas, especially since many occur on the not-very-specific general appropriations measures (Ringelstein 1989).

Abortion is a domestic issue that has prompted many vetoes in recent years. Indeed, ten of George Bush's forty-four vetoes dealt with abortion and contentiousness on abortion continued under Bill Clinton. Legislation to ban "partial birth abortions" encompassed multiple threats, actual vetoes, override attempts, and further legislation during 1996 and 1997. Clinton vetoed a bill passed in April 1996 because it failed to include an exception for the health of the mother. Republicans could not override his veto, but passed similar legislation in 1997 by a clear veto-proof margin in the House and just three votes shy of the two thirds needed to override in the Senate. The new bill had gained supporters, such as newly elected pro-choice Senator Mary Landrieu (D–La.), because it contained more moderate language and some protections not in the previous bill. The legislation even obtained the rare endorsement of the American Medical Association, in part because it contained protections against prosecuting the doctors who abort to protect the mother's health. Even Senate Democratic leader Tom Daschle (S. Dak.), who had pressed for a compromise measure that failed, supported the ban. The scramble toward moderation left Clinton in an awkward position, especially when it appeared increasingly likely that his anticipated second veto would be overturned. However, he vetoed the 1997 bill as well and it still failed to be overridden in the Senate in 1988.

For the veto, unlike the other three interactions (position taking, support, and budget agreement), we run into a rather difficult problem due to the small number of cases. The considerable deference given to presidents in the sphere of foreign policy might suggest they have little need to veto such legislation. Such vetoes do occur, but as categorized by Ragsdale, they are rare and, since we will show that no vetoes occur at all for five years, even more missing data occur when we examine those in foreign policy only. We think, therefore, that whatever patterns we observe for veto propensity overall will be mirrored in the domestic realm because it comprises most vetoes. To the extent we are able to uncover differences by policy area, we expect that the executive environment will be more important for foreign and the legislative environment more influential in the domestic realm. Here again, this is because we anticipate greater deference to presidents in the foreign sphere, and we expect that popularity and staff resources will be more important in foreign policy, but that presidents' party margin and workload will dominate veto propensity overall and in the domestic realm.

RESULTS

The reader will recall that we examine presidential position taking and legislative support for the House only as a result of data availability. In explaining veto propensity and budget agreement we consider the entire Congress. Thus, House-only independent variables used for chapters 4–5 (staff size and presidents' party margin) are converted into full-Congress variables for the analyses in chapters 6–7. Obviously many excluded variables could influence each of these four interactions uniquely but had to be excluded for parsimony. We strongly assert the view that a more general model, such as our multiple perspectives approach, is more valuable for broader theory building than simply picking idiosyncratic explanatory variables. Thus, we have endeavored to explain four different presidential-congressional interactions with the same three environment models.[5]

Trend Analysis

It is clear from figure 6.1 that the propensity to veto legislation fluctuates dramatically on a yearly basis, confounding any clear trend. However, the lag veto variable is statistically significant. Veto propensity ranges from none for Democratic presidents but Kennedy in their first or second year to a high of twenty-six in 1974 under Gerald Ford. The year 1974 reflects a split presidency between Nixon and Ford, but the record number of vetoes is due almost entirely to the latter. Nixon, who was preoccupied with Watergate, issued just two vetoes during slightly more than half of 1974 while all the remaining vetoes were issued by

Ford. The vast majority appear to be minor bills (e.g., upgrading benefits for U.S. marshals and animal health research). Ironically, Ford
vetoed HR 11897 that would have named a federal office building after
himself in his home town of Grand Rapids, Michigan. Perhaps his most
important veto that year was on increasing funding for federal health
programs (*Congress and the Nation* 1977, 1117–19). Ford also issued
eleven pocket vetoes and four of his public bill vetoes in 1974 were overridden by the required two thirds vote of both chambers of Congress.
The next greatest veto issuance in the modern era was George Bush in
1992, a surprisingly assertive president whom Spitzer (1997) calls the
"veto king." Of Bush's forty-four vetoes over four years, the only one to
be overridden was the Cable Television Act, which occurred in October
of 1992, just before his election defeat to Bill Clinton.

We have already observed that absolutely no vetoes occurred during
five years of our forty-seven year time period. Not surprisingly, all but
one of those years occurred under Democratic presidents who had par-

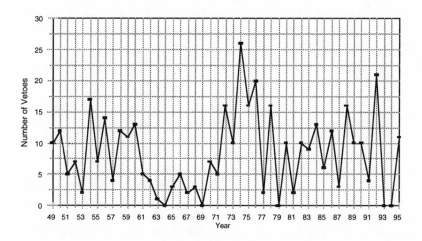

FIGURE 6.1
Veto Propensity, 1949–1995

Note: Veto propensity refers to the number of regular, public bill vetoes per
year.

Trend Analysis

	B	Sig T	
Count	.71	.306	Adjusted R² = .04
One-Year Lag	.66	.000	Adjusted R² = .21

tisan majorities in both houses of Congress. The lone exception was Richard Nixon in 1969 during his honeymoon (first) year in office. Clinton is the only modern president failing to issue a veto during any two years of a presidency and, for Clinton, this experience occurred during his first two years, 1993–94. We will see in the concluding chapter that Clinton stepped up veto usage significantly during subsequent years when Republicans gained control of both chambers of Congress and were quite unified in their opposition to his policies.

As expected, presidents do issue many more vetoes at the end of a Congress than at the beginning, largely because most laws are finally adopted in the second rather than the first session of a two-year Congress. This tendency is reflected in our statistically significant one-year lag variable reported in figure 6.1. Most often, the first year is devoted more to committee hearings and legislative markup and the second session to floor voting, both amendments and final passage. We observe no influence of time on veto propensity from the count variable. Thus, although veto propensity is not random, it is not patterned by a steady increase or decrease as characterized the first two presidential-congressional interactions. Accordingly, no trend appears in the propensity to veto (adjusted $R^2 = .04$).

Political Time

The results of the regression analysis for political or historical era revealed in table 6.1 show that this variable explains none of the variance in veto propensity. As we could have predicted from trend, nearly eight vetoes occur on average during the earlier period but no appreciable difference in veto propensity occurs after 1974. Democrats do average fewer vetoes than do Republican presidents on a yearly basis, although party explains just 21 percent of the variance in veto propensity. The obvious explanation for greater Republican assertiveness is that they always faced a hostile Congress (in at least one branch). However, none of the Democratic presidents faced an opposition Congress (before Clinton in 1995). Although the veto, like other assertive actions, probably costs the president political capital, presidents will take this presumably more costly risk (than, say position taking) as a last resort effort to prevent enactment of legislation that they oppose.

Somewhat more variance in veto propensity is explained by selected years in presidential terms of office. Here we observe that presidents issue on average fewer vetoes during their first (honeymoon) than during the non–theoretically important "other" (or constant) years. This finding was as hypothesized, although part of the explanation may be due to an earlier result that presidents almost never veto as many bills during the first year of a Congress as they do during the second year. Thus, presidential honeymoon years, which are always in an odd-numbered year, also correspond exactly with the first year (session) of a new Congress. Presidents do issue more vetoes during last and, especially, reelection years, as hypothesized. Reelection year is statistically significant in the regression model.

The final control for political time is by individual president, where the assertive Truman serves as the constant. Only Ford issued more vetoes on a yearly basis but was, of course, in office just two and one half years. As evident in both the plot in figure 6.1 and in table 6.1, Democrats Kennedy, Johnson, Carter, and Clinton issued fewer vetoes than their Republican counterparts. Only Truman and Johnson among Democrats and Ford among Republicans reveal statistically significant differences in veto propensity among the individual presidents. For all of

TABLE 6.1
Veto Propensity and Political Time Controls

	Unstandardized Coefficient	Adj. R^2
Historical Era		
Political Era, Post-1974	1.37	−.01
constant (1974 and before)	7.73***	
Select Year in Presidential Term		
First Year	−3.82	.22
Last Year	1.82	
Reelection Year	7.74**	
constant	7.93***	
Individual President		
Harry Truman (constant)	7.97***	.31
Dwight Eisenhower	2.19	
John Kennedy	−4.52	
Lyndon Johnson	−5.86*	
Richard Nixon	2.43	
Gerald Ford	11.48**	
Jimmy Carter	−1.23	
Ronald Reagan	.97	
George Bush	2.97	
Bill Clinton	−4.03	

*   Significant at the .05 level
**   Significant at the .01 level
*** Significant at the .001 level

Reagan's bluster about Congress, it is a bit surprising that he issued so few vetoes among these contemporary presidents. Of course, Republicans controlled the Senate for his first six years in office. In any event, individual president was a useful control. Perhaps because it includes ten categories rather than only two (for political era) or four (for year in term), individual president explains more of the variance (but still only an adjusted R^2 of .31%) in veto propensity than either of the other two controls for political time.

The fact that Clinton issued no vetoes at all during his first two years in office does not mean that his major initiatives were approved. Once the Republicans took over control of both chambers of Congress during the elections of 1994, he did utilize this prerogative power. We observed that Clinton issued eleven vetoes in 1995, one of which was overridden but none of Clinton's six vetoes in 1996 were overturned. The House overrode his veto of late-term abortions but it was upheld by the Senate. Another successful veto was on legislation limiting product liability. CQ asserts that "Although Clinton failed to achieve any landmark personal victories, he also managed to escape devastating defeats" ("Presidential Support," *AllPolitics*.com, 1996, 5). The CQ organization lists the several override attempts that failed in that year. We saw earlier that in 1997 Clinton again vetoed legislation outlawing partial birth abortions.

General and Policy Models

As we have done in the other chapters, we now provide multivariate explanations for veto propensity based upon the three environments. Overall, the nine variable model explains 61 percent of the variance in general veto propensity (adjusted R^2) after correction for autocorrelation. Table 6.2 reveals that several variables are unimportant in the general model. Minor speeches, employees in EOP, legislative staff size, and all of the three exogenous variables are insignificant in explaining overall veto propensity. However, presidents' popular approval from the executive environment is significant and in the predicted negative direction. That is, presidents do issue more vetoes when they are unpopular. Thus, just one of the variables from the executive environment was important for veto propensity. We had expected greater explanatory power from this environment for this discretionary action by presidents.

In contrast, the legislative environment is quite important, with two of its component variables being statistically significant at the .01 level or better. Of these three determinants, workload (number of public laws enacted) was most important, confirming an earlier expectation that the pure volume of legislation brings increased prospects for veto usage. Its importance in the model shows that earlier studies of the veto should have utilized such a workload variable but only Hoff (1991) incorporated it in research. The presidents' party margin is also significant and indicates that presidents do veto more when they are vulnerable politically. This finding, of course, is consistent with earlier research but presidential party margin as a resource variable is not as important as the activity, number of public laws enacted. Legislative staff size did not matter at all.

The findings for the first two environments reveal that the legislative environment is more important than the executive environment but both play a role in veto propensity. However, the exogenous environment also performed contrary to expectations. We had anticipated that the economic situation (deficit or surplus/outlays) and the size of government (number of civilian employees) would have dampening effects on veto propensity but the results are insignificant. Also, president's legislative support (the process variable) was negatively related to veto usage as expected, but this influence too had a minimal effect on veto

TABLE 6.2
General and Policy Models for Veto Propensity

	General Model	*Domestic Model*	*Foreign Model*
Executive Environment			
Popular Approval	–.19***	–.13**	–.53**
Employees in EOP	–.36	.32	–.34
Minor Speeches	.55	.86	–.11
Legislative Environment			
Committee Staff	–.33	–.16	–.52
Party Margin	–.27**	–.25**	–.16
Workload	.33***	.28***	.38*
Exogenous Environment			
Economic Situation	–2.56	–5.19	2.35
Size of Federal Govt.	–.24	–.23	–.38
Legislative Support	–.17	–.16	–.19
constant	37.83**	31.09**	7.06
Adj. R^2	.61	.60	.19
LaGrange Multiplier	2.07	8.25	6.48

*   Significant at the .05 level
**   Significant at the .01 level
*** Significant at the .001 level

propensity. Thus, legislative support is not the powerful predictor of veto usage that some have assumed (Watson 1993).

Our next step is to divide the vetoes into the two policy areas as a further control in this research. Because so many of our vetoes occur in domestic policy, we expected this issue area to closely mirror what occurs for overall veto propensity. The results in table 6.2 find this to be the case, with nearly as much of domestic veto propensity explained (60% adjusted R^2) as for overall vetoes. Two variables from the legislative environment are statistically significant in the model, with workload again being paramount. Presidents' congressional party margin is as important for domestic vetoes as it was for overall vetoes, while presidential popular approval (executive environment) remains significant at a slightly lower confidence level. The Lagrange multiplier is within acceptable limits revealing that autocorrelation is not present in the model of domestic veto propensity.

We again express caution in interpreting the presidents' propensity to veto in the sphere of foreign policy due to the limited number of cases. We have discussed the notion of legislative deference to presidents in foreign policy, which likely explains some of this lower foreign veto propensity. We are able to explain very little of the propensity to issue foreign policy vetoes, just 19 percent adjusted R^2. As anticipated, the executive environment becomes more important in this policy area; indeed, popular approval was significant at the .01 level in explaining the issuance of foreign policy vetoes. Workload is the only variable from the legislative environment that remains significant in vetoing foreign policy legislation. As with the general model, a correction for autocorrelation is necessary in the foreign policy model of veto propensity.

To summarize the findings for the three models, we were able to explain substantial variance in general and domestic veto propensity with relatively few independent variables. Thus, our three significant variables are highly parsimonious. We found that it is the legislative environment (composed of party margin and workload), not aspects of the executive environment (except for the single influence of popular approval) that best explain veto propensity. The same variables were important in both models. When examining foreign policy veto propensity, the model composed of three environments does a poor job of explanation which, in part, results from the limited number of observations. As anticipated, executive variables become more important in the foreign sphere than they were for domestic and overall vetoes. However, as anticipated by our multiple perspective, all three models required explanation from more than one environment. The limited ability of the exogenous environment to contribute to explanation of veto propensity overall or by policy area was not surprising.

SUMMARY AND CONCLUSION

The veto is the only one of our four direct presidential-congressional interactions that is specifically provided in the Constitution. As such, it is also the only one of the four dependent variables for which data exist since the beginning of our nation's history. Indeed, position taking, support, and budget agreement appear for just the modern period. Several scholars have considered the veto to be an important check and balance of our democratic system of governance (Spitzer 1988, 1; Sundquist 1986). At the same time, it is a tool that the Founding Fathers apparently believed would be used sparingly as "a last resort" (Spitzer 1988). Nevertheless, its increased use in the nineteenth and into the twentieth centuries corresponds with increasing presidential involvement in legislative policymaking. Although modern presidents no doubt have been more assertive in the legislative arena than their predecessors, this growing assertiveness has not necessarily occurred in veto usage. Much of the reason for this phenomenon is the decline in private bills and, thus, less presidential need to veto them. We also conclude that regular and pocket vetoes are truly unique and should be studied separately when examining veto propensity. Finally, the short-lived item-veto is now history as another dimension of presidential-congressional relations.

In controlling for political time, we find no upward trend toward regular, public bill vetoes among post–World War II presidents. Thus, no difference appears before 1974 and after in veto propensity. We believe this is due partly to the reduction of private bills and also to the availability of other devices for contemporary assertive presidents to further their policy preferences. Even though no trend occurs in veto propensity, other elements of political time provide useful explanations of veto usage. Year in presidential term provides only a slightly better control than historical era for veto propensity, but none of the year designations were statistically significant. Individual presidents provided the best political time control for veto propensity. Ironically, the relatively passive Gerald Ford was not so in veto propensity. Clearly, this was one area of high assertiveness for him compared to other presidents, especially and surprisingly, Ronald Reagan. However, unlike his Republican counterparts as president, Reagan could count on a supportive Senate during six of his eight years in office. Democrats during this period had relatively little need to veto legislation. Except for John Kennedy, each subsequent Democrat had at least one year (Clinton had two) when he issued not a single regular, public bill veto.

Most important theoretically in our analysis is the prediction of vetoes by three different environments: executive, legislative, and exogenous. Although presidents have great discretion in veto usage, the limited explanatory power of presidential characteristics implies that the president must respond to outside forces. Only the personal resource from the executive environment, popular support, had any influence on overall veto propensity. For regular vetoes, the president depends on the ability of his party to control Congress and legislative workload variables in using the veto. In short, some of our hypotheses were confirmed but others were not. We found that legislative environmental variables were more important but executive and exogenous variables were less influential than we had presumed. As expected, our three environments explained domestic and foreign policy vetoes differently.

Some might think that the idiosyncratic nature of legislation means scholars should focus attention on more specific characteristics of the legislative battle. Variables like the vote margin and party cohesion on final passage of bills could be important to veto propensity (Hoff, 1991). Public or interest-group issue salience may also be a cue for the president in making this decision. For example, a jobs bill can be more easily vetoed in good economic times than bad. But such a design of specific unique determinants for the veto defeats our larger purpose of seeking general variables to explain a number of presidential-congressional interactions. Thus, overall explanatory power of our models remains high even though we have not purposely selected particular idiosyncratic variables that we suspect would inflate explanatory power for particular presidential-congressional interactions.

CHAPTER 7

Budget Agreement

NATURE OF BUDGET AGREEMENT

The history of budgeting reflects a course of changing authority fluctuating between the president and Congress (Fenno 1966; Cox et al. 1993). According to the Constitution, Congress bears the responsibility for providing a budget for the nation. However, Congress yielded authority to the executive branch with the Budget and Accounting Act of 1921, thereby shifting the responsibility for preparing the initial budget document to the president. The intent of the act was to shift criticism for budget decisions away from Congress toward the president (Wildavsky 1988). However, this structural change permitted assertive presidents, beginning with Franklin Roosevelt, to set the budget agenda while Congress was left to a reactive role in the budget process. Later, Congress regained some power from the executive branch through the numerous elements of the Budget Impoundment and Control Act of 1974 (Kettl 1992). As a result, Congress and the president now share more equally in the budget making process; however, the president still controls the preparation of the initial budget document thereby setting the agenda for budget negotiations.

Recent presidents and Congresses have been unable to effectively deal with the growing deficit problem throughout the 1980s and early 1990s. Congress attempted to impose sanctions on both itself and the president to ensure across-the-board budget cuts if neither party was willing nor capable of making such reductions on its own. These efforts were directed at cutting the federal deficit, which had soared to unprecedented heights. Although this legislation was initiated by Congress itself, the nature of the legislation was such that if Congress did not respond to the deficit, automatic spending cuts would go into effect. Because these cuts occurred automatically in the absence of congressional activity, they can be considered external constraints even though the legislation was formulated by Congress. Ultimately, Congress changed the legislation (generally known as Gramm-Rudman) three times in five years, revealing the difficulty both Congress and the president faced in actually reducing spending. Both actors realized that they were not capable of

113

making the painful political decisions necessary to reduce the deficit and balance the budget. Thus, they placed themselves at the mercy of legislation that would take effect via their own inaction. Such automatic cuts were politically tolerable because they diffused responsibility for budget cuts away from specific members of Congress. The courts, however, took the bite out of early attempts at such legislation by declaring the automatic budget cuts in Gramm-Rudman I unconstitutional (Wildavsky 1988; Kettl 1992). Additionally, Congress was equally imaginative at both circumventing such legislation and scaling back deficit targets in later legislation during 1991–92. Although the many variations of budget reform did provide for some deficit reduction, gains were nominal at best and, ultimately, Gramm-Rudman was a failure (Kettl 1992).

Most contemporary budgeting has been characterized by increased conflict between the president and Congress over their budget preferences. The Democratically controlled Congress was a consistent source of consternation during the Republican presidencies of Ronald Reagan and George Bush. With the election of Democratic President Bill Clinton and the subsequent 1994 congressional elections that put the Republicans in charge of the House and Senate, the political climate was reversed from that of the 1970s and 1980s (Republican president and Democratic Congress). Although the roles have been reversed, partisan politics over the budget have continued unabated through to the present. In 1995, Clinton and the Republican Congress clashed sharply over the federal budget to the point that the government shut down on at least two occasions; however, the Republican Congress was saddled with most of the blame (*CQ Almanac* 1995). Despite the settlements reached in 1996 and 1998, discussed later in this chapter, budgeting since Richard Nixon has been much more contentious than previously. This conflict is due to congressional attempts to check presidential power in the Congressional Budget Act of 1974 and to the fact that most of this period has been characterized by divided government (Thurber 1996).

Conceptually, budget agreement reflects the efforts that have occurred over time for both the president and Congress to shape and enact their preferences via the power of the purse. Specifically, budget agreement is measured as the final appropriations by Congress as a percentage of the funds requested by the president. As such, budget agreement reflects the level of fiscal consensus that exists between the president and Congress. If budget agreement is high, near 100 percent, then both the president and Congress have probably reached consensus regarding their respective budget preferences. However, if budget agreement is low, it is doubtful that the president and Congress have reached agreement on their preferences and Congress is undoubtedly acting to curtail the preferences of the president by denying funds to his preferred programs.

One of the problems we encountered is that even if budget agreement is 100%, it is arguable whether this is 100% of presidents' requests or 100% of Congress's adjustments to the presidents' requests. Also, the question remains, is 100% better than 103% or is 103% better than 100%? Initially, one might consider that anything over 100% must be better. Presumably though, President Reagan would consider 100% better than 103% due to his fiscal conservatism. For our purposes, we consider 100% optimal and anything over 100% as suboptimal but better than less than 100%.[1] For example, building a scale where A = budget agreement over 100%, B = 100% budget agreement, and C = budget agreement less than 100%, we would order the scale from best to worse as B, A, C. While 100% budget agreement may reflect only presidential requests, over 100% likely includes almost all funding requested by the president and additional legislative preferences, which could make presidential-congressional relations more harmonious. Still, we will only consider appropriations up to the amount of his requests as optimal.

Some additional conceptual and measurement problems occur with the aggregate budget agreement variable. First, one is not able to distinguish exactly whose preferences are being enacted. It is possible that Congress might rearrange presidents' total budget requests and appropriate funds as they see fit. In this situation, the variable of appropriations as percent of requests might appear to show a high degree of consensus when in reality, money for presidential preferences has been reallocated to reflect congressional preferences. While this situation is a distinct possibility, it seems unlikely given the president's ability to veto a congressional budget that is not to his liking. Conversely, the president will not opt to use the veto lightly since it has meant vetoing the entire bill, not just a specific component. Certainly, the political costs of vetoing an entire budget prevent the president from indiscriminately vetoing budgets that do not exactly match his requests (Kieweit and McCubbins 1988). Yet the threat of the veto prevents wholesale revision of presidential requests by Congress. Consequently, while there are discrepancies between presidential requests and congressional appropriations, such discrepancies should be minor. However, even considering these measurement problems, this budget agreement variable provides a unique and heretofore unexplored avenue for examining and understanding the relationships that exist between the president and Congress.

The year 1997 seemingly marked a new era in budget agreement. No longer was it necessary for the president to veto the entire budget. Rather, he could make specific line-item vetoes, a device that would provide the president with a significant increase in power. Clinton first used the line-item veto on three tax breaks in the early fall of 1997. However, a negotiated settlement with Congress made a congressional override attempt unnecessary on two of the measures. In a defense appropriation bill in October of that year, Clinton line-item vetoed thirty projects, worth an estimated $287 million. One commentator argued that the president was careful to apportion the cuts roughly equally between Democratic and Republican legislators (*New Orleans Times Picayune*, October 7, 1997, A-4). Clinton also avoided calling the projects "pork barrel" but instead emphasized the need for fiscal discipline to balance the budget by 2002. Clinton claimed to "set objective criteria and take politics out of the decision making process, " but vetoed less than 1 percent of fiscal 1998 appropriations. As mentioned in chapter 6, the item-veto was short-lived.

Another measurement issue with our percentage variable budget agreement is that it does not possess a high degree of variation. In fact, only about 20 percent variation occurs between the lowest value (83.73) and the highest value (102.16), with a mean score of 96.89. Although one would prefer continuous variables, regression continues to prove robust even as its assumptions are violated (Cohen and Cohen 1983). Additionally, political actors operate on a calendar year basis while budgeting itself occurs in fiscal years. Despite these problems, we feel that budget agreement is an important variable and its use and study herein contribute significantly to the literature on presidential-congressional interactions. We know of no other variable that taps presidential and congressional preferences in this way that does not also possess problems and limitations. Also, since both requests and appropriations appear to tap actor preferences (Kiewiet and McCubbins 1988), our combining them gets at the proximity of preferences, despite its aggregated nature.

As in the previous chapters, we follow a standard format in presenting our expectations and results. First, we offer expectations for the trend and the political time control variables (historical era, select year in presidential term, and individual president). We then posit influences for our three environments (executive, legislative, and exogenous), the process model, and by policy area. Next, we present the results for the general model overall and by policy area. Finally, we present a summary and then develop our conclusions regarding budget agreement.

EXPECTATIONS

Trend

Our summary of the modern budgeting process in the United States suggests a pattern of congressional dominance (prior to 1921), followed by a period of growing presidential dominance (after 1921), followed finally by a period of presidential-congressional conflict (after 1974). Since our time series begins in 1949 during growing presidential dominance, we expect to find an overall declining trend in budget agreement. That is, budget agreement in the early years of the time series should be high or near the 100 percent mark. Following Nixon and the Budget Act of 1974, we expect to find that budget agreement takes a downward turn, with greater divergence between presidential requests and congressional appropriations during the most recent years.

Although we anticipate a downward trend since the early 1970s due to increasing divided government and ideological conflict, we expect to find an incremental effect in budget agreement overall. That is, the one-year lag of budget agreement should exercise both a strong and significant effect over the current years' level of budget agreement. We predict this incremental effect, despite Wildavsky's (1988) claim that we have entered a new era in budgeting in which entire programs may be subject to budget gutting. Evidence suggests that even where budget cutting is substantial, such as in the Environmental Protection Agency (EPA) under Reagan, these are short-term reductions from which agencies can recover (Wood and Waterman 1993). Additionally, even in the case of the somewhat extreme automatic cuts intended in Gramm-Rudman I, the legislation would have implemented across the board cuts such that no one program or agency would have borne the brunt of the budget cutting axe. Thus, there should be an incremental effect with the lag variable and little effect from the count variable since we anticipate only a slight decrease in budget agreement.

Political Time

We have several expectations when examining our three political time controls (historical era, select year in presidential term, and individual president). First, we have already anticipated that frequently divided government leads to greater conflict between Congress and the president. We expect then that in looking at our historical era variable, the post-1974 period should reveal a negative coefficient, indicating that budget agreement has generally decreased since Nixon.

Second, we anticipate more budget agreement in the first than in reelection and last years. It is in the honeymoon year that the president possesses his greatest amount of political capital as well as general goodwill and appeal to popular mandate (Pfiffner 1996). Such general deference to the president during his honeymoon year should produce greater budget agreement. Last years should also reveal substantial budget agreement since the current president is leaving office and may experience a gesture of good will from Congress. Reelection years, however, pose an interesting problem. When the president and Congress are controlled by the same party, one would expect greater budget agreement in the interest of furthering the reelections of both; however, if divided government exists, it is possible that budget agreement will decrease with each party attempting to stall a budget resolution in hopes that the other party will receive the blame for the lack of a budget and thereby end up losing out at the polls (*Congressional Quarterly Almanac* 1995). However, such action is risky at best since it is difficult to discern how the general public will react in such situations. Regardless though, we expect budget agreement to be lower in reelection years than in first or last years.

Finally, for individual presidents, we expect the following effects. The presidencies of Gerald Ford, Jimmy Carter, Reagan, and Bush should have a negative effect on budget agreement. Although Carter served in conjunction with a Democratic Congress, his outsider status hurt his ability to effectively deal with Congress (Jones 1988) and, as a result, his overall budget agreement should be lower. Strong ideological positions by Presidents Reagan and Bush on social welfare programs often pitted them against a Democratically controlled Congress and resulted in numerous budget clashes. Consequently, the control for their terms in office should have a negative impact on budget agreement.

Although Clinton was never the political outsider that Carter was, he did not experience solid support from the Democratic Congress during his first two years. He then faced the first Republican controlled Congress in forty years during his second two years and into his second term. Budget clashes were inevitable as Republican legislators rushed to take full advantage of their new majority status, which continued though at reduced levels after 1996. Thus, Clinton's term should also exert a negative influence on budget agreement. Finally, beyond the individual aspect of each of these presidents, a collective reason exists for expecting these presidents in particular to exert a negative effect on budget agreement. All of the presidents discussed above held office following the Congressional Budget Act of 1974. Thus, in addition to any individual presidential characteristics that influence budget agreement, this more conflictual recent period of budgeting should emerge in this aspect of political time.

The year 1997 had the potential for considerable budget disagreement between President Clinton and the 105th Congress, which had enlarged its Republican majority in both chambers during the 1996 elections. Clinton's large electoral margin over former Republican Senate Majority Leader Bob Dole (R–Kans.), along with more conservative Senate leadership under Trent Lott (R–Miss.), suggested considerable potential for deadlock in presidential-congressional relations. However, gridlock was avoided when both sides compromised in May 1997 over the 1998 budget by both cutting taxes and agreeing to balance the budget within five years. Both parties took credit in closing the deal, which provided something for both liberals and conservatives, yet neither side was completely satisfied. However, compromise was easier because both sides wanted to avoid the government shutdowns that had occurred during 1995–96, and because the economy continued to be healthy, allowing $200 billion more in revenue over five years than had been anticipated.

In seven of the last nine years, Congress had failed to pass all of the necessary budget resolutions on time by the October 1 beginning of the fiscal year. Many disagreements occurred between President Clinton and the Republican Congress during the summer and early fall of 1998 as the latter sought to capitalize on the Clinton sexual scandal with Monica Lewinski and the upcoming midterm congressional elections. Despite all the maneuvering, which resulted in another late budget, a continuing robust economy allowed the protagonists to achieve the first balanced budget in thirty years—and do it several years prior to the 2002 deadline. It was an amazing feat that allowed both sides to claim victory and, after dividing up about $20 billion of the surplus for favored programs, still adopted a budget $50 billion in the black. The general public bought into the good times by electing many incumbents but also rewarding Democrats more than Republicans. Indeed, it was the first time since 1822 that the president's party gained seats in the House during the sixth year in office.

Environmental Influences

Consistent with the fundamental argument presented herein, we expect to find that all three environments (executive, legislative, and exogenous) have some influence on budget agreement. Within the executive environment resources should influence budget agreement more than activities. Additionally, both congressional resources and activities should have some effect because Congress makes the final determination regarding appropriations. Concerning exogenous factors, economic situation should exert a strong effect on budget agreement since public concern and scrutiny over federal spending appears to fluctuate with overall economic prosperity (Wildavsky 1988, 216–17; Kettl 1992; Frendreis and Tatalovich 1994). Also, size of federal government should influence budget agreement indirectly since employees have to be paid. As nondiscretionary expenditures increase discretionary expenditures decrease. Such situations should lead to less budget agreement since there are fewer funds to allocate to each actor's preferences.

Although we expect influences from all three environments, budget agreement proves more difficult than the other interactions in discerning the most influential environment. Since a lengthy period of presidential dominance has occurred during the time series under examination, one might contend that executive variables would be more important. However, recent attempts by Congress to reassert itself in the budget process argue for a more mixed interpretation, with variables from neither environment taking dominance over the other. Indeed, the external conditions may be the most important for budget agreement, more so than for our other three interactions. This is due to the importance of the economy as a whole in making budget decisions, particularly in recent years when deficit spending has threatened to upset the national economy. We now turn to more specific expectations for the individual variables.

Executive. Beginning with the executive environment, presidential activity in the form of speech making should have little direct influence on budget agreement. Any discernable effects should be positive in that the president may take important elements of his budget on the road with him and use rhetoric to gain widespread popular support for his preferences. However, it is far more likely that the outcome of the budget process will hinge on negotiations with legislators and not with appeals to the general public. If anything, a more complex relationship exists in that speech making influences overall popularity (Brace and Hinckley 1992) and not budget agreement directly.

Presidential popularity should have a positive influence on budget agreement. Initially one might think that popularity would have a strong effect on budget agreement since popularity (rightfully or wrongfully) is equated with mandates; however, room for doubt exists. Although a high popularity speaks well for presidents and their influence, it may entice them to ask for too much from Congress (Brace and Hinckley 1992, 7). Thus, if the president becomes overconfident and requests too much, low popularity could produce less budget agreement. However, we still feel that popular approval should have a positive effect since Congress should be more indulgent of the president if his popularity is high rather than low. Budget agreement then should increase as presidential popularity increases.

Presidents' staff resources in the size of the EOP variable present a mixed bag of expectations. On the one hand, a larger staff may increase the resources available for developing the budget. Since the early 1970s the OMB has acted to coordinate and better develop budget proposals to reflect presidential preferences (Wildavsky 1988; Kettl 1992). However, it does not necessarily hold that increased resources or the coordination introduced by the OMB will make a "better" budget or a budget that is more appealing to Congress. In fact, the creation of the Congressional Budget Office (CBO) in 1974 was intended as a check against the OMB (Kettl 1992). As such, our expectations for the EOP staff variable are somewhat open. This research helps to provide (albeit in an empirical sense) whether or not the oft discussed staff resource of the OMB (the largest section of the EOP) contributes or detracts from the president's ability to influence budget agreement.

Legislative. Turning to the legislative environment, we again deal with activities first. Congressional activity in the form of workload should have a strong effect on budget agreement. A hard working Congress with a heavy agenda should devote less time to specific budget considerations and negotiations. The one notable exception to this expectation would be two recent Republican Congresses (1995–98). Having been the minority party in the House for the past forty years and only occasionally gaining the majority in the Senate, one would expect the Republican majority not only to press forward with a heavy workload (number of public laws) but also to pay careful attention to presidential budgets. However, this exception applies primarily to the fact that Republicans have long been denied the majority position in congressional affairs. If the Republicans continue to hold their majority in Congress, it is likely that time considerations will quell their present enthusiasm and provide a constraint on their behavior.

Congressional staff resources present a problem similar to presidential staff resources. Although, increased legislative staff would provide additional manpower to assess, review, and revise the budget, there is no guarantee that such additional committee staff resources will make it a better or, more importantly, a more appealing budget to the president. If anything though, congressional staff would have a negative effect on budget agreement since the addition of staff resources would permit Congress to challenge the presidents' budget requests more frequently. However, even the smaller congressional staff of 1995 was assertive in budgeting. Again, though, this aggressiveness is likely attributable to the overall enthusiasm of Republicans as the majority party.

In contrast, House party margin should have a stronger effect on budget agreement. As the House party margin of the president increases so should budget agreement. Such congruence should follow intuitively; however, there is some reason to expect it to have slightly less of an effect than one might think. Obviously, as the presidents' party margin increases, the preferences of both the president and Congress should more closely resemble one another. This congruence should lead to increased budget agreement since preferences are similar. However, the fact that the president and Congress possess different constituencies argues for a milder effect. That is, preferences become more congruent when the House party margin of the president increases but that does not entail a 1:1 mapping of each actor's preferences. Thus, the varying constituency interests possessed by each actor could still lead to disagreement over the budget, such as during the Carter administration, despite possessing large partisan majorities in Congress.

Exogenous. Prior scholarship has observed the influence of several of our variables on budget decisions made by both presidents and Congress. Indeed, external conditions seem more likely to influence budgeting than other presidential-congressional interactions. Certainly exogenous economic conditions should be paramount but events may also be important. Donald Kettl (1992, chapter 1) shows how the Iraq War in 1991 forced George Bush to request a tax increase when he had said that he would not do so in the famous "read my lips" speech. The veto has been shown to influence budget decisions. Roderick Kieweit and Matthew McCubbins (1988) show that the veto can restrain greater spending by Congress than presidents desire but cannot exact additional funds for presidential preferences. Thus, presidential vetoes could be an important influence on degree of budget agreement by creating an atmosphere of hostility.

Economic situation should have a positive effect on budget agreement. As the economic situation worsens there is less room for compromise between the president and Congress. With less discretionary money available overall, neither Congress nor the president can "buy" the other actor's support. That is, one is less able to obtain support for one's own projects by funding the other's projects. As such, when the economic situation worsens, a gain for one actor entails a loss for another, whereas previously, it may have been possible for both actors to win to some degree. These stakes tend to raise the level and seriousness of the conflict surrounding budget agreement and argue for a positive relationship between economic situation and budget agreement. That is, as the economic situation worsens, budget agreement decreases.

As size of government (the number of federal government employees) increases, budget agreement should also increase. This expectation is due to the fact that, as the number of employees goes up, the amount of money necessary to compensate these employees also increases. Presumably, increases in salaries and wages for employees (a high portion of total spending) must be offset by decreases in discretionary spending. Thus, as more of the federal budget is spent on salaries and wages, less money is available for discretionary programs. As such, both the president and Congress have less room to ask for increases or decreases.

Since less opportunity exists for either the president or Congress to impose their particular desires, an increase should occur in the budget agreement between the two actors.

Process

As a device of last resort, vetoes indicate a breakdown in negotiations between Congress and the president. The more the president uses the veto, the less one can expect Congress and the president to be in accord. Thus, veto propensity should have a negative relationship with budget agreement. That is, as the president increases his use of the veto, budget agreement should decline. Clearly, if the president has to rely on the veto, conflict exists between himself and Congress. Thus, the veto indicates that negotiations have broken down and that compromise is a less likely option. That neither party is willing to negotiate or compromise signals a serious gap in the preferences of each actor. If such controversy ensues, there is little reason to expect that either actor's preferences should be more congruent regarding the allocation of fiscal resources in the budget. Thus, one should expect that as the use of the veto increases, budget agreement decreases.

Policy Effects

Although domestic and foreign policies often diverge, we anticipate less of a policy distinction in examining budget agreement than in the other dependent variables we have examined. Both the executive and legislative environments should influence domestic budget agreement, but we expect presidential variables to be more important in foreign policy since Congress may defer to the president in these matters. However, such deference often involves legislation or actions that do not necessarily require resource expenditures. It is a much different matter when money is at issue for foreign aid and national defense. Congress is less likely to support presidential requests for money for foreign than domestic policy for two reasons: (1) money spent on foreign affairs could be spent on domestic projects that could translate into votes, and (2) defense expenditures are typically the largest pool of discretionary spending available to Congress. Consequently, unless there is a major security threat to the United States (whether perceived or real), Congress can use defense expenditures to fund other programs. Ronald Reagan may be the exception in being able to generate moderate support for defense spending (Kamlet et al. 1987). Although we expect to find presidential variables dominant for most foreign policy distinctions, in terms of budget agreement, we anticipate that congressional variables also play a role in determining foreign budget agreement.

RESULTS

Trend Analysis

Figure 7.1 shows the time trend for the budget agreement variable. Although we anticipated a slight increased trend since the early 1970s due to frequently divided government and ideological conflict, we also expected to observe little change in budget agreement overall. Examining the trend line in figure 7.1 shows a statistically significant effect from the one-year lag of the variable (.38 regression coefficient) and a significant effect from the count variable (.08 coefficient). These findings indicate that an incremental effect occurs in budget agreement such that the previous year's values influence the current year's values and also confirm that a slight monotonic process is involved in budget agreement.

Recall that very little variation occurs in the budget agreement variable, under 20 percentage points in the range over our 47 year time period.

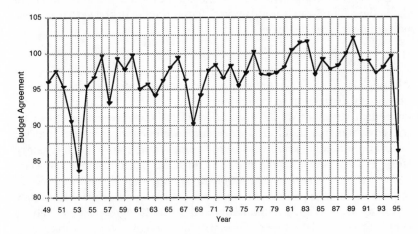

FIGURE 7.1
Budget Agreement, 1949–1995

Note: Budget agreement refers to total appropriations by Congress as a percentage of the total funds requested by the president.

Trend Analysis

	B	Sig T	
Count	.08	.024	Adj. R^2 = .11
One-Year Lag	.38	.022	Adj. R^2 = .11

Therefore, even the two spikes that appear are relatively modest, especially when one observes that the left axis for budget agreement is in units of only five percent, thereby magnifying the changes observed. The low value is 1953 when newly elected Dwight Eisenhower—the first Republican president in twenty years—received substantially lower appropriations (only 84 percent) of what he had requested. What could account for this phenomenon during a popular president's honeymoon year? Upon entering office Eisenhower declared "the first order of business is eliminating the annual deficit" (*Congress and the Nation* I 1965, 361). He reduced many appropriations requests, especially in defense, over what Truman had requested and the Republican-controlled 83rd Congress cut spending even further. This may have been due to the poor state of the economy, in part a result of the mid-1952 steel strike. Although disavowing general price controls, Eisenhower maintained controls over scarce materials as well as some rent controls. He also put off a planned tax cut to deal with the looming recession that hit the country hard by August 1953.

The highest value (102 percent) for budget agreement occurs in 1989 under President Bush. Although this year possesses the highest value in the series, budget negotiations during 1989 were less than civil. Congress had hoped to pass all appropriations by the October 1st deadline but failed to do so. Also, three appropriations bills were vetoed by Bush because they contained items that were contrary to his anti abortion position. This interesting facet of budget negotiations over a single controversial issue area threatened a government shut down. Thus, Congress had to resort to stop gap continuing resolutions to maintain funding at existing levels. After mounting an unsuccessful veto override attempt against the President's first veto, Congress on the last day of the session actually passed appropriations reflecting Bush's preferences. Although Congress deferred to Bush, they actually approved slightly more than he requested, thereby satisfying some (if only a marginal amount) of their own preferences.

Political Time

Our first political time control, historical era, has a very small effect on budget agreement, explaining just 12 percent of the variance. A small but significant difference appears between the overall percentage of budget agreement prior to 1975 and the percentage of budget agreement after 1974. As can be observed from scanning Figure 7.1, budget agreement is actually slightly higher during the later than the earlier period (2.47*). Therefore, budget agreement has not declined since the 1974 Budget Act, the deep drop in 1995 for Bill Clinton notwithstanding.

Select year in presidential term exhibits a non-existent relationship with an adj. R^2 of .05 and none of the selected years in term attain significance. Acknowledging for a moment that statistical significance is a relative construct (conventional levels merely indicate varying degrees of confidence that the relationship(s) found in the data does not occur at random), the unstandardized coefficients all possess the predicted direction. Honeymoon and, particularly, last years possess negative coefficients (–1.16 and –2.09 respectively). Oddly enough, budget agreement appears highest in reelection years. Contrary to recent experiences then, reelection years may be the most agreeable years in terms of budget agreement. However, it should be reiterated that these coefficients are not statistically significant at conventional levels and again the overall model is insignificant. Thus, budget agreement is not influenced by whether or not it is the president's first year, last year or reelection year.

Turning to individual presidents, the results in Table 7.1 also indi-

TABLE 7.1
Budget Agreement and Political Time Controls

	Unstandardized Coefficient	Adj. R^2
Historical Era		
Political Era, Post-1974	2.47*	.12
constant (1974 and before)	95.78***	
Select Year in Presidential Term		
First Year	–1.16	.05
Last Year	–2.09	
Reelection Year	.92	
Constant	97.17	
Individual President		
Harry Truman (constant)	94.88***	.25
Dwight Eisenhower	.79	
John Kennedy	.11	
Lyndon Johnson	1.13	
Richard Nixon	1.88	
Gerald Ford	3.81	
Jimmy Carter	2.45	
Ronald Reagan	4.55*	
George Bush	4.45	
Bill Clinton	–.22	

*   Significant at the .05 level
**   Significant at the .01 level
*** Significant at the .001 level

cate that the individual president model is insignificant and explains twenty five percent of the variance. The individual dummy variables are also insignificant, with the exception of Ronald Reagan, who obtained the greatest budget agreement of all the modern presidents. Therefore, while individual president explained more variance (R^2 = 25%) than political era and, especially year in term variables, none were very important. Therefore, we do not have much confidence for the results of our political time controls in explaining budget agreement.

We conclude that budget agreement is only modestly a function of political time; its one year lag and the count variables. That is, there is an incremental effect in which the previous year's level of budget agreement influences the current year's level of budget agreement and an ever so slight, almost imperceptible, monotonic increase in budget agreement is occurring. Although we found statistical significance in the post 1974 period, political era explained the least amount of the variance in budget agreement among our three political time controls. None were very impressive. We now turn to our general model of three environments as an explanation of budget agreement.

General and Policy Models

We originally anticipated that all three environments would have some effect on budget agreement but that the exogenous environment was probably the most important. The results in table 7.2 indicate that for the general model, both the executive and exogenous environments have an effect but that variables in the legislative environment do not. Although not all three environments are important for the general model of budget agreement, the fact that two of the three environments have some effect and in particular, that one of them is the exogenous (i.e., noninstitutional) environment, lends support to our multiple perspectives approach. The overall model does a very good job of explaining budget agreement, .86 adjusted R^2. We consider this finding particularly important based on the limited variation present in the variable.[3]

We now discuss some of the individual variables, first for the general and then for the policy models. The results show that there is no relationship for minor speeches and employees in the EOP with budget agreement. This finding confirms our expectation that neither speech making nor presidential staff (employees in EOP) would have much of an effect on budget agreement. As per our expectations, presidential popular approval is significant and possesses the correct sign, positive (.26). This indicates that as presidential popularity increases, budget agreement also increases. Our expectation was that as popular approval increased, the president could point to his popularity as a mandate for his programs and thereby increase his influence with Congress. This finding reveals that presidents are able to make use of their popular opinion when negotiating over the budget.

Within the legislative environment, we anticipated finding that there would be no relationship between congressional committee staff size and budget agreement and the results bear out this expectation. However, we did anticipate a positive relationship with congressional party margin and a negative relationship with workload on budget agreement. Although, the coefficients possess the correct direction for both variables, neither of them approaches significance at the .05 level. Consequently, the results show that none of the variables from the legislative environment have an effect on overall budget agreement.

In examining the results for the exogenous variables for the full general model, we find mixed results. Economic situation possessed the correct direction (25.23) and while it approached significance at the .05 level, it did not attain significance. However, we feel comfortable that as more data points become available, future research will reveal this rela-

TABLE 7.2
General and Policy Models for Budget Agreement

	General Model	Domestic Model	Foreign Model
Executive Environment			
Popular Approval	.26***	−.48	.83
Employees in EOP	.71	−.69	−.87
Minor Speeches	.18	−.41	−.29
Legislative Environment			
Committee Staff	.11	−.12	.78***
Party Margin	.22	.66	.34
Workload	−.31	−.12	.26
Exogenous Environment			
Economic Situation	25.23	267.45***	7.06
Size of Federal Govt.	.21***	.53***	.21***
Veto Propensity	.38	−.55	−.36
Constant	9.23	19.11	8.35
Adj. R^2	.86	.32	.69
Lagrange Multiplier	.18	323.25	9.68

*   Significant at the .05 level
**   Significant at the .01 level
*** Significant at the .001 level

tionship and show that economic situation does affect budget agreement due to the variables' theoretical relevance. Size of the federal government also possesses the predicted positive direction (.21) and attains statistical significance. This confirms our expectation that as the number of employees increases, then so will budget agreement as fewer discretionary funds are available to debate. Finally, our process variable, veto propensity, neither attained statistical significance nor possessed the predicted direction.

Table 7.2 also differentiates the results by domestic and foreign policy. The explanatory power of the domestic model is .32 adjusted R^2, perhaps indicating that other factors may affect domestic policy budget agreement. In this model, we find that only the exogenous environment has an effect. None of the legislative variables emerge as significant in looking at the domestic model. It appears then that neither the president nor Congress is able to influence domestic budget agreement with their institutional resources; however, exogenous factors proved important. One of the exogenous variables that is significant in the general model is also significant in the domestic model (number of federal government employees); economic situation is also significant at conventional levels. As anticipated then, economic situation and size of government possess an effect on domestic policy allocations.

In foreign policy we find that the legislative and exogenous environments have an affect on foreign policy budget agreement. Contrary to our expectation, the regression coefficient (.78) for committee staff reveals that when congressional staff increases, foreign policy budget agreement also increases. We anticipated that increased staff would increase the level of oversight regarding foreign policy requests, which would in turn lead to less budget agreement. Again though, size of government both attains significance and possesses the predicted direction (.21). Oddly enough, however, economic situation is no longer significant. While foreign funding is distinguishable from domestic funding, one would have expected the perceptions of the domestic economy to influence how much Congress would appropriate of what the president requests. Compared to the general model, the foreign policy model also possesses considerable explanatory power with a .69 adjusted R^2.

Overall, the findings for budget agreement are quite strong. Our multiple perspectives approach is supported by the fact that at least two environments are necessary in explaining budget agreement and one of those environments was the exogenous environment. Probably the only disappointment was that we expected at least one congressional variable to attain significance in explaining domestic budget agreement. Overall though, we did anticipate that the exogenous environment should be the most important environment when considering budget agreement and we find that size of the federal government is significant with the predicted directions across the general, domestic, and foreign models. The other exogenous variable, economic situation, is also significant in the predicted direction in the domestic model and approaches significance in the predicted direction in the general model.

SUMMARY AND CONCLUSION

The Budget of the United States is a political document and therefore a primary battleground for conflicts between presidents and Congress (Thurber 1996, 209). The budget process reveals an important interaction between the two modern institutions due to the fact that, as mentioned in chapters 1 and 7, Congress requires a budget document from modern presidents. We also indicated that this device gives presidents a leg up on the legislature because of the unified nature of the executive branch. Numerous studies document the changes in presidential-congressional relations brought about by the various reform efforts since the 1921 Budget Act (Thurber 1996; LeLoup 1980; Schick 1986). Scholars generally agree that the 1974 Act changed Congress's own practices rather than those of the executive (Marini 1992, 8). It centralized decision making more in Congress but shifted power somewhat between the two institutions. Allen Schick (1986, 15) contends that the 1974 Act constrained both actors and made them even more independent. Howard Shuman (1992, 16) argues that, although presidents set the budget agenda, they influence subsequent decisions only marginally.

Unlike our other three interactions, budget agreement is neither a consistently increasing nor decreasing phenomenon; rather, the trend analysis indicates that it is an incremental process. Additionally, budget agreement is not influenced by historical era, select year in presidential term, or individual presidents (see table 7.1). The trend line as well as the post-1974 coefficient reveal that somewhat more budget agreement has occurred in more recent years. This finding provides counterevidence that divided government may have detrimental consequences on budgeting.

The three (general and two policy) models show that only the executive and exogenous environments influence the general model. Only the exogenous environment influences the domestic policy model and both the legislative and exogenous environments influence the foreign policy model. Although, we have consistently anticipated that all three environments should have an effect on the interactions, the fact that two environments influence budget agreement in the general and foreign policy models supports our thesis that no single perspective (i.e., a

Congress- or president-centered approach) is adequate to fully understand presidential-congressional interactions.

Although only two of the environments proved to have a contributing influence on budget agreement, the strong effects of the exogenous environment make considerable sense. Most of the funds that the president and Congress deal with each year are already obligated and, therefore, basically uncontrollable. However, when the economy is improving with deficits decreasing, one would expect Congress and the president to have more flexibility in their negotiations and for Congress to possess a greater willingness to fund the budget requests made by the president. This compromise attitude should derive from less concern over fiscal discipline and less public scrutiny.

The one thing we know with a great deal of certainty is that budget agreement does not vary by huge amounts either from year to year or across many years. Other than times of crisis, the post–Korean war (1953 spike) and enormous deficits (1989 spike), budget agreement ranges from the low 83 percent to just a little over 102 percent. Neither Congress nor the president is able to change much of what must be allocated to pay personnel, fund programs, and pay interest on the debt. Thus, the president and Congress wrangle over discretionary dollars that seem like much to the general public, but which are relatively small when compared to overall federal expenditures. Although budget agreement varies little, we explain a considerable portion of the variation in this important presidential-congressional interaction.

CHAPTER 8

Conclusion

OVERVIEW OF BOOK

Previous research tends to follow one of two directions when examining presidential-congressional relations. First, most scholars examine these relationships from only a single institutional perspective, arguing either presidential or congressional dominance. The nature of subfield specializations within the discipline may contribuite to these perspectives. Such research typically focuses on explaining presidential-congressional relations either from a largely presidential (Neustadt 1990; Spitzer 1993; Mezey 1989) or congressional perspective (Bond and Fleisher 1990; Jones 1994, 1995). While these efforts have contributed to our understanding of presidential-congressional relations, they fail to illuminate the greater complexity inherent in studying their interactions. Some authors argue that the nature of modeling is to reduce complexity through abstraction and, therefore, increasing the complexity of a model is not always worthwhile (Huckfeldt, Kohfeld, and Likens 1982). Although, we do not necessarily disagree with this view, to ignore the greater complexity inherent in presidential-congressional relations leaves a gaping hole in such research.

One of the most promising responses to single institutional perspectives has been Mark Peterson's tandem institutions approach to studying presidential-congressional relations. Peterson (1990) contends that it is necessary to examine presidential-congressional relations from the point of view of both political institutions, that neither institution alone explains their interactions. Other authors find this approach useful (LeLoup and Shull 1999; Thurber 1996). While we both applaud and commend Peterson's efforts in this direction, we find that even this dual explanation does not tell the entire story. We contend that presidential-congressional interactions are affected not only by the respective institutions but that exogenous (or environmental) factors can have important effects on either constraining or facilitating presidential-congressional relations.

The second tendency in presidential-congressional relations research is to study a single interaction. Typically, research to date has examined only CQ's support or success scores (Edwards 1980, 1989; Bond and Fleisher 1990). Having chronicled the support/success debate in earlier chapters, we will not recover that ground here. The important point to note regarding the tendency to focus on a single interaction is that it ignores other aspects of presidential-congressional relations in which both actors attempt to assert their respective preferences. Again, research that takes such a one-dimensional focus fails to capture not only the complexity but the diversity of presidential-congressional relations.

We examine four different presidential-congressional interactions in order to better illuminate diversity inherent in such relations in adopting public policy. Even Peterson's tandem institutions approach investigates only a single dependent variable. It seems almost all too obvious that presidential-congressional interactions must be multifaceted and take place across a number of different phenomenon, such as the ones we present herein (presidential position taking, legislative support, veto propensity, and budget agreement). Consequently, we break new ground by incorporating four direct interactions as separate dependent variables in our analysis of presidential-congressional relations.

In addition to institutional and exogenous influences, it is highly likely that the interplay of these interactions influence each other as well. Although we are limited by using year as the unit of analysis in picking out the reciprocating effects among the interactions within a single year, we attempt to capture some of this process by using the interaction process in the current model. Although not completely clear from our research, further elaboration of the process effects of the interactions on one another may prove as entangling in reality as modeling the entire policy process (Jones 1984; Peters 1996; Ripley 1985; Shull and Gleiber 1994).

In this research, we analyze presidential-congressional interactions across the longest time series yet (1949–95). We offer sophisticated modeling, using three environments to explain these interactions in adopting public policy. We test and control for auto-correlation in the models. We also control for trend as well as for three elements of political time: historical era, year in presidential term of office, and individual presidents. Another control we employ is for policy type (domestic and foreign). Several authors have documented the changing roles of these institutions by policy areas (Hinckley 1994; Shull 1991; Ripley and Lindsay 1993; Peterson 1994). All in all, our analysis provides a more sophisticated and more comprehensive assessment of presidential-congressional interactions than has occurred heretofore.

The argument that we present is that presidential-congressional relations extend beyond a single or even a tandem institutions approach.

Rather, congressional-presidential relations need to be understood from "a multiple perspective" that includes not only the diverse elements within executive and legislative institutions themselves but also from the exogenous environment. This outside environment includes economic and human resources as well as other activities in policymaking. Our four analysis chapters show that each of the four direct interactions in policy adoption are influenced by at least two if not all three environments (executive, legislative, and exogenous).

Additionally, presidential-congressional relations do not occur at a single moment in time defined by a single interaction, such as legislative support for presidents. Rather, these interactions are better understood as an ongoing process in which each actor is continuously engaging the other in attempts to enact particular preferences. Thus, the president may take a position on a particular piece of legislation in order to enhance its possibilities of making it through the legislative process while at the same time vetoing a piece of legislation that Congress has just passed. Similarly, Congress may withdraw support from presidential preferences or decide to cut out money from presidential requests, either to deny the president his preferences or to further congressional preferences. Thus, a temporal process of policy adoption often within a single year is occurring.

SUMMARY OF FOUR INTERACTIONS AND RESULTS

We examine four direct presidential-congressional interactions that are related but not identical. They are all part of the policy adoption process in that they are government activities that seek to facilitate or constrain the enactment of legislation. As such they could be viewed as a temporal subprocess to the larger policy process. Once the agenda has been set and different proposals formulated to address the agenda, then the process of interactions begins in order to effect adoption of a particular formulated preference. That is, given varying preferences over policy formulation, the president and Congress attempt to adopt their preferred positions, from earlier position taking and support to later vetoes and budget agreement. Our research demonstrates complexity within what is commonly viewed as a single stage (adoption) in the policymaking process. In the next section we summarize our results for the general models of presidential-congressional relations.

Presidential Position Taking

Position taking is measured as the number of times the president takes a position on roll call votes in Congress each year. As such, position taking does not define the domain of the presidential agenda but rather reflects a subset of the overall legislative agenda. By taking a position on a particular vote, the president is attempting to insert his preferences into the legislative arena. The president possesses political capital (Light 1982) that he can expend to achieve his preferences. One of the ways the president expends political resources is by taking positions on votes on legislation in Congress. When a president takes a position he risks political capital in the sense that if the bill fails, then it may hurt the president's professional reputation and thereby also affect his ability to influence legislators in future situations.

Not only does taking a position involve an initial investment but it also entails a certain amount of future commitment to a piece of legislation. That is, having invested in a piece of legislation, it will probably be necessary to stake further resources into that same legislation in the future through such devices as negotiating for passage with legislators and appealing to the general public through speeches and addresses. Certainly, presidents are not obligated to continue to advocate positions that they have already taken and, in fact, they may find it necessary to abandon some positions. However, as a general rule, it would be wasteful to invest in legislation via positions and then not follow up with further efforts for the legislation. Finally, presidents are likely to only take positions on those pieces of legislation that reflect their preferences since political assets are finite. That is, presidents have a certain amount of exhaustable resources that prevent them from indiscriminately taking positions on legislation.

We find that all three environments influence whether or not the president decides to take a position on roll call votes: the executive, legislative, and exogenous environments. Within the executive environment, presidents are more inclined to take a stand on legislation when they are unpopular with the general public. We documented a decline in popular approval but an increase in position taking over time. Thus, presidents' standing with the public places pressure on the president to resolve problems. Clearly, since presidents take positions on legislation that is already in Congress, it makes sense that they would be influenced by congressional factors as to whether or not to take such positions. The particular variable that influences presidential position taking in the legislative environment is presidential party margin. A strong party margin facilitates the support of presidential preferences and thus the president engages in more position taking. Conversely, a weak party margin constrains the enactment of presidential preferences and, thus, presidents take fewer positions on House roll call votes.

Although not of the same magnitude as the variables in the two institutional environments, the size of government variable in the exogenous environment is also statistically significant for position taking. We recognize that size of government may have a spurious relationship with position taking but suggest that more people require more government programs to sustain them. Thus, as the size of government increases, the scope of government must as well and any increase in the amount of legislation appears to precipitate an increased response in position taking by presidents. All in all, a single variable from each of our three environments did a good job of explaining the number of presidential positions on roll call votes in Congress.

Legislative Support

More quantitative research has been conducted on legislative support of presidents' vote positions than for any of the four interactions covered here. Chapter 5 compared support with success and influence in order to clarify the meaning and measurement of this frequently used concept. Support in this context refers to the average percent House member agreement with the presidents' publicly stated positions on each roll call vote. We use support rather than a somewhat related congruence measure in part because Lyn Ragsdale (1996) provides these values overall and when disaggregated by policy area, making them compatible to our other interaction variables. It is important to remember that unlike the old (box score) measure of success, support need not indicate presidential agenda preferences. Rather, the votes reflect matters on Congress's agenda, with the president being a reactor rather than an initiator. We agree with others that support measures agreement or congruence rather than influence or leadership (Pritchard 1983; Edwards 1991; Bond, Fleisher, and Krutz 1996; Shull 1997; Sullivan 1991c). Nevertheless, we have argued that support constitutes an important interaction between the president and Congress.

As with position taking, we find that all three environments influence legislative support for presidents' vote positions. In the executive environment, we observe employees in the EOP influencing support. The size of presidential staff should influence relations between the executive and legislative environments. That is, the president is not able to negotiate and deal with each legislator himself; rather, presidents often must utilize their staffs as the communication and negotiation link between themselves and the legislature. The more staff available to the president overall, the more resources that can be devoted to legislative liaison. Thus, as employees in the EOP increase, legislative support of presidents' vote positions tends to increase. The fact that presidential popularity was insignificant for support squares with other research (Brace and Hinckley 1992; Collier and Sullivan 1995). However, this presidential resource was important in each of the remaining three presidential-congressional interactions.

In the legislative environment, we find that presidents' House party margin is important and also influences legislative support; again, this finding makes intuitive sense. Because of the ideological similarities within the same party, interparty preferences should be more closely aligned. Party therefore entails similar preferences. If the margin of the president's party increases, there should be more overall support for presidential preferences. We find that this is the case. As House party margin increases, so does legislative support in that body. In our analysis, party margin was highly significant, congruent with other research showing the pervasiveness of this variable for presidents' legislative relations (Edwards 1989; Bond and Fleisher 1990).

Finally, in the exogenous environment, we find that the process variable is important. For support, the most directly related process variable is position taking. As position taking increases, our analysis reveals that support goes down. This finding indicates that as the president continues to take positions, Congress is less likely to support presidential preferences. Congress may view the president as asking for too much; that is, if the president continues to take positions to support his preferences, Congress will back away from supporting the president and in turn support its own preferences. Presidents should choose their positions with care, but a low-risk strategy could be frustrating to an activist president. However, presidents should use their political capital as constructively as possible and taking too many positions wastes political capital since support declines as position taking increases.

Both of the other exogenous variables are also significant in explaining presidents' legislative support. Economic activity (measured as surplus or deficit/outlays) and size of government (number of civilian employees) both were associated positively with support. Presidents' support from Congress then is dependent upon both institutional environments, but also quite strongly affected by outside influences as well. Legislative support was the only interaction for which all three variables in the exogenous environment were significant.

Veto Propensity

The veto represents one of presidents' most decisive powers. As a tool to secure executive policy preferences, presidents use the veto to block legislative action that they oppose. As such, it is a negative tool of last resort, often used out of weakness rather than strength. The veto does not directly help to secure presidential preferences but is used primarily to thwart the preferences of Congress. In that capacity, it can also be used as a negotiating tool wherein threats may encourage legislative compromise (Spitzer 1988). Knowing that the president can resort to the veto if necessary, Congress is put into a position of having to acknowledge and consider presidential preferences.

In this research, we measure veto propensity as the number of times per year that the president uses the regular veto on public legislation. While there are other interesting aspects of the veto, such as congressional overrides or override attempts, these variables pose particular problems. The veto itself occurs infrequently and we find that in some years no vetoes exist at all. Therefore, it is difficult to further disaggregate the veto by policy area beyond the simple domestic/foreign dichotomy because of the small number of cases. Indeed, so few foreign vetoes occur, that examining subissues of only domestic and economic—not foreign—legislation is feasible.

We find in our results that both institutional environments influence presidents' decisions on whether or not to issue a veto. From the executive environment, presidential popular approval is highly significant; however, in being negative, it possesses the wrong direction. That is, as popular approval increases, the number of vetoes decreases. One would expect that as popular approval increased, then so would the number of vetoes. With strong popular approval, the president should feel more comfortable attempting to enact his own preferences over those of Congress. It may be though that as popular approval increases, so does the perception of popular mandate. Although high approval certainly does not guarantee support, it could prompt legislators to work with presidents instead of against them. Thus, if support increases with popular approval, the president would not need to issue as many vetoes. However, unpopular presidents may use the device to show the public that they are trying to lead Congress.

In the legislative environment, both party margin and workload are significant and possess the predicted direction. Obviously it is the presidents' prerogative whether or not to issue a veto, but it certainly makes sense that they would consider legislative factors in making such a decision. Party margin should play an important part in determining whether or not the president will have to issue many vetoes. If party margin is high, then it is likely that the president and Congress will agree on many of their preferences and, consequently, the president should not be required to issue many vetoes. However, if party margin is low then it is much more likely that presidents will have to turn to the veto to assure that their preferences are taken into account by Congress. Conversely, legislative workload relates strongly to the incidence of vetoes since, the greater the number of public laws, the more work Congress is engaged in, and thus, the prospects for veto usage are greater. The president could also gain in this circumstance in that a busy Congress will have less time to devote to action necessary to override the veto.

Finally, the exogenous environment contributes no significant explanation to the number of annual public bill vetoes by presidents. Although this finding was disappointing, it is not surprising given that position taking and veto propensity were the least well explained of our four presidential-congressional interactions in policy adoption. Despite explaining over sixty percent of the variance in veto propensity, such explanation presumably involves political influences within rather than outside the two institutional environments.

Budget Agreement

For our purposes, budget agreement is measured as the percent of the president's overall budget requests appropriated by Congress. A problem with this interaction variable is in knowing whose preferences are enacted in the final budget agreement. While 100 percent agreement may occur, it is possible that Congress is replacing the president's requests with its own. This book does not deal with whose budgetary preferences are achieved but only the concurrence of preferences. The concern here is to show which environments influence the ways in which both the president and Congress attempt to enact their preferences. Consequently, it is not important to know who wins but rather to show whether institutional or exogenous environments influence the variation in this interaction.

Although we do not find that all three environments influence budget agreement, both the executive (popular approval) and exogenous environments (economic situation and size of government) are important. Similar to veto propensity, we again find that at least two environments are important; however, for budget agreement, we find that at least one of the relevant environments is the exogenous environment. This again highlights the fact that a single institution or even a tandem institutions approach to understanding presidential-congressional interactions is deficient in that exogenous factors rarely are taken into account (but see Peterson 1990). Thus, a multiple perspectives approach such as utilized here is needed to attain greater understanding. In fact, our approach works quite well considering how little variation occurs in budget agreement.

In the executive environment, we find that presidents' popular approval is an important determinant of budget agreement. However, the direction of the coefficient is negative, which is counterintuitive. One would expect budget agreement to increase with popular approval. That is, Congress should defer more to presidential preferences as their popular support increases. Regardless though, the relationship between popular approval and budget agreement suggests that it needs to be included in a fully specified model. Budget agreement was the only one of our four interactions for which presidential party margin in Congress was not important.

In the exogenous environment, we find that economic situation and size of government are significant predictors of budget agreement. Certainly, economic situation should play a very important part in influencing budget agreement. As the economic situation increases (improves) then so should budget agreement due to the fact that economic situation, as measured by Mayhew (1992), is intimately connected to the level of the surplus/deficit. If the deficit improves, more resources are available to both parties. If more resources are available, then more of the preferences of each actor can be accommodated by the budget and so agreement should increase. As economic situation worsens then budget agreement should also decrease as well due to the fact that as less resources are available, both Congress and presidents will have to fight harder to enact their policy preferences.

The size of government variable is also important for budget agreement and was signficant in three out of four of our presidential-congressional interactions. This result stands to reason since the largest item in the federal budget is personnel and neither presidents nor Congress are inclined to fire federal employees. We strongly urge subsequent scholars to utilize this variable, which has heretofore not been incorporated in studying presidential-congressional interactions. That we were able to explain 86 percent of a variable (budget agreement) that varies so little is a testament to the multiple perspectives approach.

Assessment

Our model outlined earlier in the theoretical framework of chapter 2 views both the president and Congress as working to achieve their separate preferences. It is not important to us what their individual preferences are, but rather, whether such preferences are adopted through the process of their interactions with one another. However, determinants within the various institutional (executive and legislative) and exogenous environments both enable and constrain each actor in attempting to achieve its preferences. In the past, scholars have typically relied on either a presidential or congressional perspective that caused them to focus on variables in only one environment. Peterson (1990) included both presidential and congressional (or tandem institutions) approaches. Our concern has been to show that all three environments play a part in influencing presidential-congressional interactions. Thus, we offer an even more encompassing multiple perspective toward understanding presidential-congressional relations.

Table 8.1 presents a summary of the effects of the independent variables within each environment used herein on the general model of our four interaction dependent variables. This table clearly shows the guiding focus of this work: namely, no one environment is capable of fully explaining any of the four presidential-congressional interactions. In examining position taking and support, all three environments are influential. For veto propensity, the two institutional environments were important but it was the only interaction for which the exogenous environment was insignificant. Finally, for budget agreement, both the executive and exogenous environments come into play. Ultimately then, the multiple perspectives approach is necessary to capture the complexity

TABLE 8.1
General Model across Four Interactions

	Position Taking	Legislative Support	Veto Propensity	Budget Agreement
Executive Environment				
Popular Approval	✓		✓	✓
Employees in EOP		✓		
Minor Speeches				
Legislative Environment				
Committee Staff				
Party Margin	✓	✓	✓	
Workload			✓	
Exogenous Environment				
Economic Situation		✓		
Size of Government	✓	✓		✓
Process		✓		

Legend

Significant effect, .05 or better = ✓

No Significant effect = blank

and diversity of presidential-congressional interactions.

We selected three variables from each environment, one activity (or process in exogenous environment) and two resource variables, in an attempt to better capture the full dimension of that environment. We find that of our two classes of variables (activities and resources) that resources are more important across the models. Obviously, only three variables do not exhaust the domain of potential measures for any of these three environments and, as such, other variables could have been used in conjunction or in place of these. In fact, we initially examined but rejected other variables to eliminate multicollinearity among the set of nine independent variables in our model. The point here is that the particular set or overall effectiveness of any one variable over the four dependent interactions is not necessarily all that important. These results indicate that a multiple perspective, our expansion of the tandem institutions approach, is necessary for a fuller explanation of presidential-congressional relations in the complex process of adopting public policy.

POLITICAL TIME AND POLICY CONTROLS

We made use of two sets of controls in this analysis: controls for elements of political time and a control for the two presidencies policy distinction. We would have preferred to incorporate our time controls into our models; however, they were already quite extensive and the addition of more variables would have used up valuable degrees of freedom. Consequently, we presented separate models using our time and policy controls. We ran separate equations for the controls in order to determine whether groupings of our data by time or policy indeed had effects on the dependent variables (interactions). Although this exercise does not tell us about the combined effects of the three environments and controls, it does allow us to estimate whether or not these control variables are relevant and whether their inclusion warrants further investigation.

Political time was used as a control in three ways, ranging from historical era as the most aggregated (only two categories) to selected years in presidents' term (four groupings) to the least aggregated control of examining each of the ten presidents separately. All three sets of controls have some benefit and are widely used in scholarly literature (Kessel 1984; Lewis and Strine 1996; Nuestadt 1980; Light 1982; Shull 1983, 1997). In order to test for the domestic/foreign policy distinction, we had to disaggregate the four dependent interactions by policy area. Fortunately, the data were available to do this across the four interactions largely because we were able to use Ragsdale's 1996 data for three of them. Thus, each interaction was disaggregated by policy area and then used as the dependent variable in the respective equation. For example, position taking was split into number of positions per year each on domestic and foreign policy. The general model is the combination of domestic and foreign positions.

Utility of Political Time

Divisions of political time provide interesting dimensions for investigation. Similar to exogenous variables, political time variables operate external to the institutions of government themselves and indicate broader environmental trends. Research on both the presidency and party realignment has speculated that there may be broad generational trends in control of the presidency and cycles of political party dominance (Skowronek 1993; Lews and Strine 1996; Schlesinger 1986; Barber 1980). The research herein has focused on one long and two shorter spans of political time and they reveal interesting results. We examine three political time controls: historical era, selected year in presidential term, and individual president. All three of these controls contribute to understanding the four presidential-congressional interactions under investigation with varying degrees of success.

A very broad cycle of dominance occurs between the executive and legislative institutions. For the better part of the nineteenth century, Congress was the dominant actor, but during the early twentieth century, the president began to overtake Congress in policymaking (Sundquist 1981). Since 1974, it appears that Congress is trying to turn back the tide of presidential dominance (LeLoup and Shull 1999); however, it remains to be seen whether or not this power shifting is in fact taking place, especially in foreign policy (Hinckley 1994). More than a shift in dominance, it seems that we have entered an era of increasing conflict (Shull 1997, chapter 5). However, that increased institutional conflict could signify a realignment in institutional dominance between Congress and the president.

Table 8.2 presents the summary effects for our political time controls. Historical era and individual presidents appear to be the most useful controls. The constant (prior to and including 1974) for historical era is significant across all four interactions and the post-1974 period is significant for position taking, support, and budget agreement. We chose 1974 as our break point because it represents a reassertive Congress and, therefore, the end of an era of presidential dominance (LeLoup and Shull 1999; chapter 2). Consequently, we expected to see stark differences for our interactions between these two time periods. As expected, position taking has increased; support has declined severely; vetoes have increased; and budget agreement has increased slightly since the earlier period of the study. Thus, recent presidents are finding that they have to be far more active, that is, take more positions and use the

TABLE 8.2
Political Time Controls across the Four Interactions

	Position Taking	Legislative Support	Veto Propensity	Budget Agreement
Historical Era				
Post-1974	✓	✓		✓
1974 and Before (constant)	✓	✓	✓	✓
Select Year in Presidential Term				
First Year	✓			
Reelection Year			✓	
Last Year				
Other Years (constant)	✓	✓	✓	
Individual President				
Harry Truman (constant)*		✓	✓	✓
Dwight Eisenhower		✓		
John Kennedy	✓			
Lyndon Johnson	✓		✓	
Richard Nixon	✓	✓		
Gerald Ford	✓	✓	✓	
Jimmy Carter	✓	✓		
Ronald Reagan	✓	✓		✓
George Bush	✓	✓		
Bill Clinton	✓	✓		

Legend

Significant effect, .05 or better = ✓

No significant effect = blank

* Truman is the constant for all models; see discussion in chapter 7.

veto more, while congressional support of the president is profoundly decreasing in terms of support. Congruence of fiscal preferences as represented in budget agreement is improving marginally. These findings by the two time periods indicate not only growing contentiousness but also increased assertiveness by both actors to assert their individual policy preferences and institutional prerogatives.

Select years in presidential term, however, does not appear to be all that useful (see table 8.2). First year is only significant for the position taking models. Reelection year is significant only for vetoes and last years are never important for any of the four interactions. Thus, we feel confident that the particular year in term has little to do with presidential-congressional interactions. The fact that the theoretically unimportant "other" years (a residual category of all remaining years not fitting into one of the three designations) is significant in three models makes us cautious about this particular control (see Shull 1997).

Finally, individual presidents appear to have some effect across all four of the models (see table 8.2). Although the presidential dummy set does not always account for much variation in the dependent variable, these findings do support the argument that one cannot ignore the individual within the larger institution when examining the presidency. That is, characteristics regarding individual presidents are important in their ability to interact with Congress. Considerable debate has occurred over whether to study the individual president (N = 1 problem; Heclo 1977) or whether to study the institutional president and largely ignore individual characteristics. Scholars like Richard Neustadt (1960) and Theodore Lowi (1985) focus on the former, while Ragsdale (1996), Bert Rockman (1984), and Joseph Pika (1979) emphasize the latter. Greg Hager and Terry Sullivan (1994) show that both matter and need attention in scholarly research. Also, the evidence here suggests that both the individual (through the presidential dummies) and institution (through variables like size of EOP) are important.

Using political time in this volume goes beyond standard treatments. It represents a new way of thinking about presidential-congressional relations according to recurring cycles instead of purely chronological time. The concern is more with understanding patterns and meaning in relationships between the two institutions. In addition to historical era and individual presidents, selected year within president's term of office facilitates comprehension of stability and change in agendas and activities. Political time allows for a more sophisticated and extended analysis than chronological time alone provides. We reiterate the utility of such controls, especially historical era and individual president, and we provide the longest time series yet incorporated for these controls on presidential-congressional interactions.

Utility of Policy Areas

The roles and influence of both the president and Congress vary considerably by policy areas and several such divisions have been used to study presidential-congressional relations (Shull 1997). For a dichotomy, the two presidencies thesis retains some utility after more than thirty years of research. The recent decision by CQ to include an economic dimension, instead of just domestic and foreign, has been suggested by others (e.g., Manning 1977; LeLoup and Shull [1979] 1991). Presidents do not appear to be more foreign policy oriented, taking relatively fewer positions in that domain. However, Congress does appear more domestic oriented, by challenging presidents with less support in that issue area. Very few vetoes appear in foreign policy but budget agreement is lower in that issue area. All in all, the two presidencies typology provided a valuable control in our analysis.

Table 8.3 shows the summary effects for disaggregating each interaction by policy area. Overall, the two policy areas had somewhat mixed results in examining presidential-congressional interactions. First, separating by policy area confirms the findings that no single environment is capable of explaining any of the interactions. The only counterexample is in domestic policy for position taking, where only one environment is relevant; however, these circumstances are largely anomalous and probably the result of chance factors. In each of the other seven interactions, at least two environments are necessary and in three of the eight total interactions, variables from all three environments provide significant explanatory power.

Disaggregating by policy area was clearly useful due to the presence of discernable patterns differentiating domestic and foreign policy. Although some of the same variables are important in both the domestic and foreign policy categories, usually considerable differentiation occurred. Overall, except for veto propensity for which few foreign interactions occur, foreign policy interactions were better explained by our three variable models than were domestic interactions. Probably the most differentiation occurs in position taking, where domestic policy is affected only by legislative factors and foreign policy is affected by variables from all three environments. Domestic and foreign support and foreign position taking obtain explanatory power from all three environments. Both types of veto propensity are institutionally based, while both domestic and foreign policy budget agreement depend heavily on the exogenous environment. These findings reveal the discriminating power of even this crude two presidencies dichotomy of public policy.

Although congressional influence in foreign policy does not yet match its power domestically, Congress is increasing its role considerably. The issue area where Congress has had the least influence has been in defense (Hinckley 1994). Wars and crises in the twentieth century have led to substantial growth of presidential power. Yet even here Congress is asserting itself, particularly when presidents are thought to have exceeded their authority and encroached into areas where Congress also maintains constitutional responsibilities. Thus, while presidential powers have grown enormously, Congress appears to be catching up (Ripley and Lindsay 1993). There is no evidence, even when Congress and the president are of the same party, that this trend will

TABLE 8.3
Domestic and Foreign Models across the Four Interactions

	Domestic				Foreign			
	PT	LS	VP	BA	PT	LS	VP	BA
Executive Environment								
Popular Approval			✓		✓		✓	
Employees in EOP		✓				✓		
Minor Speeches						✓		
Legislative Environment								
House Staff	✓							✓
Party Margin	✓	✓			✓	✓		
Workload		✓			✓	✓		
Exogenous Environment								
Economic Situation				✓	✓	✓		
Size of Federal Govt.		✓		✓		✓		✓
Process		✓			✓	✓		

Legend

Significant effect, .05 or better = ✓

No significant effect = blank

PT = Position taking.
LS = Legislative support.
VP = Veto propensity.
BA = Budget agreement.

reverse itself in the near future. The two-presidencies distinction appears less empirically obvious than it did in the 1960s. Yet the phenomenon still exists, if more so for Republican than Democratic presidents. Although theory has been limited, considerable research has worked toward this end (Shull 1991, 1994; Lindsay and Steger 1993), and it is parsimonious.

IMPLICATIONS

The first implication to be drawn from the results contained herein is that no single environment is sufficient by itself to explain presidential-congressional relations. For any of the interactions we examine, at least two environments are necessary for understanding presidential-congressional relations. Additionally, all three environments were roughly equal in importance with each (executive, legislative, and exogenous) environment contributing to at least three interactions. Consequently, not only is a multiple perspectives focus necessary but also those multiple perspectives cannot consist simply of variables from either institution. Rather, exogenous variables beyond the institutions themselves act in conjunction with the institutions to facilitate or constrain the interactions of both the president and Congress.

The second implication is that no single variable captures the domain of any of the environments. We chose three variables to represent each environment that modeled elements of both activities and resources. We did this to try to better represent each environment and allow for a full range of effects from different variables in each environment. Unfortunately, including additional variables beyond three threatened our degrees of freedom and thus, we limited the analysis to three variables in each environment.

The third implication we draw is that no single variable is important across all of the interactions. However, popular approval (executive), party margin (legislative), and size of government (exogenous) were significant in three out of four of the general models. Thus, neither the president nor Congress can rely on any one resource or activity in dealing with each other. Rather, they must continuously look to the myriad of resources, internally and externally, that affect their behavior in order to enact their preferences. Another important implication of this work is that the executive environment appears to play a larger role in the policy adoption phase than has previously been suggested (Bond and Fleisher 1990; Jones 1994). Admittedly, two of our dependent variables are largely discretionary presidential activities (position taking and veto propensity). However, seen from the context of policy adoption (that is, strategically using these decisions to enact preferences) and in conjunction with the fact that the executive environment was important in all four of the general models, it appears that the president plays a major, perhaps coequal role in the adoption of public policy. Next, we discuss some very recent events within our four activities and speculate on what they may mean for presidential-congressional relations.

Prospects

Presidential-congressional relations have been observed empirically for over forty years through the Congressional Quarterly (CQ) measures utilized in this volume. Presidential position taking, a basis for most of these measures, has received surprisingly little scholarly attention in its own right. Obviously, success and support have been used extensively; however, sometimes they are used interchangeably and become confused. Although much research has occurred on the presidential veto, it has been treated in isolation as have the other three interactions included in this volume. Finally, almost no one has compared budget agreement between the two institutions, at least over an extensive time period. In this section we speculate on the prospects for congressional-presidential relations.

Recall that presidential *position taking* may not necessarily reflect the president's agenda because positions are based on votes before Congress. Some of these matters may also be on the presidents' agendas but they do not control Congress's agenda or the bases for the votes themselves. Still, assertive presidents will take positions to further their own agenda preferences. One could conclude that it might be better for presidents if they did not take so many positions because their support is likely to suffer. They should probably adopt a focused rifle (e.g., Reagan) rather than a broader shotgun approach (e.g., Carter; Pfiffner 1996), and prioritize their preferences in lower position taking, especially since other presidential activities and resources (such as speeches or employees) seem to have little effect on this activity. That recommendation is particularly apt in the foreign realm where lower popularity increases position taking. As with each of the other interactions except budgeting, a partisan party majority encourages position taking. This relationship occurs only in the foreign policy realm when a good economic situation also facilitates foreign policy position taking.

We have seen that *legislative support* is dependent upon position taking and recommended that presidents de-emphasize the former to enhance the latter. Somewhat inexplicably, a larger staff size also contributes to support. Also, simply having more of the president's partisans in Congress is the crucial determinant. Messages in the foreign realm and size of the EOP in both policy areas are somewhat manipulable by presidents and they may want to keep this finding in mind. Although the president presumably can do little about gaining more partisan supporters, it might be in presidents' best interests to exert more effort in congressional elections. A backup plan would be to spend much energy to mitigate the party effect by appealing to members of Congress across the aisle from presidents' own partisans, such as Bill Clinton has done on trade and welfare matters.

Earlier in this volume we suggested that *veto propensity* indicates presidential weakness rather than strength. An unpopular president presumably uses the veto more to persuade the general public and Congress that he is assertive. Since presidents are usually held in higher regard than Congress (LeLoup and Shull 1993, 95), it may be in presidents' interests to assert this prerogative to present an appearance of leadership or to make a strong public criticism of the Legislature. Presidents obviously need their partisans to preclude an override (at least in the domestic sphere) and also have less need to use the veto when less legislation is passed by Congress. Both presidents and Congress should think about the implications of these findings for their own policy preferences.

Our final presidential-congressional interaction is *budget agreement*. In the recent period of the study, presidents appear to have the upper hand in budgeting. This is because legislative appropriations more closely reflect presidential requests than occurred previously. This finding may be yet another indication that divided government may not affect policy adoption very much (Mayhew 1992). The item veto, available only during fiscal 1998 seemingly made budget congruence closer and, presumably, more closely reflected presidential than congressional preferences. Budget agreement is the unusual instance where legislative variables matter little in either foreign or domestic budget agreement. Only in foreign budget agreement is a legislative variable important and, more than any other of our four interactions, exogenous circumstances largely explain this presidential-congressional interaction.

Recent events suggest that, despite divided government and resultant partisan differences, compromise rather than deadlock usually results. None of the indicators separately tell the whole story of executive-legislative interactions. For example, Clinton's very low legislative support score in 1995 masked the fact that he took many positions and succeeded in preventing much Republican legislation from being enacted into law. At the same time, Clinton's high marks in 1994 belie the failure of his number one priority (health care) even to make it to the floor of Congress. However, Congress overrode only one of his eleven 1995 vetoes (he issued none during 1993–94). In the end, Republicans even gave up on their proposal to balance the federal budget in seven years

(*CQ Weekly Reports*, January 27, 1996, 213). Yet, despite continued divided government and partisanship, deadlock in policymaking did not occur, as evident in the budget agreements during 1997 and 1998. Eventually, the balanced budget and several other fiscal goals (such as reductions in Medicare) were adopted. Indeed, that circumstance of budget agreement may have resulted from low public regard for past conflict and expectations for government performance despite partisan rancor.

Future Research

One of the most important directions for future research is to develop more parsimonious and elegant models. Multicollinearity was an important factor in determining which variables we included in our three environments. We had to exclude some variables from our equations based on their high correlation with one another; other models might improve on the ones that we have presented here. The results indicate that presidential minor speeches and congressional staff size are prime candidates for dropping altogether. The former was significant in only one of the models but the latter was the *only* significant variable for domestic position taking (see table 8.3). Therefore, they should not be abandoned too quickly. Certainly presidential popular approval and party margin in Congress should be retained since they were important in three of the four general models and four of the eight policy models. Although not always as significant as party margin, workload and EOP staff variables possess theoretical interest and are therefore candidates for retention.

In the exogenous environment, it undoubtedly will prove difficult to develop better economic measures. Traditionally, unemployment and the consumer price index are used as indicators; however, separately they are highly collinear, and at least in our analysis, combining them into a factor score diminished their explanatory power. They also proved troublesome due to their high colinearity with many of our other variables. However, Mayhew's (1992) measure, which we call economic situation, presents itself as a good measure of the state of the economy, but, of course, would be expected to relate more to budget agreement than the other three interactions. In addition, a process variable (along with two resources in the exogenous environment) was significant in three of the eight policy models and thus needs to be considered in time series research.

More parsimonious models could allow for the inclusion of control variables directly into the model, but since so many variables were significant, degrees of freedom would be reduced considerably. If possible, such models would reflect an advance on what we have presented since we were not able to incorporate our control variables directly into our models. Thus, any effects from the control variables are somewhat speculative since they are not included in the primary models. One way to accomplish more parsimonious models could be through the use of factor scores for each environment. Factor analysis would permit multiple indicators for each environment while keeping the overall number of variables (resulting factor scores) in the model to a minimum. Oblimin rotation would provide for an additional check on the research by ensuring that all of the variables included for a particular environment actually were indicators for that environment and, therefore, independent of other environments.

Another avenue for future research is to better explore and more fully develop the idea of a temporal process across the different interactions. We employ a rather simple conception of process among the interactions that follows almost a linear progression, wherein the interactions are somewhat related, usually within the same year. Additionally, this process conceptually fits into the general policy process model under the adoption phase. All four interactions are part of the interplay that leads to the enactment of legislation. As such, this interaction process can be viewed as a subprocess of the adoption phase of the general policy process. Further elaboration of how these processes fit together and complement one another would be an important contribution to understanding the overall policy process.

We see some particular data needs for further research on presidential-congressional relations. Ragsdale (1996) should provide scholars with the numerators (raw numbers of times Congress as a whole or actual number of members approving of the presidents' vote positions). We are exceedingly grateful for those data she provides and she incorporated more data (including some of our own) in the next edition of her invaluable book. Such raw numbers are needed for both indicators rather than simply reporting the resulting percentages by year. As it now stands, scholars are limited to averaging mean percents when aggregating the data beyond the particular calendar year.

Where do we go from here with research on presidential-congressional relations? Within Congress, scholars should consider committee voting and tracking the legislative history of bills to see if presidents influence these activities. We need better ways of ascertaining whether bills (and their roll call votes) are part of the president's legislative agenda. That requires collecting the CQ boxscore (dropped in 1975) so that scholars are less dependent on presidents' vote positions for both the organization's current success and support scores. We need better data on the president's ability to shift votes in Congress, thereby tapping presidential leadership or influence rather than simple congruence of positions (Pritchard 1983; Sullivan 1991b; Mouw and MacKuen 1992).

Improved measures of presidential success and failure with Congress, including explanations other than public support and party margin, would lead to better theory. Perhaps measures of presidential-congressional ideology less related to party are possible (Gleiber and Shull 1992). Finding better ways of studying interactions between the first two branches of the national government more systematically is the most pressing problem for scholars of American political institutions.

Contributions

This work makes a number of important contributions to the study of presidential-congressional relations that enhance our understanding of both of these institutions and how they interact with one another. First, it presents a unique data set that has not heretofore been available. Second, it makes use of sophisticated multivariate time series analysis to estimate these interactions across the largest time series yet. Third, it expands the scope of scholarly research on presidential-congressional relations by examining four interactions instead of only one. Finally, it presents a broader multiple perspectives approach to understanding presidential-congressional relations that goes beyond a tandem institutions approach, more fully revealing the complexity of congressional-presidential interactions.

Our data set is the longest one ever used to study all but one of our presidential-congressional interactions. Extending from 1949 to 1995, our analysis provides a comprehensive examination of presidential-congressional interactions and goes beyond the data sets others use (Edwards 1989; Bond and Fleisher 1990; Peterson 1990). Not only has this data set contributed to our analysis but it presents itself as a useful tool for other scholars. Of particular note are the variables for House committee staff and congressional appropriations, which we have compiled for this entire time period. Previously, the staff variable was only available from 1970 to 1995 in secondary sources. Using House committee records and *Congressional Quarterly Almanac*, we were able to collect the values for these two variables back to 1949. Likewise, we extended position taking and support backward in time to 1949 and found comparable budget agreement that heretofore has not been researched.

Additionally, this analysis makes use of sophisticated multivariate techniques to assess the presidential-congressional interactions. Previous volumes have undertaken extensive descriptive studies of presidential-congressional relations (Shull 1997). And in fact, such research contributed to our desire to engage in more sophisticated analyses (see methodological appendix). By using multivariate time series analysis, we are able to go beyond descriptive groupings of data to assess the presence of relationships among variables and determine the nature and magnitude of relationships (either positive or negative). While some scholars have employed similar sophisticated techniques (Bond and Fleisher use logit analysis and Peterson employs probit), they have not had as extensive a data set available nor have they examined as many interactions or environments.

One of the most important contributions of this research is the expansion of the study of presidential-congressional relations to the four interactions we investigated. We certainly do not claim to have covered the range of all possible interactions; however, this work breaks new ground by shifting the focus of presidential-congressional relations away from single interactions to multiple interactions. No one variable can capture the interactive process that occurs around the adoption of legislation. Congress and the president engage each other in a contest of wills and resources and attempt to see their respective preferences enacted at the other's expense. Proceeding from position taking to support to the veto and finally to budget agreement, we have laid out a temporal linear process among these variables that is supported by the influence of these variables across the models. Although we acknowledge that a linear process is too neat and cannot fully capture the reciprocity that occurs among these interactions, it establishes a basis from which to more fully investigate such processes. Being related to the enactment of preferences, these four direct interactions are all part of the adoption phase of the general policymaking process.

Finally, perhaps the most important contribution of this work and its raison d'être is its multiple perspectives approach to understanding presidential-congressional interactions. Albeit building on the tandem institutions research, our multiple perspectives approach goes well beyond the tandem institutions by emphasizing the importance of not only the two institutional environments but also the exogenous environment. Our results show that the complexity of presidential-congressional relations is fully revealed only by incorporating all three environments in the analysis. The fact that multiple environments prove significant across all four of the interactions we examine contributes further evidence that the multiple perspectives approach is necessary to fully understand presidential-congressional interactions.

METHODOLOGICAL
APPENDIX

In this appendix, we lay out a more detailed discussion of the data and the analysis techniques that we utilized in *Explaining Congressional-Presidential Relations*. In particular, we discuss the data that we used and any modifications that we made to other scholars' data. We also present the analysis techniques that we employed and a discussion of the decision to use ordinary least squares regression (OLS) rather than other methodologies. We also present the particular descriptive statistics and procedures used to test and correct for auto-correlation.

DATA

The data for this analysis are drawn from a number of sources as discussed in chapter 3. The unit of analysis is the year, consisting of forty-seven years (1949–95). Some might contend that congressional session or elections (two-year cycles) or presidential term (four-year cycles) are more theoretically meaningful measures of political time. However we have chosen to stay with a yearly examination for three reasons: (1) to change the unit of analysis to either congressional session or presidential term would reduce the number of cases to the point of limiting statistical analysis; (2) for studying presidential-congressional relations it does not appear intuitively obvious which cycle one would choose over the other (see Shull and Gleiber 1995); and (3) each year, the president and Congress express preferences on legislation and attempt to see those preferences enacted into law. Certainly, legislation may carry over from one legislative session to another; however, since our analysis is not focused on the particulars of what either the president or Congress desires, it matters little whether a piece of legislation from a previous year is reintroduced in the current year. Our concern is with studying how the president and Congress interact to attain their preferences and what factors influence those interactions.

The time period 1949–95 represents the longest time series to date to study presidential-congressional relations. Although a number of our

157

variables were fairly easy to attain, we present at least two variables that have heretofore been unattainable for this entire time series in a single secondary source. The first variable is House staff size. We use this variable to obtain our measure of change in House staff size on most of our interactions. Although, *Vital Statistics on Congress* (1996) carries this variable, it is only available in five-year increments prior to 1970. The second variable is budget agreement, which is composed of measures of presidential budget requests divided by congressional budget appropriations. Neither of these variables are easily acquired for this entire time period. Secondary sources provided only spotty reporting of both variables for years prior to the 1970s. Such reporting seems odd when considering the heavy emphasis on quantification in the field and, the fact that we found data available for every year, as far back as 1949, when examining original source material.

However, we have uncovered data for budget agreement that are consistent over our entire time period. *CIS U.S. Serial Set* vol. 14038 (Senate Document no. 102-11, p. 750) provides extensive documentation allowing comparison of budget estimates (called requests) and appropriations. Page 749 of this source provides these two variables for fiscal 1966–94, congruent with Ornstein and coauthors (1996). We uncovered a similar Senate document for the years beginning in fiscal 1946 and we have confidence they are equivalent since the few overlapping years of both sources provided the exact same values. In that source the compilers point out that the concepts and measures differ and change across time (*CIS U.S. Serial Set* vol. 12760, Senate Document no. 58, p. 743). They state on p. 1025 that "figures include permanent appropriations for refund of taxes and sinking fund and other debt retirement accounts." Editions prior to the 86th Congress included such data for all fiscal years through 1958. Other comparisons by fiscal year are provided in detailed footnotes to both volumes.

We now consider each of our variables in turn. In addition to the following, characteristics of all the variables are presented in table A.1. Both presidential position taking and veto propensity are count variables. Position taking varies from as few as ten positions per year to as many as one hundred and forty-three. Veto propensity ranges from zero to twenty-six in a single year. Support and budget agreement are both percentages. Mean support in the House varies from as little as 42 percent to as much as 84 percent and is an average measure of support calculated for the entire year. Budget agreement is the percent of total presidential requests that are actually appropriated by Congress. Budget agreement ranges from as little as 84 percent of requests appropriated to as much as 102 percent of requests appropriated (that is two percent more than the president requested were funded).

TABLE A.1
Descriptive Statistics of Dependent and Independent Variables

	Range	Minimum	Maximum	Mean
Dependent Vars.				
Position Taking	133	10	143	75.11
Legislative Support	42.27	41.20	83.47	59.54
Veto Propensity	26	0	26	8.34
Budget Agreement	18.43	83.73	102.16	96.89
Independent Vars.				
Popular Approval	50	26	76	54.04
Employees in EOP	4,643	1,078	5,721	2,220.70
Minor Speeches	35	1	36	11.38
House Staff	1153	−800	353	21.49
House Party Margin	34.7	33.1	67.8	49.19
Congressional Party Margin	33.30	34.60	67.90	50.19
Workload	550	88	638	344.89
Economic Situation	.42	−.26	.17	−9.17E−02
Size of Federal Government	1,542,842	1,960,708	3,503,550	2,783,610.8

One might question whether or not budget agreement and the economic situation variable we use are reciprocal. It seems unlikely though that such an endogeneity problem exists between these two variables. Certainly, overall levels of budget appropriations affect the surplus or deficit, which are components of the economic situation variable. However, percentage of budget agreement provides no indication of the amount of funds actually appropriated. For example, 98 percent or 102 percent budget agreement could each occur in a year when there is extreme spending or in a year of fiscal restraint. Only the amount of funds appropriated should have an influence or determining effect on the surplus/deficit value contained in the economic situation variable. As such, budget agreement should not be reciprocally related to economic situation.

We admit that our budget agreement variable constitutes a gross aggregation but contend that it is probably as good as any single indicator of congruence available. The aggregation bias is evident when examining even just two component elements: defense and nondefense agreement. Obviously the lack of variation in the variable overall is masking considerable disagreement by these two policy areas. This finding illustrates the need for disaggregation by political time and policy areas as we have done for each of our four presidential-congressional interactions.

In the executive environment, minor speeches and number of employees in the Executive Office of the President (EOP) are both count variables. Minor speeches range from as few as one speech in a year to as many as thirty-six in a year (see table A.1). Employees in the EOP vary from 1,078 to 5,721. Presidential popular approval is the percent value that is averaged for the entire year and ranges from as low as 26 percent approval to as much as 76 percent annual public approval. This discussion reveals the mixture of count and percentage variables in our models and warrants caution in the interpretation of the analysis.

In the legislative environment, our staff variable is a change measure, party margin is a percent score and workload is a count variable. Congressional staff is a change measure calculated by subtracting the previous year's staff size from the current year's staff size to see how much of an increase or decrease occurred. Change in staff size ranges from −800 to 353. Party margin is a percent variable that measures the percentage of the presidents' party in Congress. It varies from as few as 33% to as much as 68% in the House and 35% to 68% in Congress as a whole. Finally, in the exogenous environment economic situation is calculated as a proportion and size of federal government is a count variable. Economic situation is calculated as surplus or deficit as a percentage of government outlays and ranges from −.26 to .17. Size of federal government measures total civilian employees in the federal government and ranges from 1.9 million to 3.5 million persons (see table A.1).

REGRESSION ANALYSIS

We began our analysis of the data using SPSS 6.1 for windows; however, a number of informal reviewers felt that the Lagrange Multiplier (LM) statistic was more appropriate than the Durbin-Watson for assessing auto or serial correlation in the models. As a statistical package, SPSS does not provide the Lagrange Multiplier. Consequently, we turned to Shazam 7.0. Shazam provides the same statistical capability as SPSS while also allowing for a number of additional algorithms and descriptive statistics such as the Lagrange Multiplier.

The first consideration that we dealt with in our regression analysis was whether or not to use ordinary least squares regression (OLS) or a two-stage least squares regression model (2SLS). The reason for this concern is the well-documented reciprocity problem that exists between position taking, legislative support, and popular approval. Essentially, the problem is that not only does presidential popular support affect each of the dependent variables but each dependent variable also influences popular support. This of course violates the causal structure of the model (Brace and Hinckley 1992) and raises questions about how the hypotheses should be stated (i.e., causal direction).

The standard correction for this reciprocity problem is the use of two-stage least squares regression. However, 2SLS becomes problematic in its own right because the coefficients are difficult to interpret. They are hard to interpret meaningfully because the first stage of the 2SLS method uses an endogenous variable (typically a lagged variable) to predict the independent variable that may be reciprocally related. From this first equation, the 2SLS saves the predicted values and then uses these values in the second stage equation that is predicting the actual dependent variable. The coefficient is unwieldy because it no longer has substantive meaning. This situation is similar to the use of factor scores and interactive terms where again, modified variables lack a particularly substantive meaning and therefore are difficult to interpret.

In addition to this problem with 2SLS, we chose to use OLS for a number of other reasons. First, although our data present reciprocity problems that are best corrected with 2SLS, other scholars have found that applying the 2SLS technique often makes little difference in terms of the final estimates obtained (Jacobson 1985, 1990). This is particularly the case in the Jacobson (1990) and Green and Krasno (1990) debate over campaign finance expenditures. Jacobson finds that the estimates obtained in 2SLS do not differ greatly from results obtained in OLS. We feel that this is likely due to the fact that the measures used in political science (as well as the social sciences in general) are relatively crude at this point in time. Consequently, the use of more refined statistical techniques makes little sense if the measures involved do not match the level of refinement found in the statistical technique. Secondly, only two of our four models would have required correction using the 2SLS. Because we are interested in comparing the four models in our summary in chapter 8, the use of 2SLS in two of the models and OLS in the others would have presented problems in comparing the four different models and the relative merits of individual variables across the models. We would no longer be comparing apples with apples because the two different regression techniques possess different assumptions.

Finally, in addition to the 2SLS problem, two of our dependent variables can be considered count variables. This raises the question of whether or not to use King's (1989) generalized event count regression (GEC model) or a form of poisson regression to analyze these two variables. Again, we chose to proceed with OLS for two reasons: (1) due to the fact that such specific techniques often offer few differences when compared to estimates obtained with OLS, and (2) in order to maintain comparability across the four interactions. Ultimately, standard OLS proves quite robust even in the face of the violation of its underlying assumptions (Cohen and Cohen 1983). Its robust properties hold true even when dealing with more refined analysis techniques. Quite often, the results of 2SLS, event count regression, logit, and probit models mirror the results obtained in OLS equations using the same data.

Indeed, we demonstrate in table A.2 the similarity between the poisson regression technique (used for count data) and the OLS analysis that we conducted for the position taking general model. Initial examination may conclude that there is a wide difference in the two models based on the unstandardized coefficients; however, we strive to place little emphasis on the magnitude of the coefficients. Inadequate measurement creates an environment in which the unstandardized coefficients of even the most well-specified models are suspect. Rather, our emphasis is on the sign and the significance of the coefficients. The comparison column reveals that the signs are similar between the OLS and poisson regression in all but one case. Also, the variables attain statistical significance in four of the nine variables. Obviously, there is some discrepancy between the OLS and poisson regression regarding the significance levels. As such, this left us in a situation of making a choice. We chose to rely on the robustness of the OLS estimates (which are quite close in terms of sign and significance) in order to use the same technique to analyze all four interactions.

We take issue with some who argue that the lack of statistical significance does not permit an inference of support for a hypothesis. The standard significance levels $p > .05$, $.01$, and $.001$ indicating 95, 99, and 99.9 percent confidence respectively, are arbitrary levels and, in fact, only demonstrate the degree to which the null hypothesis, that no relationship exists in the particular random sample, can be rejected (Henkel 1976). As such, one could relax the confidence interval to $p > .10$ or a 90 percent confidence interval and still be reasonably assured that any hypothesized relationship found at this confidence level exists in the data. Thus, there is no magic number at which a relationship exists where before it did not; rather, significance merely indicates the degree of confidence we have in rejecting the *lack* of a relationship. We are not suddenly convinced of the confirmation of a hypothesis if the significance is $.049$ instead of $.051$, and we feel it is perfectly appropriate to discuss the potential existence of a relationship even if a variable does not attain significance at the standard levels. Actually, there is only slightly greater confidence that we can reject the null hypothesis. However, since throughout the text, the standard $.05$, $.01$, and $.001$ signifi-

TABLE A.2

Comparison of OLS and Poisson Regression Analysis for Position Taking

	General Model OLS	General Model Poisson	Comparison
Executive Environment			
Popular Approval	−.65*	−.00	sign
Employees in EOP	.21	.00***	sign
Minor Speeches	−.54	.00	
Legislative Environment			
Committee Staff	−.46	−.00	sign
Party Margin	.82*	.01***	sign/sig.
Workload	−.34	−.00	sign
Exogenous Environment			
Budgetary Situation	−100.16	−1.35***	sign
Size of Federal Govt.	.25*	7.06***	sign/sig.
1yr Lag of Budget Agreement	.34	.04***	sign
Constant	−.311	−1.89**	sign
Adj. R^2	.60	.41	

* Significant at the .05 level
** Significant at the .01 level
*** Significant at the .001 level

cance levels were used for our hypothesis tests, we acknowledge whenever we deviate from a strict assessment of the confirmation of hypotheses regarding these significance levels.

Ultimately we felt that because we wanted to use the same multiple perspectives approach to examine all four dependent variables, we had to compromise to keep the analysis truly comparable. Also, while we realize that two of our interactions are interrelated and that reciprocity problems may occur, there is no theoretical reason to expect such reciprocity problems in the other two interactions. Thus, we encounter a problem of comparison if we treat two of the dependent variables differently from the other two. Consequently, in order to maintain comparability across the four models, and for the reasons stated above, we have chosen to use OLS throughout our analysis, correcting for time series problems where necessary.

We used the Lagrange Multiplier (LM) statistic to detect correlation (both autocorrelation inherent in time series data and spatial correlation; White et al. 1990). The LM chi square values are listed in the respective tables. In addition to using the Lagrange Multiplier, the autocorrelation functions (ACF) and the partial autocorrelation functions (PACF) for the residuals from the equations were examined for other than first order autoregressive processes. No, second or higher order processes were detected. Based on the first order nature of these processes, we chose to forgo the more complex ARIMA modelling and deal with the autocorrelation in these models using the Cochran-Orcutt autoregressive technique (Ostrom 1990; Cromwell, Labys, and Terraza 1994; McDowall, McCleary, Meidinger, and Hay 1980). Where correlation was detected, we employed a Cochran-Orcutt technique to correct for autocorrelation with a Prais-Winsten transformation to recapture the data point lost in the Cochran-Orcutt equation (Norusis 1994; White et al. 1990).

Because our unit of analysis is year, we are not able to simply add a dummy variable to control for policy content. Rather, we disaggregated the data by the foreign/domestic policy split and thereby created two substantive policy dependent variables for every interaction (e.g., general presidential position taking is the composite of presidential position taking on domestic policy and presidential position taking on foreign policy). For example, in looking at position taking, we originally estimated the general model using overall position taking. We then disaggregated position taking by positions on domestic roll call votes and positions on foreign roll calls and then reestimated the regression equations using the two new policy-specific dependent variables. The following are the regression equations used to obtain the estimates used in the general and policy models.

Equation for Presidential Position Taking:

$$PT = a_1 + PSX_1 + EOPX_2 + MSX_3 + CSX_4 + PMX_5 + WX_6 + ESX_7 + FEDX_8 + LagBAX_9 + e$$

Where:

PT   Position taking, dependent variable

PS   Popular support
EOP   Number of employees in the Executive Office of the President
MS   Number of presidential minor speeches
CS   Change in House committee staff
PM   Presidential party margin in House of Representatives
W   Congressional workload
ES   Economic situation
FED   Number of employees in the federal government
LagBA One-year lag of budget agreement

Domestic and foreign position taking were substituted for PT in the respective policy models.

Equation for Legislative Support:

$$LS = a_1 + PS1X_1 + EOPX_2 + MSX_3 + CSX_4 + PMX_5 + WX_6 + ESX_7 + FEDX_8 + PTX_9 + e$$

Where:

LS   Legislative support, dependent variable

PS   Popular support
EOP   Number of employees in the Executive Office of the President
MS   Number of presidential minor speeches
CS   Change in House committee staff
PM   Presidential party margin in House of Representatives
W   Congressional workload
ES   Economic situation
FED   Number of employees in the federal government
PT   Position taking

Domestic and foreign legislative support were substituted for LS in the respective policy models.

Equation for Veto Propensity:

$$VP = a_1 + PS1X_1 + EOPX_2 + MSX_3 + CSX_4 + PMX_5 + WX_6 + ESX_7 + FEDX_8 + LSX_9 + e$$

Where:

VP   Veto Propensity, dependent variable

PS   Popular support
EOP   Number of employees in the Executive Office of the President
MS   Number of presidential minor speeches
CS   Change in House committee staff
PM   Presidential party margin in Congress
W   Congressional workload
ES   Economic situation
FED   Number of employees in the federal government
LS   Legislative support

Domestic and foreign veto propensity were substituted for VP in the respective policy models.

Equation for Budget Agreement:

$$BA = a_1 + PS1X_1 + EOPX_2 + MSX_3 + CSX_4 + PMX_5 + WX_6 + ESX_7 + FEDX_8 + VPX_9 + e$$

Where:

BA   Budget agreement, dependent variable

PS   Popular support
EOP   Number of employees in the Executive Office of the President
MS   Number of presidential minor speeches
CS   Change in House committee staff
PM   Presidential party margin in Congress
W   Congressional workload
ES   Economic situation
FED   Number of employees in the federal government
VP   Veto propensity

Domestic and foreign budget agreement were substituted for BA in the respective policy models.

We would have preferred to include our political time controls with the multiple perspectives model in a single regression equation but found that such an exercise limits the degrees of freedom and takes away from the primary purpose of comparing each of the four interactions with the same independent variables. Clearly, different time controls would be significant for different interactions and, thus, comparability would again be compromised. Consequently, we estimated the control equations separately and presented the results at the beginning of each substantive chapter. Again, we used standard OLS and corrected for time series autocorrelation with Cochran-Orcutt and Prais-Winsten techniques where the LM statistic indicated such corrections were necessary.

We ran each dummy set of control variables against the four dependent variables. For both select year in presidential term of office and individual president, we used (G-1; where G = the number of dummy variables) sets of dummy variables. That is, in both instances one of the dummy variables was excluded from the set and the constant substantively interpreted in its place. For select year in presidential term of office the constant is substituted for "other" years, while first, last, and reelection years were included in the model as dummies. For individual president, the constant was substituted for Truman, and dummies included in the model for Eisenhower, Kennedy, Johnson, Nixon, Ford, Carter, Reagan, Bush, and Clinton. We used the following equations for political time, with budget agreement as the example:

Post–1974 and before 1974

$BA = a_1 + P74X_1 + e$

Where:

BA   Budget agreement
P74   Dummy variable, 0 = 1974 and before, and 1 = post-1974

Select Years in Presidential Term

$BA = a_1 + S1X_1 + S2X_2 + S3X_3 + e$

Where:

BA   Budget agreement
S1   First or honeymoon year
S2   Reelection year
S3   Last year

Individual President

$BA = a_1 + DEX_1 + JKX_2 + LJX_3 + RNX_4 + GFX_5 + JCX_6 + RRX_7 + GBX_8 + BCX_9 + e$

Where:

BA   Budget agreement
DE   Dwight Eisenhower
JK   John Kennedy
LJ   Lyndon Johnson
RN   Richard Nixon
GF   Gerald Ford
JC   Jimmy Carter
RR   Ronald Reagan
GB   George Bush
BC   Bill Clinton

In addition to the above, there were a number of techniques that we initially employed but ultimately rejected. We originally anticipated including best-fit models using backwards regression. The intent behind this was to eliminate statistically insignificant variables thereby reducing any suppression in the models and showing the "best fit" relationship with the three environments. What we found with the backwards regression best-fit models was, that generally, the same variables were significant and that the overall explanatory power of the models varied little. Consequently, we opted not to include what we felt was essentially redundant information.

We also found in looking at best-fit models that paring down the general and policy models to include only the significant variables produced R^2s very similar to the full general and policy models. Again, we chose not to include such information because of its redundancy; however, this finding led us to greater confidence in the somewhat high R^2 values of the overall models. High R^2 values can indicate multicollinearity in the set of independent variables. This produces models with inflated explanatory power and usually few significant variables. We were reasonably confident that by examining the correlation coefficients among our independent variables prior to regression analysis that this was not the case; yet, the high R^2 values we obtained were somewhat suspicious. However, the best-fit or reduced-form models, in which we included only the significant variables from the original models, produced similarly high R^2 values. Such findings gave us further confidence that our independent variables were not overly inflating the explanatory power of the models.

Finally, this analysis provides a sophisticated examination of the four interactions. While we do not employ the most refined statistical techniques available, our time series analysis is far more sophisticated than the often descriptive analyses that occur when examining presidential-congressional relations. As stated, we reject the 2SLS and event count techniques in favor of OLS corrected for auto and serial correlation for a number of reasons, including comparability across the four models as well as to make the book accessible to less quantitatively minded scholars and graduate students.

NOTES

CHAPTER 1. INTRODUCTION

1. Portions of this and the next section are adapted from Shull 1997, chapters 1–2.

2. Those areas of congressional influence in domestic policy initiation have been identified by Sundquist 1968, 535; Gallagher 1977; Jones 1984; Chamberlain 1946; Price 1972; Moe and Teel 1970.

3. An interesting example of dramatic agenda shift occurred with the election of the 104th Congress in 1994. The major presidential issue of health care had been fought and lost at the pre-floor level during that year, while during 1995 the congressional agenda in the House focused on the Republican "Contract with America." The battle over the "Contract" was fought largely on the floor, where much of it also died.

4. Although some authors have offered the rudiments of a multiple perspectives approach (e.g., Peterson 1990; Rohde and Simon 1985), none develop the notion as comprehensively as done herein.

5. Those arguing early on for presidential dominance in foreign policy include Dahl 1950; Koenig 1975; Robinson 1967; Donovan 1974; Clausen 1973; Destler 1974, 85. However, early studies countering that Congress has an important foreign policy role include Orfield 1975; Gallagher 1977; Chamberlain 1946; Sundquist 1968; Moe and Teel 1970; Johannes 1972a; 1972b; Fisher 1972.

6. Shull (1997) uses presidents' party as a control for political time but we incorporate party differently here, as a resource within Congress rather than a presidential characteristic (Bond and Fleisher 1990).

7. Immigration matters and individual claims against the government constitute the bulk of private bills. To limit the introduction of private bills, strict procedural rules have been established, and starting during Nixon's presidency, the number of private bills enacted have dropped from an average of 657 per Congress during the 80th through 91st Congress (1947–70) to 100 during the 92nd through 100th Congress (1971–88). Also decreasing are the number of private bill vetoes (FDR through LBJ average 19.6 per year; Nixon through Bush [1990] average .8 per year) (Oleszek 1989, 118; Ornstein et al. 1996, 266).

8. Even in the post–World War II era of greater executive-legislative conflict, only about 12 percent of all vetoes of public bills and 21 percent of all private non–pocket vetoes have been overridden. Portions of this discussion have been drawn from Shull, Gleiber, and Ringelstein (1992).

9. Planning Programming Budgeting Systems (PPBS), was introduced in the Department of Defense early in the Lyndon Johnson administration. It

requires comprehensive estimates of costs and benefits of government programs. Johnson applied its provisions to other agencies but it was quickly abandoned when such calculations proved more difficult in nondefense programs. Management by Objective (MBO) was introduced in the Gerald Ford administration to provide a less comprehensive way to plan and manage federal expenditures. It was quickly abandoned by Jimmy Carter who introduced Zero Based Budgeting (ZBB), which he had used effectively as governor of Georgia. This device proved more difficult to apply to the federal government and it, too, soon was abandoned. See Kramer 1979 for discussions of these devices.

10. Wildavsky (1988, chapter 10) is not even sure that the line item veto will reduce spending. It might allow Congress to balloon budgets thereby passing the buck to presidents who may or may not make difficult cuts that are difficult politically. Others concur that government spending may not decrease (Spitzer 1985, 616). The briefly held line-item veto in fiscal 1998 is discussed in chapter 6.

CHAPTER 2. A MULTIPLE PERSPECTIVES APPROACH

1. Such abstraction does lose sight of the fact that bureaucrats and support staff do possess their own preferences and can bring those preferences to bear at times, particularly in policy implementation. However, this analysis focuses on policy adoption, where executive actor preferences should be more congruent.

2. Conflict may exist between both the House and the Senate, and while it is important and deserving of treatment in its own right (Shull 1997, chapter 5), it is not considered in our analysis. Other treatments of the U.S. presidential system focus on the distinct split between the president and Congress without dealing with intralegislative differences (Lijphart 1992). Some of our analysis deals with House only while other portions focus on Congress as a whole.

3. However, in some cases we expect an individual variable included in the general model to have no effect. While this raises the potential for misspecification, we opted to leave such variables in the model in order to uniformly apply the same model across all interactions.

4. Studies examining veto overrides include Levin 1983; McKay 1989; Rohde and Simon 1985; Simonton 1987; Snape and Breaux 1988; Watson 1988; Hoff 1992.

5. Presidents' positions on roll call votes need not actually adopt policy. Amendments and other votes may occur before final passage (see Shull 1997, chapter 3).

6. In this context, individual refers to either the president or Congress, not to specific incumbents.

CHAPTER 3. MEASUREMENT STRATEGIES

1. Private behavior also affects their interactions, but it is difficult to discern and little systematic quantitative evidence exists (Covington 1987). Roll calls are visible and important, but not the only aspect of legislative behavior.

Presidents' legislative liaison and bargaining skill could affect legislative relations, but scholars disagree about how to measure them systematically (Edwards
1989, chapters 9–10; Bond and Fleisher 1990, chapter 8; Lockerbie and Borrelli
1989; Gleiber, Shull and Waligora 1988; Peterson 1990).

2. Reasons exist why data for the Senate were not collected and used for
position taking and support apart from being unavailable in Ragsdale's data. By
using her data rather than our own coding, we encourage replication and assure
that all data are coded similarly. Certainly we encourage her to code the Senate
in the future. Still, for most purposes, in the upper chamber, many votes are
nongermane amendments and their inclusion would be problematic as policy
adoption. Thus, our House votes for position taking and support are more likely
to adopt legislation than are votes in the Senate. This difference makes similar
analysis among the two chambers problematic.

3. Since Ragsdale (1996) does not provide the individual votes themselves
categorized by issue area, caution must be exercised in interpreting these percentages due to the differing number of votes by issue area for any given year.
Because the scores reported are aggregations (means of means of Ragsdale's
yearly percentages), some bias may appear. Also, her data seemingly contain
some inaccuracies (e.g., Clinton took two positions on agriculture votes in 1993;
Ragsdale 1996, table 8.6), but no agriculture support score is presented for him
because, presumably, no positions were taken (Ragsdale 1996, table 8.10).

4. Jackknifing provides average coefficient estimates for a series of regression coefficients that successively omit a different observation, thereby indicating the robustness of the coefficients across cases.

5. Subsequent variations of the box score that incorporate innovative
approximations of presidential agenda preferences appear in Light (1982) and
Peterson (1990). Jeffrey Cohen ([1982] 1991) provides a long historical period
for these data based on State of the Union messages only.

6. CQ changed the method of calculating individual member scores in
1987. Prior to that time, it used as the basis the total number of votes, regardless
of whether a member was present. Beginning in that year, they also provide a separate score that discounts for absences. The newer score thus assumes that member percent support and opposition add to 100 percent (*Almanac* 1987, 22-C).
The change in calculating individual legislator scores does not affect the overall
average percent support measure used here.

7. Regrettably, Ragsdale (1996) provides only a percentage figure; she
does not give the numerators (*frequency* of members voting with the president's
position) needed to calculate overall or individual party support more accu-
rately. Although CQ provides such numerators, Ragsdale fails to include them.
Accordingly, when aggregating her seven policy areas into the two presidencies
dichotomy or by political time, means of means are used, which introduce some
distortion in the resulting percentages of overall support.

8. We initially included Congressional Quarterly's measure of presidential
success in Congress but it was so highly correlated with veto use that it was subsequently dropped from the analysis in favor of legislative support to help reduce
multicollinearity. Also, override attempts were closely related with the veto
propensity variable and was also excluded.

9. Popular prestige, as manifested in the Gallup support score is "the prevalent impression of a president's public standing," setting "the tone" and defining "the limits of what Washingtonians do for him, or do to him" (Neustadt 1980, 65). Neustadt also suggests that popular prestige is more complex than the attitude tapped by the Gallup question. But we think the Gallup support score contains a large component of true variance of mass popularity and taps the reciprocal relationship between mass and elite perspectives.

10. The specification of a nonrelationship between popular support and legislative support or success continues to be controversial. Some find evidence for a linkage (Edwards 1980; Brace and Hinckley 1992; Rivers and Rose 1985; Gleiber and Shull 1992) but others find little support for a relationship (Edwards 1989; Bond and Fleisher 1990; Collier and Sullivan 1995).

11. We used the change measure because it connotes the same information as staff size but was uncorrelated with our other dependent variables. We considered but then dropped using seniority of committee members instead of staff size to measure this legislative resource because we are more interested in Congress as a whole than its subunits, such as committees.

12. Budgets are not designated foreign or domestic per se. However, we were able to closely approximate the designations by adding foreign aid to the defense figures. No separate trade designation was available. All of the residual amounts were considered nondefense (e.g., domestic). We are confident that we are examining comparable defense-nondefense budget agreement across our forty-seven years.

13. Unfortunately when examining selected years, the data points are few, especially for last (lame duck) year, which equals just four cases (1952, 1960, 1968, the latter because Johnson announced early in that year he would not seek reelection, and 1988). A potential problem is that more than half of our observations fall in the nondesignated "other" year category. Because this residual category is theoretically uninteresting, it serves as the constant in the multiple regression. Although some scholars also consider first and second terms (e.g., Neustadt 1960), the data points are few for such analysis.

CHAPTER 4. PRESIDENTIAL POSITION TAKING

1. We recognize that position taking could be influenced by presidents' legislative support or success but chose to omit this influence to maintain the symmetry of the book. This relationship is considered in chapter 5, however, with position taking as the process variable predicting support.

2. Some authors suggest that even Eisenhower may have been more active a president than once thought (Ambrose 1980; Greenstein 1982).

3. Recall that presidential ideology related highly to both presidential party and margins of partisans in Congress and, thus, was dropped from this analysis.

4. Brace and Hinckley (1992) identify a potential simultaneity problem between popular support, position taking, and legislative success and we discuss this matter more fully in the appendix.

5. We recognize that this expectation depends on the public mood. The general public seemed to agree with Harry Truman's criticism of a "do nothing" Congress in 1948 but also seemed supportive of the reduced government role under Eisenhower.

6. From a strictly theoretical standpoint, it may appear odd to include variables in the models that we feel may not have a significant effect; however, our principal aim is exploration and not a definitive statement of the most relevant variables. To that end, we desire to apply a common model across all four of the interactions that we examine. There may be instances in which we expect that a variable included in the model may have little to no effect on the various interactions.

7. Although support also relates to position taking (Brace and Hinckley 1992; Shull 1997, chapter 6), we follow our process model of including only the most directly related interaction for each dependent variable.

CHAPTER 5. LEGISLATIVE SUPPORT

1. Parts of this section are drawn from Shull 1997, chapter 6.

2. It is unclear what source CQ used prior to the publication of the *Weekly Compilation of Presidential Documents* in 1965, but in a letter to Steven Shull, Research Director Robert Cuthrell presumed that *Public Papers* and other documents were sources for initiatives. Nevertheless, it was a CQ judgment about whether an issue mentioned in a presidential message constituted an actual legislative request. If more than one presidential remark was directed toward the issue, only the most definitive statement was used to track through the legislative process.

3. This charge is not totally accurate since most major requests appear in the form of multiple initiatives (Shull and LeLoup [1981] 1991). The box scores of presidential initiatives are simply calls for legislation, not necessarily actual bills before Congress. Thus, they show whether the president follows through on his stated agenda preferences but do not assure us that the request was actually introduced in Congress.

4. A massive data collection project accumulating the box score throughout history is currently underway. Interested readers should contact Michael Malbin at State University of New York (Albany).

5. CQ began collecting support since 1953 but changed the coding rules so data from 1953–56 are not exactly equivalent to later data (Ragsdale 1996, 382). Besides, they did not code them according to easily identifiable policy categories in the earlier years (see chapter 3).

6. Rather than Hammond and Fraser's (1984a) box score, Mouw and MacKuen (1992) use the CQ key vote support score, a measure assessed by Shull and Vanderleeuw (1987).

7. Brady and Volden (1998) think that ideology provides a better explanation of voting than does divided government or even political party.

8. Recall from chapter 3 that Ragsdale (1996) provides data on position taking and support by issue area for the House only. Thus, we are limited to

using her data set for presidential position taking and presidential support thereof, focusing on the lower chamber of Congress.

9. We recognize that it may be easier to get the party in line when every vote matters. Therefore, when the presidents' party split is close to fifty-fifty, they may do better with their party support than if their margin is slightly larger. Accordingly, presidents may have greater support when their party margin is very high or when they have the minimal votes needed for their party to be in control of the chamber.

10. Recall that Reagan's Republican Party had control over the Senate during six of his eight years in office, but Ragsdale does not provide Senate votes at all, let alone designated by issue area. Presumably Reagan had higher proportions of senators than House members supporting his vote positions during those years.

11. These ten presidents served different numbers of years in office and the limited number of observations, particularly for Ford and Clinton, should be kept in mind.

CHAPTER 6. VETO PROPENSITY

1. Liberal presidents are often assumed to be activist and assertive in their relations with the Congress. Yet contrary to predictions of passivity (Barber 1992), conservative Ronald Reagan was active in the opposite direction, trying to restrict policy outcomes, particularly in domestic policy. This means that liberalism alone may not be sufficient to predict veto activity.

2. Ironically, the only two contemporary authors of book length works on the veto oppose the item veto (Spitzer 1988; Watson 1993). A variation of this device, which did not require a constitutional amendment, took effect January 1997, but was declared unconstitutional by the Supreme Court soon thereafter.

3. Party margin in Congress is a potential but very crude measure of presidents' professional reputation. Gleiber, Shull, and Waligora (1998) develop a more refined measure of this concept from the *New York Times* index.

4. Committee seniority is another potential measure of the president's not winning in Congress but we have not included this variable.

5. We assumed that presidents' prior experience with the veto will influence their decision but did not find a relationship with the lag variable. We have discussed Spitzer's (1988, 1997) interesting veto threat variable and another possibility includes override attempts. At least one previous study found that previous overrides temper the president's propensity to veto (Copeland 1983). All in all, however, veto propensity should be well explained by our broader environmental influences and their more encompassing component variables. Thus, we do not include override attempts in our general model.

CHAPTER 7. BUDGET AGREEMENT

1. We can order the preferences of the president as follows. Where $A = 100\%$, $B > 100\%$ and $C < 100\%$, the president should possess the follow-

ing preferences: A is preferred to both B and C, B is preferred only to C, and C is the least preferred outcome. Thus, anything more, is less than optimal but still better than not getting as much as requested. Obviously, strategic under or over estimates may occur but this subtle dimension of budget preferences is elusive.

2. A negative R^2 value can only occur when using the adjusted R^2 value and is essentially meaningless.

3. Although there is some concern with this R^2 value being so high, possibly indicating multicollinearity, a best-fit model with only three variables (not reported) still attains an R^2 value of .80, which indicates that these three variables produce good explanatory power even when the other variables are excluded from the model (see methodological appendix for why we do not incorporate best-fit models).

REFERENCES

Ambrose, S. E. 1982. "The Eisenhower Revival." In *Rethinking the Presidency*, ed. T. E. Cronin. Boston: Little, Brown.

Anderson, F. L., et al. 1966. *Legislative Roll-Call Analysis*. Evanston, Ill.: Northwestern University Press.

Anderson, J. E. 1975. *Public Policy-Making*. New York: Praeger.

Bailey, J., and R. O'Connor. 1975. "Operationalizing Incrementalism." *Public Administration Review* 35:60–66.

Barber, J. D. 1980. *Pursuit of the Presidency*. Englewood Cliffs, N.J.: Prentice Hall.

———. 1992. *Presidential Character*. 4th ed. Englewood Cliffs, N.J.: Prentice Hall.

Barger, H. 1984. *The Impossible Presidency*. Glenview, Ill.: Scott Foresman.

Baumgartner, F., and B. D. Jones. 1993. *Agendas and Instability in American Politics*. Chicago: University of Chicago Press.

Beck, N. 1982. "Parties, Administrations, and American Macroeconomic Outcomes." *American Political Science Review* 76:83–93.

Berry, W. D. 1990. "The Confusing Case of Budgetary Incrementalism." *Journal of Politics* 52:167–96.

Bond, J., and R. Fleisher. 1980. "Limits of Presidential Popularity as a Source of Influence in the House." *Legislative Studies Quarterly* 5:69–78.

———. 1984. "Presidential Popularity and Congressional Voting." *Western Political Quarterly* 37:291–306.

———. 1990. *The President in the Legislative Arena*. Chicago: University of Chicago Press.

Bond, J., R. Fleisher, and G. S. Krutz. 1996. "Empirical Findings on Presidential-Congressional Relations." In *Rivals for Power*, ed. J. A. Thurber. Washington, D.C.: CQ Press.

Brace P., and B. Hinckley. 1992. *Follow the Leader*. New York: Basic Books.

Brady, D., and C. Volden. 1998. *Revolving Gridlock*. Boulder, Colo.: Westview.

Budget of the U. S. Government. Annual. Washington, D.C.: Government Printing Office.

Campbell, C., and B. Rockman, eds. 1991. *The Bush Presidency: First Appraisals*. Chatham, N.J.: Chatham House.

Chamberlain, L. H. 1946. "President, Congress, and Legislation." *Political Science Quarterly* 61:42–60.

CIS U.S. Serial Set Index. Monthly, Cumulative Annually. Washington, D. C. Congressional Information Service.

Clausen, A. R. 1973. *How Congressmen Decide: A Policy Focus*. New York: St. Martin's Press.

Cohen, J. E. 1980. "Presidential Personality and Political Behavior." *Presidential Studies Quarterly* 10:588–99.

———. [1982] 1991. "Historical Reassessment of Wildavsky's 'Two Presidencies' Thesis." In *The Two Presidencies: A Quarter Century Assessment*, ed. S. A. Shull. Chicago: Nelson-Hall.

———. 1997. *Presidential Responsiveness and Public Policy-Making.* Ann Arbor: University of Michigan Press.

Cohen, J., and P. Cohen. 1983. *Applied Multiple Regression/Correlation Analysis for the Behavioral Sciences.* Hillsdale, N.J.: Lawrence Erlbaum Associates.

Collier, K., and T. Sullivan. 1995. "New Evidence Undercutting the Linkage of Approval with Support and Influence." *Journal of Politics* 57:197–209.

Congress and the Nation. Vols. 1–8. Washington, D.C.: Congressional Quarterly.

Congressional Roll Call (annual). Washington, D.C.: Congressional Quarterly, Inc.

Congressional Quarterly Almanac (annual). Washington, D.C.: Congressional Quarterly, Inc.

Congressional Quarterly Weekly Reports. Washington, D.C.: Congressional Quarterly, Inc.

Copeland, G. W. 1983. "When Congress and the President Collide: Why Presidents Veto Legislation." *Journal of Politics* 43:696–710.

Corwin, E. S. 1957. *The President: Office and Powers*, 4th ed. New York: New York University Press.

Covington, C. R. 1987. "Staying Private: Gaining Congressional Support for Unpublicized Presidential Preferences on Roll Call Votes." *Journal of Politics* 49:737–55.

Covington, C. R. et al. 1995. "A Presidency-Augmented Model of Presidential Success on House Roll Call Votes." *American Journal of Political Science* 39:1001–24.

Cox, G. W., and S. Kernell, eds. 1991. *Politics of Divided Government.* Boulder, Colo.: Westview Press.

Cox, J., G. Hager, and D. Lowrey. 1993 "Regime Change in Presidential and Congressional Budgeting." *American Journal of Political Science* 37:88–118.

Cromwell, J. B., W. C. Labys, and M. Terraza. 1994. *Univariate Tests for Time Series Models* (Sage University Paper series on Quantitative Applications in the Social Sciences, series no. 07–099). Thouasand Oaks, Calif.: Sage.

Crovitz, L. G., and J. A. Rabkin. 1989. *The Fettered Presidency.* Washington, D.C.: American Enterprise Institute.

Dahl, R. A. 1950. *Congress and Foreign Policy.* New York: Harcourt Brace.

———. 1963. *Modern Political Analysis.* Englewood Cliffs, N.J.: Prentice Hall.

Davidson, R. H. 1996. "The Presidency and Congressional Time." In *Rivals for Power*, ed. J. A. Thurber. Washington, D.C.: Congressional Quarterly.

Davidson, R. H., and W. J. Oleszek. 1996. *Congress and its Members.* 5th ed. Washington, D.C.: CQ Press.

Davis O., L. Dempster, and A. Wildavsky. 1966. "A Theory of the Budget Process." *American Political Science Review* 60:529–47.

Destler, I. M. 1974. *Presidents, Bureaucrats, and Foreign Policy.* Princeton: Princeton University Press.

Donovan, J. C. 1970. *The Policy Makers.* New York: Pegasus.

———. 1974. *The Cold Warriors.* Lexington, Mass.: D. C. Heath.

Durant, R. F. 1992. *Administrative Presidency Revisited.* Albany: State University of New York Press.

Easton, D. 1965. *Framework for Political Analysis.* Englewood Cliffs, N.J.: Prentice Hall.

Economic Report of the President. Annual. Washington, D.C.: Government Printing Office.

Edelman, M. J. 1974. "The Politics of Persuasion." In *Choosing the President,* ed. J. D. Barber. Englewood Cliffs, N.J.: Prentice Hall.

Edwards, G. C. III. 1980. *Presidential Influence in Congress.* San Francisco: W. H. Freeman.

———. 1983. *The Public Presidency.* New York: St. Martin's.

———. 1985. "Measuring Presidential Success in Congress: Alternative Approaches." *Journal of Politics* 47:667–85.

———. [1986] 1991. "Two Presidencies: A Re-evaluation." *The Two Presidencies: A Quarter Century Assessment,* ed. S. A. Shull. Chicago: Nelson-Hall.

———. 1989. *At the Margins: Presidential Leadership of Congress.* New Haven, Conn.: Yale University Press.

———. 1991. "Response to Sullivan's 'The Bank Account Presidency'." *American Journal of Political Science* 34:724–29.

Edwards, G. C. III, A. Barrett, and J. Peake. 1997. "The Legislative Impact of Divided Government." *American Journal of Political Science* 41:545–63.

Edwards, G. C. III, J. H. Kessel, and B. A. Rockman, eds. 1993. *Researching the Presidency: Vital Questions, New Approaches.* Pittsburgh: University of Pittsburgh Press.

Federalist Papers. 1956. New York: New American Library.

Federal Register. Washington, D.C.: United States Government Printing Office.

Fenno, R. 1966. *Power of the Purse.* Boston: Little, Brown.

Fett, P. J. 1994. "Presidential Legislative Priorities and Legislators' Voting Decisions." *Journal of Politics* 56:502–12.

Fiorina, M. P. 1996. *Divided Government.* 2nd ed. Needham Heights, Mass.: Allyn and Bacon.

Fisher, L. 1972. *The President and Congress.* New York: Free Press.

Fleisher, R., and J. Bond. 1983. "Assessing Presidential Support in the House." *Journal of Politics* 49:745–58.

Fox, H. W. Jr. and S. W. Hammond. 1977. *Congressional Staffs.* New York: Free Press.

Frendreis, J. P., and R. Tatalovich. 1994. *Modern Presidency and Economic Policy.* Itasca, Ill.: Peacock.

Froman. L. A. 1963. *Congressmen and Their Constituents.* Chicago: Rand McNally.

———. 1968. "The Categorization of Policy Contents." In *Political Science and Public Policy,* ed. A. Ranney. Chicago: Markham Publishing Co.

Fry, B. R., and R. F. Winters. 1970. "Politics of Redistribution." *American Political Science Review* 64:508–22.

Gallagher, H. G. 1977. "The President, Congress, and Legislation." In *The Presidency Reappraised*. 2d ed. Ed. T. Cronin and R. Tugwell. New York: Praeger Publishers.

Gibson, M. 1995. "Issues, Coalitions, and Divided Government." *Congress and the Presidency* 22:155–66.

Gleiber, D. W., and S. A. Shull. 1992. "Presidential Influence in the Policy Making Process." *Western Political Quarterly* 41:441–67.

———. 1999. "Justifying Presidential Decisions: The Scope of the Veto Message." *Congress and the Presidency* 26:forthcoming.

Gleiber, D. W., S. A. Shull, and C. Waligora. 1998. "Measuring the President's Professional Reputation." *American Politics Quarterly* 26:259–78.

Goldfinger, J., and S. A. Shull. 1995. "Presidential Influence on Major Legislation." Presented at the annual meeting of the American Political Science Association, Chicago.

Gomez, B. T., and S. A. Shull. 1995. "Presidential Decision Making: Explaining the Use of Executive Orders." Presented at the annual meeting of the Southern Political Science Association, Tampa.

Green, D., and J. S. Krasno. 1990. "Rebuttal to Jacobson's 'New Evidence for Old Arguments'." *American Journal of Political Science* 34:363–72.

Greenstein, F. I. 1982. *Hidden Hand Presidency*. New York: Basic Books.

Hager, G. L., and T. Sullivan. 1994. "President-Centered and Presidency-Centered Explanations of Presidential Public Activity." *American Journal of Political Science* 38:1079–1103.

Hammond, T. H., and J. M. Fraser. 1980. "Faction Size, the Conservative Coalition, and the Determinants of Presidential Success in Congress." Presented at the annual meeting of the American Political Science Association, Washington, D. C.

———. 1984a. "Judging Presidential Performance on House and Senate Roll Calls." *Polity* 16:624–46.

———. 1984b. "Studying Presidential Performance in Congress." *Political Methodology* 10:211–44.

Hargrove, E. C. 1974. *The Power of the Modern Presidency*. Philadelphia: Temple University Press.

Heclo, H. 1977. *Studying the Presidency*. Naugatuck, Conn.: The Ford Foundation.

Henkel, R. E. 1976. *Tests of Significance* (Sage University Paper series on Quantitative Applications in the Social Sciences, series no. 07–004). Thousand Oaks, Calif.: Sage.

Hilsman, R. 1968. *To Move a Nation: The Politics of Foreign Policy in the Administration of John F. Kennedy*. New York: Dell.

Hinckley, B. 1994. *Less Than Meets the Eye*. Chicago: University of Chicago Press.

Hoff, S. B. 1991. "Saying No: Presidential Support and Veto Use," *American Politics Quarterly* 19:310–23.

———. 1992. "Presidential Support and Veto Overrides." *Midsouth Journal of Political Science* 13:173–90.

Huckfeld, R. R., C. W. Kohfeld, and T. W. Likens. 1992. *Dynamic Modeling*. Newbury Park, Calif.: Sage.

Huntington, S. P. 1961. *The Common Defense: Strategic Programs in National Politics.* New York: Columbia University Press.

Ippolito, D. S. 1978. *The Budget and National Politics.* San Francisco: W. H. Freeman.

Jacobson, G. C. 1978. "The Effects of Campaign Spending in Congressional Elections," *American Political Science Review* 72:769–83.

———. 1980. *Money in Congressional Elections.* New Haven, Conn.: Yale University Press.

———. 1985. "Money and Votes Reconsidered: Congressional Elections, 1972–1982." *Public Choice* 47:7–62.

———. 1990. "The Effects of Campaign Spending in House Election: New Evidence for Old Arguments." *American Journal of Political Science* 34:334–62.

Johannes, J. R. 1972a. *Policy Innovation in Congress.* Morristown, N.J.: General Learning Press.

———. 1972b. "Where Does the Buck Stop? Congress, President, and the Responsibility for Legislative Initiation." *Western Political Quarterly* 25:396–415.

Jones, C. O. 1984. *An Introduction to the Study of Public Policy.* 3rd ed. Monterey, Calif.: Brooks/Cole.

———. 1988. *The Trusteeship Presidency: Jimmy Carter and the U. S. Congress.* Baton Rouge: Louisiana State University Press.

———. 1994. *Presidency in a Separated System.* Washington, D.C.: Brookings Institution.

———. 1995. *Separate but Equal Branches.* Chatham, N.J.: Chatham House.

Kallenbach, J. 1966. *The American Chief Executive.* New York: Harper & Row.

Kamlet, M. S. 1987. "Whom Do You Trust? Analyses of Executive and Congressional Economic Forecasts." *Journal of Policy Analysis and Management* 7:365–84.

Kerbel, M. R. 1991. *Beyond Persuasion: Organizational Efficiency and Presidential Power.* Albany: State University of New York Press.

Kernell, S. 1986. *Going Public: New Strategies of Presidential Leadership.* Washington, D.C.: CQ Press.

———. "Facing an Opposition Congress." In *Politics of Divided Government,* ed. G. W. Cox and S. Kernel. Boulder, Colo.: Westview.

Kerwin, C. M. 1994. *Rulemaking: How Government Agencies Write Law and Make Policy.* Washington, D.C.: CQ Press.

Kessel, J. H. 1974. "Parameters of Presidential Politics." *Social Science Quarterly* 55:8–24.

———. 1975. *The Domestic Presidency: Decision-Making in the White House.* North Scituate, Mass.: Duxbury Press.

———. 1984. *Presidential Parties.* Homewood, Ill.: Dorsey Press.

Kettl, D. 1989. "Expansion and Protection in the Budgetary Process." *Public Administration Review* 49:231–39.

———. 1992. *Deficit Politics.* New York: Macmillan.

Kieweit D. R., and M. D. McCubbins. 1988. "Presidential Influence on Congressional Appropriations Decisions." *American Journal of Political Science* 32:713–36.

King, G. 1989. "Variance Specification in Event Count Models." *American Journal of Political Science* 33:762–84.

King, G., and L. Ragsdale. 1988. *The Elusive Executive: Discovering Statistical Patterns in the Presidency.* Washington, D.C.: CQ Press.

Kingdon, J. W. 1978. *Congressmen's Voting Decisions.* New York: Harper & Row.

———. 1984. *Agendas, Alternatives, and Public Policies.* Boston: Little, Brown.

Koenig, L. W. 1975. *The Chief Executive.* New York: Harcourt Brace Jovanovich.

Kramer, F. A., ed. 1979. *Contemporary Approaches to Public Budgeting.* Cambridge, Mass.: Winthrop Publishers, Inc.

Lee, J. R. 1975. "Presidential Vetoes from Washington to Nixon." *Journal of Politics* 37:522–46.

LeLoup, L. T. 1980. *Budgetary Politics.* 3rd ed. Brunswick, Ohio: Kings Court, Inc.

LeLoup, L. T., and S. A. Shull. [1979] 1991. "Congress versus the President, 'The Two Presidencies Reconsidered'." In *The Two Presidencies: A Quarter Century Assessment,* ed. S. A. Shull. Chicago: Nelson-Hall.

———. 1979. "Dimensions of Presidential Policy Making." In *The Presidency: Studies in Public Policy,* ed. S. A. Shull and L. T. LeLoup. Brunswick, Ohio: King's Court Communications.

———. 1993. *Congress and the President: The Policy Connection.* Belmont, Calif.: Wadsworth.

———. 1999. *The President and Congress: Collaboration and Combat in National Policymaking.* Needham, Mass.: Allyn and Bacon.

Levin, M. A. 1983. "Tactical Constraints and Presidential Influence on Veto Overrides." *Presidential Studies Quarterly* 13:646–50.

Lewis, D. E., and J. M. Strine. 1996. "What Time Is It? The Use of Power in Four Different Types of Presidential Time." *Journal of Politics* 58:682–706.

Light, P. A. 1982. *President's Agenda: Domestic Policy Choice from Kennedy to Carter.* Baltimore, Md.: Johns Hopkins University Press.

———. 1992. *Forging Legislation.* New York: Norton.

———. 1995. *Thickening Government.* Washington, D.C.: Brookings Institution.

Lijphart, A. 1992. "Introduction." In *Parliamentary Versus Presidential Government,* ed. A. Lijphart. New York: Oxford University Press.

Lindsay, J. M., and W. P. Steger. 1993. "Two Presidencies in Future Research." *Congress and the Presidency* 20:103–17.

Lockerbie, B., and S. A. Borelli. 1989. "Getting Inside the Beltway: Perceptions of Presidential Skill and Success in Congress." *British Journal of Political Science* 19:97–106.

Lowi, T. J. 1964. "American Business, Public Policy, Case Studies, and Political Theory." *World Politics* 16:677–715.

———. 1985. *The Personal President: Power Invested, Promise Unfulfilled.* Ithaca, N.Y.: Cornell University Press.

MacRae, D. 1970. *Issues and Parties in Legislative Voting: Methods of Statistical Analysis.* New York: Harper & Row.

Manning, B. 1977. "Congress, the Executive, and Intermestic Affairs: Three Proposals." *Foreign Affairs* 55:306–24.

Marini, J. 1992. *The Politics of Budget Control.* New York: Taylor and Francis.

Mason, E. C. 1890. *The Veto Power, 1789–1889.* New York: Russell and Russell.

Mayhew, D. R. 1966. *Party Loyalty Among Congressmen: The Difference Between Democrats and Republicans, 1947–1962.* Cambridge: Harvard University Press.

————. 1992. *Divided We Govern.* New Haven, Conn.: Yale University Press.

————. 1995. "Clinton, the 103rd Congress, and Unified Party Control." Yale University. Mimeo.

McConnell, G. 1976. *The Modern Presidency.* New York: St. Martin's Press.

McCubbins, M. D. 1991. "Government on Lay-Away: Federal Spending and Deficits under Divided Party Control." In *The Politics of Divided Government,* eds. G. W. Cox and S. Kernell. Boulder, Colo.: Westview Press.

McDowall, D., R. McCleary, E. E. Meidinger, and R. A. Hay Jr. 1980. *Interrupted Time Series Analysis* (Sage University Paper series on Quantitative Applications in the Social Sciences, series no. 07–021). Thousand Oaks, Calif.: Sage.

McKay, D. 1989. "Presidential Strategy and the Veto Power: A Reappraisal." *Political Science Quarterly* 104:447–61.

Mezey, M. 1989. *Congress, the President, and Public Policy.* Boulder, Colo.: Westview.

Moe, R. C., and S. Teel. 1970. "Congress as Policy Maker: A Necessary Reappraisal." *Political Science Quarterly* 85:443–70.

Mouw, C., and M. MacKuen. 1992. "The Strategic Configuration, Personal Influence, and Presidential Power in Congress." *Western Political Quarterly* 41:579–608.

Mowrey, D. G. 1980. "Presidential Management of Budgeting and Fiscal Policy Making." *Political Science Quarterly* 95:395–425.

Nathan, R. P. 1983. *The Administrative Presidency.* 2d ed. New York: John Wiley and Sons.

Neustadt, R. E. 1955. "A Presidency and Legislation: Planning the President's Program." *American Political Science Review* 49:980–1021.

————. 1960. *Presidential Power: The Politics of Leadership.* New York: John Wiley.

————. 1973. "Politicians and Bureaucrats." In *The Congress and America's Future.* 2nd ed., ed. D. Truman. Englewood Cliffs, N.J.: Prentice Hall.

————. 1980. *Presidential Power.* New York: John Wiley.

Norusis, M. J. 1994. *SPSS Professional Statistics 6.1.* Chicago: SPSS Inc.

Oldfield, D., and A. Wildavsky. [1989] 1991. "Reconsidering the Two Presidencies." In *The Two Presidencies: A Quarter Century Assessment,* ed. S. A. Shull. Chicago: Nelson-Hall.

Oleszek, W.J. 1989. *Congressional Procedures and the Policy Process.* 3rd ed. Washington, D.C.: CQ Press.

Orfield, G. 1975. *Congressional Power: Congress and Social Change.* New York: Harcourt Brace Jovanovich.

Ornstein, N. J., et al. 1996. *Vital Statistics on Congress 1995–1996*. Washington, D.C.: Congressional Quarterly, Inc.

Ostrom, C. W. Jr. 1990. *Time Series Analysis, Regression Techniques* (Sage University Paper series on Quantitative Applications in the Social Sciences, series no. 07–009). Thousand Oaks, Calif.: Sage.

Ostrom, C. W., and D. M. Simon. 1985. "Promise and Performance: A Dynamic Model of Presidential Popularity." *American Political Science Review* 79:334–58.

Patterson, S. C., and G. A. Caldeira. 1988. "Party Voting in the U.S. Congress." *British Journal of Political Science* 18:111–31.

Peppers, D. A. [1975] 1991. "Two Presidencies: Eight Years Later." In *The Two Presidencies: A Quarter Century Assessment*, ed. S. A. Shull. Chicago: Nelson-Hall.

Peters, G. B. 1996. *American Public Policy*. 4th ed. Chatham, N.J.: Chatham House.

Peterson, M. A. 1990. *Legislating Together*. Cambridge: Harvard University Press.

Peterson, P. E., ed. 1994. *The President, the Congress, and the Making of Foreign Policy*. Norman: The University of Oklahoma Press.

Petrocik, J. R. 1991. "Divided Government: Is It All in the Campaigns?" In *The Politics of Divided Government*, ed. G. W. Cox and S. Kernell.

Pfiffner, J. P. 1996. *Strategic Presidency*. 2nd ed. Lawrence: University Press of Kansas.

Pika, J. A. 1979. "Beyond the Oval Office." *Congress and the Presidency* 9:17–36.

Poole, K., and H. Rosenthal, 1996. *Congress: A Political and Economic History of Roll Call Voting*. New York: Oxford University Press.

Price, D. E. 1972. *Who Makes the Laws? Creativity and Power in Senate Committees*. Cambridge: Schenkman.

Pritchard, A. 1983. "Presidents Do Influence Voting in the U. S. Congress." *Legislative Studies Quarterly* 8:691–711.

———. 1986. "An Evaluation of C.Q.'s Presidential Support Scores." *American Journal of Political Science* 30:480–95.

Public Papers of the Presidents of the United States. Annual. Washington, D.C.: Government Printing Office.

Ragsdale, L. 1984. "The Politics of Presidential Speechmaking." *American Political Science Review* 78:971–84.

———. 1993. *Presidential Politics*. Boston: Houghton Mifflin.

———. 1996. *Vital Statistics on the Presidency*. Washington, D.C.: CQ Press.

Ragsdale, L., and J. J. Theiss III. 1997. "Institutionalization of the American Presidency." *American Journal of Political Science* 41:1280–1318.

Ranney, A., ed. 1968. *Political Science and Public Policy*. Chicago: Markham.

Renka, R. D., and B. J. Jones. 1991. "The 'Two Presidencies' during the Reagan and Bush Administrations." In *The Two Presidencies: A Quarter Century Assessment*, ed. S. A. Shull. Chicago: Nelson-Hall.

Ringelstein, A. C. 1985. "Presidential Vetoes: Motivations and Classification." *Congress and the Presidency* 12:43–55.

————. 1989. "The Justifications for and the Policy Content of Presidential Vetoes." Ph.D. dissertation, University of New Orleans.

Ripley, R. B. 1972. *The Politics of Economic and Human Resource Development.* Indianapolis, Ind.: Bobbs-Merrill.

————. 1979. "Carter and Congress." In *The Presidency: Studies in Public Policy,* ed. S. A. Shull and L. T. LeLoup. Brunswick, Ohio: King's Court Communications.

————. 1985. *Policy Analysis in Political Science.* Chicago: Nelson-Hall.

Ripley, R. B., and J. M. Lindsay, eds. 1993. *Congressional Resurgence in Foreign Policy.* Ann Arbor: University of Michigan Press.

Rivers, D., and N. L. Rose. 1985. "Passing the President's Program." *American Journal of Political Science* 29:183–96.

Robinson, J. A. 1967. *Congress and Foreign Policy-Making: A Study in Legislative Influence and Initiative.* Revised ed. Homewood, Ill.: Dorsey Press.

Rockman, B. A. 1984. *The Leadership Question.* New York: Praeger.

————. 1991. "The Leadership Style of George Bush." In *The Bush Presidency: First Appraisals,* ed. C. Campbell and B. A. Rockman. Chatham, N.J.: Chatham House.

Rohde, D. W. 1994. "Presidential Support in the House of Representatives." In *The President, the Congress, and Foreign Policy,* ed. P. E. Peterson. Norman: University of Oklahoma Press.

Rohde, D. W., and D. M. Simon. 1985. "Presidential Vetoes and Congressional Response: A Study of Institutional Conflict." *American Journal of Political Science* 29:397–427.

Rossiter, C. 1956. *The American Presidency.* New York: Harcourt Brace.

Sabatier, P., and H. Jenkins-Smith. 1993. *Policy Change and Learning.* Boulder, Colo.: Westview.

Salisbury, R., and J. Heinz. 1970. "A Theory of Policy Analysis and Some Preliminary Applications." In *Policy Analysis in Political Science,* ed. I. Sharkansky. Chicago: Markham.

Schick, A. ed. 1986. *Crisis in the Budget Process.* Washington, D.C.: American Enterprise Institute.

Schlesinger, A. Jr. 1973. *Imperial Presidency.* Boston: Houghton Mifflin.

————. 1986. *The Cycles of American History.* Boston: Houghton Mifflin.

Schulman, P. R. 1975. "Non-incremental Policy Making." *American Political Science Review* 69:1354–70.

Schwarz, J. E., and L. E. Shaw. 1976. *The United States Congress in Comparative Perspective.* Hinsdale, Ill.: Dryden Press.

Shaw, T. C., and S. A. Shull. 1996. "Beyond Divided Government: Explaining Vote Controversy on Important Legislation." Presented at the annual meeting of the American Political Science Association, San Francisco.

Shull, S. A. 1979. *Presidential Policy Making: An Analysis.* Brunswick, Ohio: King's Court Communications.

————. 1981. "Assessing Measures of Presidential-Congressional Interaction." *Presidential Studies Quarterly* 11:151–57.

————. 1983. *Domestic Policy Formation.* Westport, Conn.: Greenwood Press.

———. 1989. *The President and Civil Rights Policy*. Westport, Conn.: Greenwood Press.

———, ed. 1991. *The Two Presidencies: A Quarter Century Assessment*. Chicago: Nelson-Hall.

———. 1993. *A Kinder, Gentler Racism? The Reagan-Bush Civil Rights Legacy*. Armonk, N.Y.: M. E. Sharpe.

———. 1994. "Conceptual and Measurement Concerns about Lindsay's and Steger's 'The Two Presidencies in Future Research'." *Congress and the Presidency* 21:159–62.

———. 1997. *Presidential-Congressional Relations: Policy and Time Approaches*. Ann Arbor: The University of Michigan Press.

Shull, S. A., and G. A. Franklin. 1978. "Agency Appropriations and Expenditures," *Southern Review of Public Administration* 1:529–41.

Shull, S. A., and D. Garland. 1996. "Presidential Influence Versus Agency Discretion: A Test of Three Models." *Policy Studies Review* 14:49–70.

Shull, S. A., and D. W. Gleiber. 1994. "Testing a Dynamic Process of Policy Making in Civil Rights." *Social Science Journal* 31:53–67.

———. 1995. "Presidential Cycles in Civil Rights Policy Making." *Presidential Studies Quarterly* 15:429–46.

Shull, S. A., D. W. Gleiber, and A. C. Ringelstein. 1992. "Determinants of Presidential Veto Propensity." Paper presented at the Western Political Science Association. San Francisco, March 19–21.

Shull, S. A., and M. F. Klemm. 1987. "Amendments Versus All Votes: A Comparison of Assertiveness and Controversy in Congress." *Southeastern Political Review* 15:139–58.

Shull, S. A., and L. T. LeLoup. [1981] 1991. "Comment on Lee Sigelman's 'Reassessing the "Two Presidencies" Thesis'." In *The Two Presidencies: A Quarter Century Assessment*, ed. S. A. Shull. Chicago: Nelson-Hall.

Shull, S. A., and J. Vanderleeuw. 1987. "What Do Key Votes Measure?" *Legislative Studies Quarterly* 12:573–82.

Shuman, H.E. 1992. *Politics and the Budget*. 3rd ed. Englewood Cliffs, N.J.: Prentice Hall.

Sigelman, L. [1979] 1991. "Reassessing the 'Two Presidencies' Thesis." In *The Two Presidencies: A Quarter Century Assessment*, ed. S. A. Shull. Chicago: Nelson-Hall.

Simonton, D. K. 1987. "Presidential Inflexibility and Veto Behavior: Two Individual-Situational Interactions." *Journal of Personality* 55:1–18.

Skowronek, S. 1993. *The Politics Presidents Make*. Cambidge: Harvard University Press.

Snape, K., and D. Breaux. 1988. "Toward an Integrated Model of Veto Overrides: A Multivariate Analysis of Override Attempts." Paper presented at the Western Political Science Association, San Francisco.

Sperlich, P. W. 1975. "Bargaining and Overload: An Essay on Power." In *Perspectives on the Presidency*, ed. A. Wildavsky. Boston: Little, Brown.

Spitzer, R. J. 1983. *Presidency and Public Policy*. Tuscaloosa: University of Alabama Press.

———. 1985. "The Item Veto Reconsidered." *Presidential Studies Quarterly* 15:611–16.

———. 1988. *The President's Veto.* Albany: State University of New York Press.

———. 1993. *The President and Congress.* New York: McGraw-Hill.

———. 1997. "The Veto King: The 'Dr. No' Presidency of George Bush." Paper presented at the conference on the Presidency of George Bush, Hofstra University. Hempstead, N.Y., April 1997.

Stanley, H. W., and R. G. Niemi, 1996. *Vital Statistics on American Politics.* Washington, D.C.: CQ Press.

Sullivan, T. 1991a. "A Matter of Fact: The Two Presidencies Thesis Revisited." In *The Two Presidencies: A Quarter Century Assessment,* ed. S. A. Shull. Chicago: Nelson-Hall.

———. 1991b. "The Bank Account Presidency." *American Journal of Political Science* 35:686–723.

———. 1991c. "Rejoinder to Edward's Presidential Influence in Congress." *American Journal of Political Science* 35:730–37.

Sundquist, J. L. 1968. *Politics and Policy: The Eisenhower, Kennedy, and Johnson Years.* Washington, D.C.: Brookings Institution.

———. 1981. *Decline and Resurgence in Congress.* Washington, D.C.: Brookings Institution.

———. 1986. *Constitutional Reform and Effective Government.* Washington, D.C.: Brookings Institution.

Tenpas, K. D. 1997. *Presidents as Candidates.* New York: Garland Publishing Inc.

Thurber, J. A., ed. 1996. *Rivals for Power: Presidential-Congressional Relations.* Washington, D.C.: CQ Press.

Tocqueville, A. [1835] 1990. *Democracy in America.* Trans. Henry Reeve. Ed. Phillips Bradley. New York: Vintage Books.

Towle, K. A. 1937. "The Presidents' Veto Since 1889." *American Political Science Review* 31:51–56.

Turner, J. 1951. *Party and Constituency: Pressures on Congress.* Baltimore, Md.: Johns Hopkins University Press.

Uslaner, E. M., and R. E. Weber. 1975. "The 'Politics' of Redistribution: Toward a Model of the Policy-Making Process in the American States." *American Politics Quarterly* 3:131–69.

Watson, R. A. 1988. "The President's Veto Power." *Annals of the American Academy of Political and Social Science* 499:36–46.

———. 1993. *Presidential Vetoes and Public Policy.* Lawrence: University Press of Kansas.

Wayne, S. J. 1978. *Legislative Presidency.* New York: Harper & Row.

Wayne, S. J., et al. 1979. "Advising the President on Enrolled Legislation: Patterns of Executive Influence." *Political Science Quarterly* 94:303–17.

Weekly Compilation of Presidential Documents. Washington, D.C.: Government Printing Office.

White, K. J., S. D. Wong, D. Whistler, and S. A. Haun. 1990. *Shazam.* New York: McGraw-Hill.

Wildavsky, A. 1964. *Politics of the Budgetary Process*. Boston: Little, Brown.

――――. [1966] 1991. "Two Presidencies." In *The Two Presidencies: A Quarter Century Assessment*, ed. S. A. Shull. Chicago: Nelson-Hall.

――――. 1979. *Speaking Truth to Power: The Art and Craft of Policy Analysis*. Boston: Little, Brown.

――――. 1988. *New Politics of the Budgetary Process*. 2nd ed. New York: HarperCollins.

Wilson, W. 1885. *Congressional Government: A Study in American Politics*. Boston: Houghton Mifflin.

――――. 1908. *Constitutional Government in the United States*. New York: Columbia University Press.

Wood, B. D., and R. A. Waterman. 1993. *Bureaucratic Dynamics*. Boulder, Colo.: Westview.

Woolley, J. T. 1991. "Institutions, the Election Cycle, and the Presidential Veto." *American Journal of Political Science* 35:279–304.

Zeidenstein, H.G. 1983. "Varying Relations between Presidents' Popularity and Their Legislative Success." *Presidential Studies Quarterly* 13:530–50.

INDEX

Abortion issue, veto propensity and, 103, 108

ACF. *See* Autocorrelation functions

Active presidency, 61, 76

Actor relations, 2; activities/resources and, 58

Agenda preferences, 11–12, 76, 175n3

American Medical Association, 103

Analysis: discussion of, 157; framework for, 23–31

Approval ratings, 62; position taking and, 71–72. *See also* Popularity

ARIMA modelling, 164

Articles of Confederation, veto propensity and, 95

Assertiveness, 28, 61; by conservative presidents, 59; policy preferences and, 81; position taking and, 150; support and, 85; veto and, 98, 111

Autocorrelation functions (ACF), 157, 164

Automatic spending cuts, 113, 114, 117

Balanced budget, 119, 151, 152

Barber, James David, 8

Beck, Nathaniel, 33

Best-fit models, 168, 177n3

Big government: active presidency and, 61; exogenous environment and, 53

Bivariate analysis, 5, 12

Bond, Jon: logit analysis and, 155; multivariate analysis by, 5

Bork, Robert, 88

Borrelli, Stephen: on skill/legislative success, 84

Box scores, 27, 28, 43, 44, 137, 175n3; collecting, 153; data base from, 78; success and, 77, 79–80; and support score compared, 13, 79

Brace, Paul: on major speeches/legislative relations, 83

Brady, David, 30

Budget agreement, xi, 2, 14–16, 18, 26, 29–31, 35, 36–37, 42, 43; calculating, 158; conceptual/measurement problems with, 115; described, 46–47, 104; domestic, 37, 123, 147, 148 (table), 166; equation for, 166, 167; foreign, 37, 123, 147, 148 (table), 166; general/policy models for, 127–30, 128 (table), 142 (table); as incremental process, 130; indicators of, 46–47; nature of, 113–16; during 1949–1995, 124 (table); one-year lag of, 48, 66, 73, 74; operationalizing, 57; position taking and, 48, 49, 65; preferences in, 114; presidents and, 74, 115, 120, 151; process of, 123; studying, 16, 124–25; variance in, 116, 127, 144; veto propensity and, 41, 47, 111, 123, 129

Budget and Accounting Act (1921), 15, 113, 130

Budget cuts, 15, 113, 117

Budget Impoundment and Control Act (1974). *See* Congressional Budget Impoundment and Control Act

Budgeting process, 6, 19, 43, 55, 118, 125; authority in, 113;